# Pentecostal Insight in a Segregated US City

New Directions in the Anthropology of Christianity

*Series editors:*
Naomi Haynes, Jon Bialecki, Hillary Kaell, and James S. Bielo

Emphasizing ethnographic depth and theoretical innovation, *New Directions in the Anthropology of Christianity* showcases the work of a fresh generation of researchers, as well as outstanding senior scholars, to provide researchers at all levels with rich sources of comparison and new analytical frameworks. The series publishes monographs and edited volumes on a range of topics on Christianity around the world, focusing on a few key themes: Politics and Christian nationalism; Economic development and humanitarianism; Engagement with religious others; Gender and sexuality; and Environment.

Prioritizing the comparative study of Christianity, the series strengthens a global network of scholars with overlapping interests, while providing a unique vantage point on the growing subfield of anthropology of Christianity.

*Christianity, Politics and the Afterlives of War in Uganda*
Henni Alava

*Mediating Catholicism*
Edited by Eric Hoenes del Pinal, Marc Loustau and Kristin Norget

# Pentecostal Insight in a Segregated US City

*Designs for Vitality*

Frederick Klaits with LaShekia Chatman and Michael Richbart

BLOOMSBURY ACADEMIC
LONDON • NEW YORK • OXFORD • NEW DELHI • SYDNEY

BLOOMSBURY ACADEMIC
Bloomsbury Publishing Plc
50 Bedford Square, London, WC1B 3DP, UK
1385 Broadway, New York, NY 10018, USA
29 Earlsfort Terrace, Dublin 2, Ireland

BLOOMSBURY, BLOOMSBURY ACADEMIC and the Diana logo are
trademarks of Bloomsbury Publishing Plc

First published in Great Britain 2022
This paperback edition published 2024

Series design: Toby Way
Cover image: Royalty Free Aerial stock photo of Seneca, One Tower skyscraper and the
city's downtown skyline at twilight; Downtown Buffalo, New York © Axiom Images

A catalogue record for this book is available from the British Library.

Library of Congress Control Number: 2022932186

ISBN: HB: 978-1-3501-7588-4
PB: 978-1-3503-2981-2
ePDF: 978-1-3501-7591-4
eBook: 978-1-3501-7590-7

Series: New Directions in the Anthropology of Christianity

Typeset by Newgen KnowledgeWorks Pvt. Ltd., Chennai, India

To find out more about our authors and books visit www.bloomsbury.com
and sign up for our newsletters.

# Contents

# Acknowledgments

I have received so much help with this project. My most profound thanks go to all the church members who assisted me in so many ways, especially in the manner they most appreciate, namely helping me to feel the Holy Spirit in my body. Given the importance they so rightly attach to public expressions of recognition and appreciation, it is a pity that I cannot thank them by their actual names here. In addition to expressing my deep gratitude to the people about whom I have written, I wish to express equal thanks to all those who generously took time to speak with me about their circumstances but whose stories I could not include in this book. Their narratives have greatly enriched my understanding, and I hope to be able to relate them elsewhere.

This text has benefited enormously from the generous help given to me by my longtime mentors Gillian Feeley-Harnik and Richard Werbner. It has been my great good fortune to have worked with these two extraordinary scholars over the years, and words really fail me here. I am equally thankful to Hillary Kaell, whose careful reading of each chapter draft prompted and sustained me over the course of the writing, and to Carl Nightingale and China Scherz, who both gave me inspiring feedback on an early draft of the manuscript. Two anonymous reviewers for Bloomsbury Press performed superb work, and this book is infinitely better for their efforts. At Bloomsbury, Lalle Pursglove and Lily McMahon have provided unstinting support and encouragement.

Many colleagues have provided transformative suggestions at conferences and other venues where I have presented earlier versions of this material. I would particularly like to thank Jon Bialecki, James Bielo, N. Fadeke Castor, Simon Coleman, Omri Elisha, Gillian Feeley-Harnik, Gareth Fisher, Marla Frederick, Angelique Haugerud, Naomi Haynes, Brian Howell, Michael Lambek, Susan McKinnon, Amira Mittermaier, Robert Orsi, Elizabeth Pérez, China Scherz, Don Seeman, Yang Shen, Jacqueline Solway, Todne Thomas, Rose Wellman, and Onaje Woodbine. I am especially grateful to the Anthropology Department at Brandeis University for inviting me to deliver the Benson Saler Lecture in the Anthropology of Religion in 2015, as well as to the Anthropology Department at the University of Wisconsin-Madison where I spent a portion of a sabbatical, unfortunately cut short by the Covid-19 pandemic, as an Honorary Research Fellow in the spring of 2020.

Without the important support of colleagues and research assistants at the State University of New York at Buffalo (UB), this project would never have gotten off the ground. I wish to extend special thanks to Shay-Akil McLean, who helped me become acquainted with the neighborhoods of the East Side of Buffalo and suggested many important research directions. At UB, I have relied heavily on the advice and encouragement of my colleagues Don Pollock and Peter Biehl in the Anthropology Department. Numerous other colleagues at UB and in the Buffalo community have given me important feedback at various stages of this work, in particular James Bono, Erika Haygood, James Holstun, Laura Mangan, Carl Nightingale, Michael Rembis, Erik Seeman, Marla Segol, Gary Steeves, Phillips Stevens, Marion Werner, and Victoria Wolcott, together with many students, including Devon Asmus, Rebekah Kimble, Rosaleen McAfee, and Jewels White. I wish to express special gratitude to LaShekia Chatman and Michael Richbart, students whose ongoing engagements appear in this text as commentaries on my ethnography.

I have received essential institutional support from a number of UB organizations: the Center for Civic Engagement and Public Policy; the Cultures and Texts Strategic Strength; the Office of the Vice President for Research; and the Humanities Institute, in which I served as a Faculty Fellow during the 2014–15 academic year. I am grateful as well to the Wenner-Gren Foundation, which awarded me a Post-PhD Research Grant for the years 2014–16.

Portions of this text have appeared in previous publications, and I am grateful for the permission of the publishers to reproduce them. These publications are as follows:

Klaits, F. (2016), "Insult and Insecurity: Discernment, Trust, and the Uncanny in Two U.S. Pentecostal Communities," *Anthropological Quarterly*, 89 (4): 1143–73.

Klaits, F. (2017), "Asking in Time," in F. Klaits (ed.), *The Request and the Gift in Religious and Humanitarian Endeavors*, 1–24, New York: Palgrave Macmillan. Reprinted by permission of Springer Nature.

Klaits, F. (2017), " 'Catch the Word': Violated Contracts and Prophetic Confirmation in African American Pentecostalism," *HAU: Journal of Ethnographic Theory*, 7 (3): 237–60.

Klaits, F. (2017), " 'We All Ask Together': Intercession and Composition as Models for Spiritual Kinship," in T. Thomas, A. Malik, and R. Wellman (eds.), *New Directions in Spiritual Kinship: Sacred Ties across the*

*Abrahamic Religions*, 131–49, New York: Palgrave Macmillan. Reprinted by permission of Springer Nature.

Klaits, F. (2018), Review of Judith Casselberry, "The Labor of Faith: Gender and Power in Black Apostolic Pentecostalism," *Anthropological Quarterly*, 91 (3): 1143–8.

Klaits, F., and S. McLean (2015), "Valuing Black Lives: Pentecostalism, Charismatic Gifts, and Human Economies in a U.S. Inner City," *American Ethnologist*, 42 (4): 610–23.

My father Joseph Klaits has always been a role model and a source of strength for me. Last but most importantly, I want to thank Laura, who has been with me every step of the way—for thirty years to the day, in fact, as of this writing—and without whom none of this would have been possible.

F. K.
Buffalo, New York
October 26, 2021

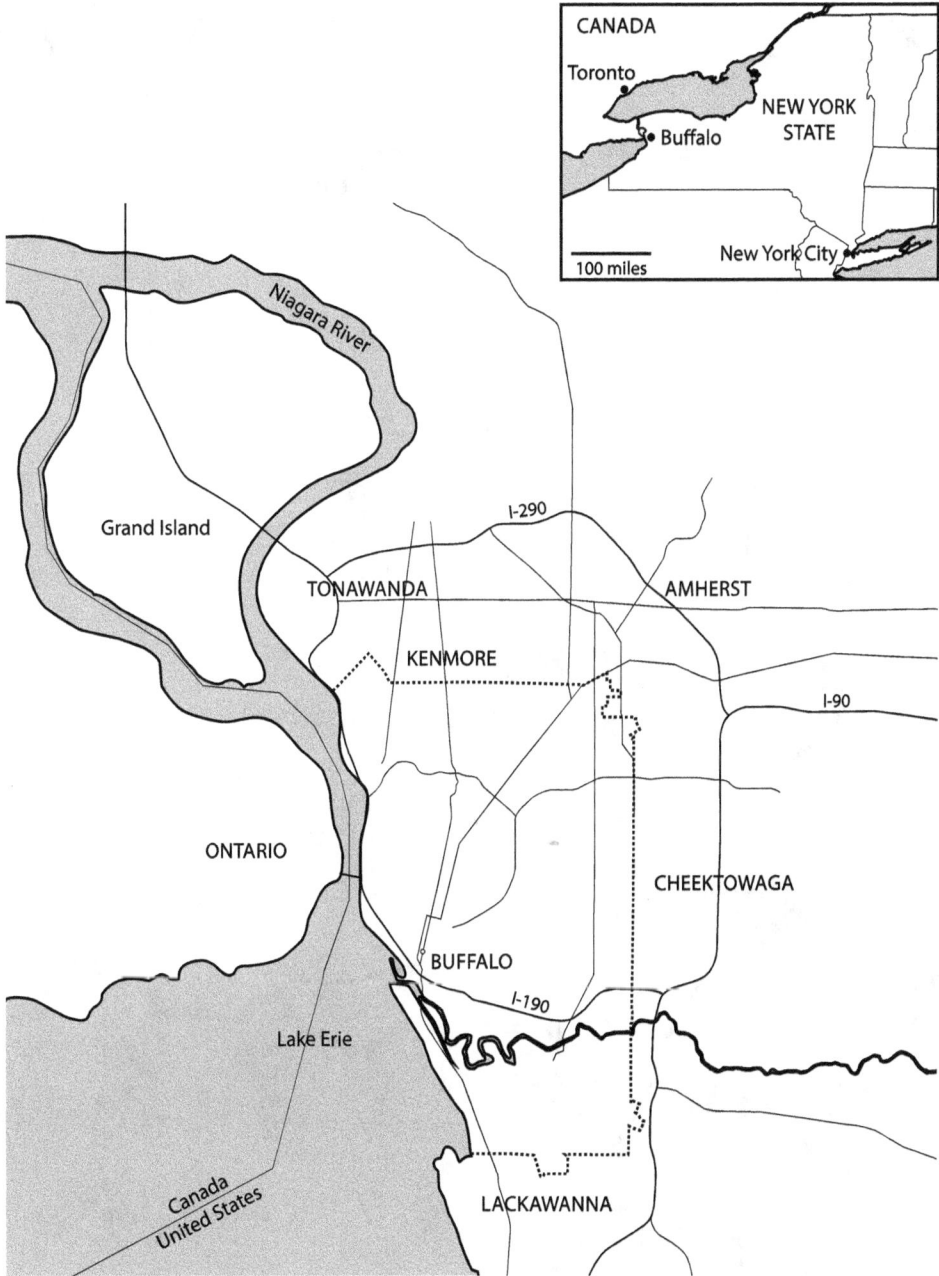

CANADA

Toronto

NEW YORK
STATE

Buffalo

100 miles

New York City

Niagara River

Grand Island

I-290

TONAWANDA

AMHERST

KENMORE

I-90

ONTARIO

CHEEKTOWAGA

BUFFALO

I-190

Lake Erie

Canada
United States

LACKAWANNA

Buffalo and suburbs. Maps courtesy of Buffalo Design & Printing.

1 mile

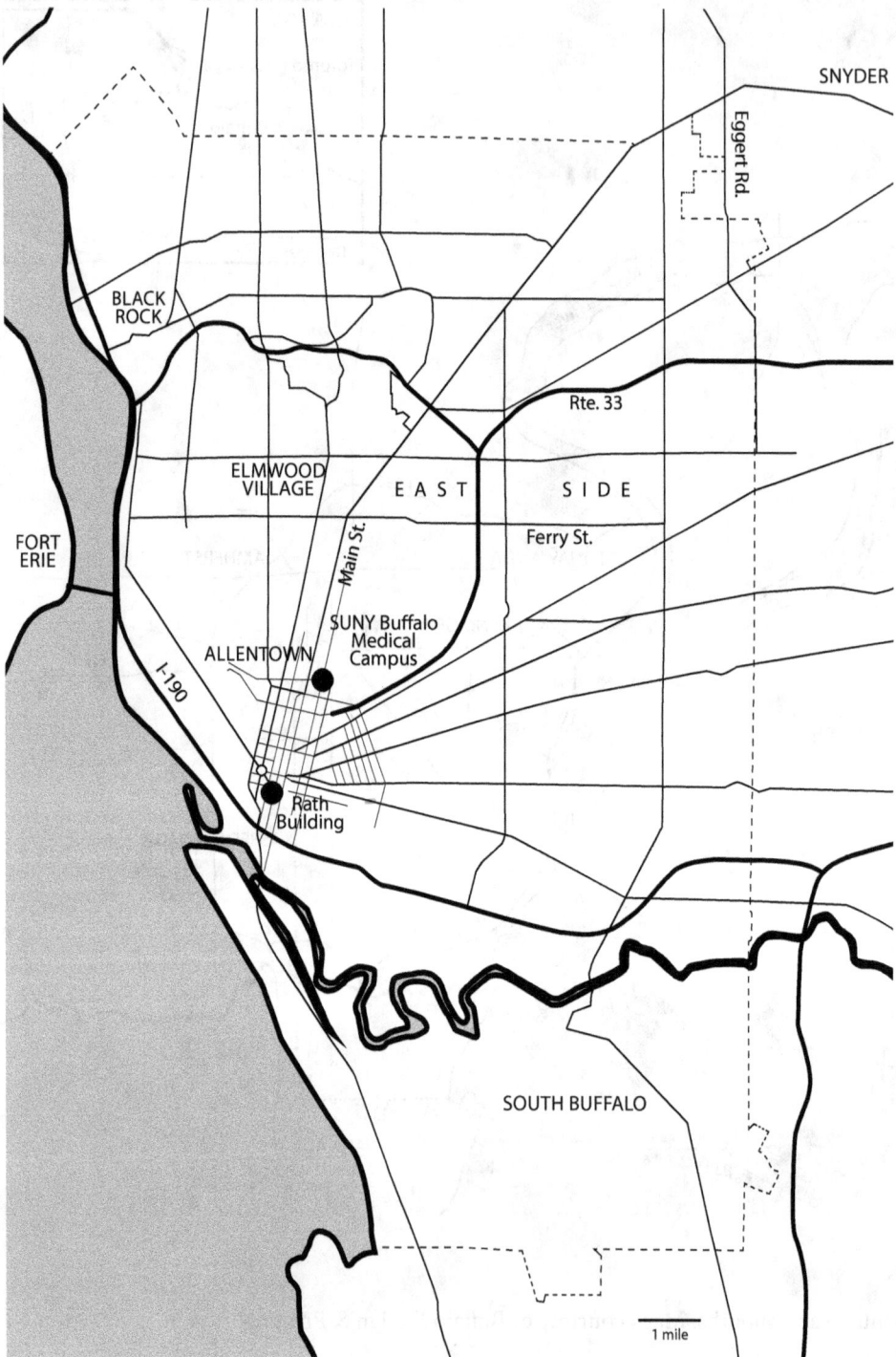

Buffalo city.

# Designs for Vitality

For Pentecostal Christian believers, communicating with God places many things in a new light. Arlene, a middle-aged woman who attends a majority white Pentecostal church in suburban Buffalo, New York, explained to me how she felt when God revealed to her decades previously, soon after she had been saved, that her husband had been unfaithful.[1] She had heard God tell her to look in her husband's briefcase, where she found a notebook full of the names of the women with whom he had been sleeping. She was devastated by the realization that she would have to become a single mother: "Did you ever drive on a highway and you see the highway for a long time straight, and you just see fields and you just see the road going forever? That's how I saw my life, like no end in sight. No end, and I didn't want to go down that road." Her vision of single parenthood as a journey without destination, as empty time, was accompanied by grief for a loss of self: "I wanted to be Susie homemaker and raise my kids; Susie homemaker is going out the door." To be a married homemaker had been the basis of Arlene's hopes for emotional and material security, and "part of me wanted God to be magical, to just make things right." God did not fix her marriage; instead, he wanted Arlene to depend on him alone.[2] "God has created us to have a relationship with us, to communicate with us," she told me. "We are the bride, the Lord is the bridegroom, that close intimate relationship is what He desires. When you enter into a marriage covenant, you're forsaking all. Children are the fruit of that relationship, and in the spiritual realm, bringing others into a relationship with God is the equivalent." Anyone in the various churches Arlene has attended whom "God has used me to plant a seed in," she said, is one of her own "spiritual children."

Pastor Hadley, a woman who leads an African American Pentecostal church located closer to the downtown area of Buffalo, spoke to her congregation about how God had acted in her own marital troubles. Decades previously, when she had been "in the world" as an unsaved single woman, she had known that she should not be in a relationship with a married man. Still, she had become romantically involved with such a man, physically touching but not having sex. "And what made it worse was that I knew his wife." Later on, after she got married and was subsequently saved, she "went to God" in prayer "because I didn't want what would've happened to her [the married man's wife] to happen to me." Nonetheless, her husband eventually cheated on her. "I said to God, 'But I didn't sleep with him!'"—that is, the married man she had been with previously.

> But God said to me, "You never get it back the way you planted it." I didn't sleep with him, but I slept with him in my heart. It's like a merry-go-round, first slow then fast. Everything we do in our life is like a seed. The world says, "What goes around comes around" while God says, "You reap what you sow." It's just a difference of vocabulary.

Pastor Hadley went on:

> It was the next day God told me: "Go tell your husband you forgive him. You forgive him, and watch how you say it." The old Hadley, I would have changed my son's name away from his. But God used me to bring him [her now ex-husband] into the kingdom, and used him to sharpen me in the kingdom. I don't have no problem preaching alongside his wife at revivals. It let people know, surely there is a God—because I would never have forgiven before.

This book compares the kinds of knowledge that Pentecostal believers receive from God about their own and other people's lived circumstances in one majority white and two African American congregations in Buffalo. Like many other Pentecostal, Charismatic, and evangelical Christians, these believers speak with wonder of how a personal relationship with God gives them "discernment," citing the biblical passage "For the word of God is quick, and powerful, and sharper than any two-edged sword, piercing even to the dividing asunder of soul and spirit, and of the joints and marrow, and is a discerner of the thoughts and intents of the heart" (Heb. 4:12). Discernment is both a learned skill and a gift of the Holy Spirit, and many believers assess their maturity in faith by the extent to which they feel that their discernment—for example, their understandings of scripture, or a prophetic ability to hear and convey God's word—has developed. Furthermore, they often promote discernment as a practical ability to assess their own and other people's motives, and therefore as necessary for avoiding a range of moral and physical perils. To "have discernment" is to be attentive to the divine voice, which believers may apprehend as an audible utterance or more commonly as a thought that is not their own.

Why should believers consider it important to receive knowledge from and about God? The answer to this question may seem obvious. As T. M. Luhrmann (2012) demonstrates, many North American Christians engage in exercises of communicating with God so that they may receive evidence of a spiritual realm that cannot be directly apprehended. Of course, as Bruno Latour (2005) points out in reference to Christianity in general, they do not desire merely evidence. If the spiritual realm were like the neutrinos of particle physics—that is, existing but not interacting with people at all—believers would see no reason to gain knowledge about its operations. God's existence is important to believers because he is an active presence in their lives, yet what specifically matters to them about his activities is not something that can be known in advance. On a related point, there has been much debate over whether anthropologists studying religion can do justice to the views of the people they write about if they avoid taking a position on believers' claims concerning the existence of spiritual beings (Bialecki 2014; Scherz 2018; Wood 2020). My own position, as I describe later, is that God exists. Such an assertion usually elicits questions from secularists about the nature of evidence ("How do you know?") or how evidence is generated (as Luhrmann [2020] asks, "How does God become real?"). Yet it might also prompt a different question, of interest to secularists and believers alike: "So what, exactly?"

In this book, I refer to discernment as "Pentecostal insight" as a way of highlighting the critical dimensions of this "So what?" question. Communications from God matter to Pentecostal believers because they entail critical claims that people *should* pass beyond what are considered ordinary forms of perception, feeling, movement, and comprehension so that they may conform with God's intentions. Messages from God induce believers to question accustomed forms of interaction and knowledge, and to create novel relationships and institutional arrangements in the process— in ways that differ significantly among the three congregations I discuss. It is this passing beyond the ordinary that I gloss as "insight"—for lack of a better term; the visual is not always key. To be clear about how believers' concepts are related to my own, when they speak of discernment they usually have in mind a gift or skill, for instance the ability to prophesy or to identify a false preacher. Less often, they speak of discernment to refer more broadly to what God causes them to apprehend. My own concepts of "insight" and "discernment" parallel this second, more general usage, inasmuch as believers understand knowledge derived from God as helping them pass beyond the ordinary.

As Arlene's and Pastor Hadley's accounts make clear, believers' insights profoundly shape their understandings of time, care, and personal value.

Arlene's description of an endless road and Pastor Hadley's metaphor of a merry-go-round—together with their shared images of seeds that are planted and then sprout—conveyed their insights into the patterns in which events have unfolded over time. Both reflected likewise on how God's patterning of events has bestowed particular kinds of value upon their lives. Communicating the word of God has given Arlene "spiritual children" in the face of marital disappointments. For Pastor Hadley, speaking publicly about how God shaped the ways she understood and responded to marital infidelity has made her a witness to God's power to instill the disposition to forgive. Finally, each of them reflected on how developing a "relationship with God" reframed their sense of responsibility to God and to other people. Arlene had to come to terms with the divine demand that she depend on God rather than a husband. Pastor Hadley, concerned about how she was relating to other women through men, worried that she might suffer the same injury she had caused another man's wife, and ended up rethinking how to respond to her husband's offense.

There are some suggestive differences, too, between the images through which Arlene related her disappointment—traveling along a road without landmarks or a destination—and Pastor Hadley reflected on her guilt, namely riding a merry-go-round that goes slowly and then rapidly. Each is a chronotope—that is, a spatial image that conveys time—but one involves stasis-in-duration, the other rhythm (with, maybe, an echo of the blues: "You never get it back the way you planted it"—about which more later on).

In this book, I ask: how are such Pentecostal insights shaped by the ways life chances are distributed across multiple intersections of class, race, and gender in a postindustrial, highly segregated US city? Conversely, how are believers' life chances affected by the ways they discern God's intents? To provide a brief example: what made it conceivable for Arlene to use an image of empty time to express her disappointed aspiration to be a nonwage-earning homemaker is that such an ambition was plausible for white women during the period when she was growing up in a working-class suburb of Buffalo in the 1960s and 1970s, much more so than it has ever been for African American women (Coontz 1992; Mullings 2001). At the same time, Arlene's decision to remain single after becoming saved hinged on what she called her "close intimate relationship" with God, which she implied to me took precedence over the expectations of many in the various churches she has attended that she should remarry. Arlene's narrative illustrates how social conditions give form to the predicaments that shape believers' felt needs for discernment, as well as how discernment shapes their awareness of how it is possible to flourish under those conditions.

## Insights into Designs

Over the course of this study, I take believers' imagery of time, care, and value, together with their images of space and place, as a guide for comparing the different kinds of critical distinctions they make between the conditions necessary for a good life and those that might frustrate its prospects. One source of the critical potential of Pentecostal and Christian Charismatic movements is their emphasis on a specific yet open-ended version of personhood, namely a split between virtuous aspects of the self that are willingly obedient to God, and sinful aspects that are unwilling and rebelliously willful. Writing of the largely middle-class Vineyard Charismatic movement in the United States, Jon Bialecki (2017) points out that as believers recognize the convergences and divergences between God's will and their own, they become less liable to attribute events solely to their own "individual causative agency" (97). It becomes important for them to gain insight into God's activity by grasping the meanings of scripture (Bielo 2009, 2011) and by cultivating awareness of God as an external presence within their own consciousness (Brahinsky 2012; Luhrmann 2007, 2012, 2020).

Another reason that Pentecostalism provides a useful avenue for exploring critical awareness is that the wonder—or in the case of the devil, the uncanniness—that believers experience as they engage with spiritual beings compels them to distinguish those beings' artful designs from ordinary happenings. Believers are not surprised when the Holy Spirit works, but their wonder at how the Spirit operates beyond the ordinary never goes away. James K. A. Smith (2010) remarks: "One of the reasons Pentecostal spirituality is so often linked to spontaneity is that Pentecostal worship makes room for the unexpected. Indeed, we might say that, for Pentecostals, the unexpected is expected, the surprising coming as no surprise" (33). Similarly in *Blackpentecostal Breath*, Ashon Crawley (2017) recounts hearing the first word of his auntie's song during a service: "We knew, with that word, that the power of the Lord was sure to come down. The surprise would be in how we got there, not in the fact of us getting there because *there* was determined as achievable and achieved before she began" (264, emphasis added). Christians commonly say that spiritual beings have plans for humanity, but they may not point out as explicitly that the artful content of those plans prompts them, as during the song Crawley describes, to cultivate insight into the ways those beings shape their life possibilities. Such aesthetics elicit particular kinds of discernment: believers are compelled to look for the un/expected, for the surprising path to the destination to which they already know God has designed them to arrive.

Crawley deploys the concept "aesthetics of possibility" to distinguish Blackpentecostal aesthetics from the racialized sensory hierarchies, articulated most systematically by Immanuel Kant, that have played important roles in shaping white "aversion" toward Blackness, with profound social consequences (see, for instance, Mills 1997; Muhammad 2010; Rothstein 2017). For Crawley, the aesthetics of possibility constitute "pure immanence" (Deleuze 2001) in the face of systemic anti-Black violence, aesthetics that operate in musical "enfleshment"—breath, sound, and noise.[3] Foregrounding God's perceived intents to a greater extent, I would stress that Pentecostal aesthetic forms are designs that promote discernment of other artful designs—those of God, the devil, and other people—which shape believers' life possibilities (in the plural). Such possibilities include blessings, breakthroughs, reassurance, intimacy, bodily integrity, and salvation, but also forms of moral and physical peril, for instance sin, rejection, improper interpersonal connection, and damnation. As outcomes of intentional designs, these possibilities of well-being and ill-being themselves possess aesthetic qualities that both shape and emerge from ritual and narrative expressions.

In the pages that follow, I argue that Pentecostal believers take *designs for vitality* as a principal object of their discernment. In writing of vitality, I am introducing my own gloss on the Christian concept of life articulated in the ubiquitously quoted scripture "I have come that they may have life, and that they might have it more abundantly" (Jn 10:10). Baptist minister T. W. Hunt, author of *The Mind of Christ* (1995)—a devotional manual that inspires Evangelist Clarice, who attends Pastor Hadley's church—recalls the epiphany he experienced when reading "In him was life" (Jn 1:4): "I knew that I could not say that. My life was dependent on air, water, and food. I must have an environment. Divinity was dependent on nothing for its continuation" (54). From this perspective, faith involves passing beyond an unreflective attitude toward one's existence in order to develop critical awareness of the conditions that God has designed for one's life on earth and in eternity.[4] In discerning the designs of God and the devil, then, believers aim to locate various life-promoting and destructive possibilities in words, places, texts, objects, and bodies. Importantly, they must learn to identify human roles as well in these designs, because God and the devil operate through people.

For my own part, though, in writing of vitality I differ from most Christians in that I do not refer to an individual's vital essence. I find the concept of vitality useful because it connotes but is not confined to human flourishing. As I understand it, a suffering body has vitality; suffering and endurance are forms of vitality. The concept of vitality, then, refers in open-ended ways to a range of tensions and overlaps between flourishing and affliction. These tensions and overlaps provide avenues for conceptualizing how believers understand God's role in permitting or even designing suffering, and for grasping their thinking about its unequal distribution. A key reason, then, for taking this comparative approach to Pentecostalism—indeed for exploring Pentecostalism at all—is to ask how different ways of developing insight into the sources and nature of vitality may provide grounds for divergent ethical and political visions.

## The Churches

Within the three congregations I describe, believers deploy Pentecostal forms of expression to make different sorts of critical claims about the good life and the moral perils that threaten it. In a suburban, majority white working-class congregation of about three hundred members that I call Eternal Hope affiliated with a national first-wave Pentecostal denomination,[5] believers hope to achieve a good life by admitting their incapacities to God, receiving God's love, and extending that love as a gift to others. This outlook underpins a right-wing political stance that values people for their willingness to acknowledge their dependence upon God, and that is critical of what is taken to be elite secularist insistence on personal self-sufficiency. Congregants in two smaller-scale, nondenominational African American churches in the inner city that I call Victory Gospel and Heaven's Tabernacle—one led by a male pastor, the other by a female pastor—hope to receive blessings by involving themselves in "God's system," which they understand as subverting the exploitative "world's system." Their approaches combine critical stances toward racialized inequalities with prophetic worship styles that stress healing and prosperity. They emphasize how a good life requires attention to the conditions under which they may receive and extend blessings by remaining "obedient" to God.

In Chapter 2, I relate how these churches are situated in wider environments of Buffalo. Briefly here, many members of Eternal Hope, including its leader Pastor Charles, have forebears who lived in the same neighborhoods of the East Side of Buffalo where Victory Gospel and Heaven's Tabernacle are now located.

Their families moved to working-class suburbs during a period of mass white migration from the East Side extending from the 1950s through the 1990s. In addition, the church has a substantial minority of African American and Latinx members, with a few interracial unions. The dozen adult members of Eternal Hope with whom I carried out extended interviews were engaged in a range of blue-collar occupations, office work, and educational and care professions, or were homemakers. About half of these interviewees hold four-year college degrees. Many church members were raised Catholic in Italian, German, or Polish neighborhoods, and converted to Pentecostalism as the result of the proselytizing efforts of a married couple who founded Eternal Hope in the 1970s. An especially important consequence of their conversion has been a transformation in their understandings of sainthood. While they had been brought up to pray to the Catholic saints, they now understand themselves as "saints of God" with the power to "intercede" by laying hands on people praying at the altar.

While Eternal Hope is an established congregation some of whose members have known one another for decades, Victory Gospel and Heaven's Tabernacle were both founded around 2010. They are located in what are now some of the poorest urban neighborhoods in the United States, whose predominantly African American residents must contend with many injurious manifestations of systemic racism. Pastor Hadley and Pastor John, the leaders of Heaven's Tabernacle and Victory Gospel respectively, were called more explicitly than were the founders of Eternal Hope to minister to the suffering and marginalized. (Hadley, John, and Charles are all pseudonymous surnames.) Pastor Hadley's nearly all-female ministry grew out of a prayer group for women contending with substance abuse or domestic violence. Pastor John ministered to young men in prison or involved in drug dealing before founding Victory Gospel, which comprises a majority of women but a substantial number of men as well. Currently in her fifties, Pastor Hadley was raised in Baptist and Church of God in Christ (COGIC) congregations, fell away and was subsequently saved at age twenty-one. Pastor John, now in his early forties, had less exposure to church in his upbringing but after being saved at age nineteen became a disciple of a bishop in Pentecostal Assemblies of the World (PAW), which like COGIC is a large African American Pentecostal denomination. Pastor John and Pastor Hadley distinguish sharply between what "the saints of God" are supposed to do and the activities of "the world," which they identify largely with the informal economies of "the street." The approximately fifty members of Victory Gospel and twenty members of Heaven's Tabernacle are of varied class standing. There are substantial numbers of skilled nurses and caregivers, a few hold other professional positions or are retirees, and many have low-wage jobs and are in other precarious circumstances. Both of the pastors have spent some time in college. There are a few African immigrants in Victory Gospel's congregation, and a Euro-American family joined for a period toward the end of my fieldwork.

I wish to stress that these churches are all very similar to one another in matters of basic doctrine. All the committed believers whom I describe insist on the need to be born again—a condition signified by the Holy Spirit's gift of the ability to speak in tongues—as well as on the principle that God has established a moral order that is violated by individual sin, which in the absence of willingness to accept Jesus leads inevitably to eternal damnation. The churches are all emphatically heteronormative. In addition, these believers draw on a shared multiracial tradition of gospel music, as well as on both Christian and secular self-help literature. Although these churches have nothing to do with each other, their members would undoubtedly recognize one another as fellow saved Christians. It is the fact of basic similarity that makes the differences of emphasis and social circumstance illuminating.

## True and Distorted Recognition

In order to explore how believers' unequal social circumstances shape their insights into God's designs for vitality, I need to make an excursion into what some anthropological writers on ethics have said about the practical and ideal endpoints of people's efforts to foster "the good," and then return to consider design in a new register. My argument in this opening chapter unfolds in three stages: (1) I take work on ethics as an invitation to reflect on how Christian faith has shaped and has been shaped by dynamics of personal recognition and distorted recognition in the United States. (2) Believers' felt needs to understand how they appear in the eyes of God prompt me then to compare some of the different ways in which members of these Pentecostal congregations envision the temporal trajectories of care that God has designed for his people. This comparison provides me an opportunity to introduce the important theme of linkages between the vital and the ethical. (3) According to believers, I finally argue, God has designed discernment to be a form of vitality in its own right. As a result, discernment constitutes not simply knowledge of God's presence but a set of abilities to locate and draw upon sources of life.

Joel Robbins (2013) has influentially argued that "to study the good as anthropologists, we need to be attentive to the way people orientate to and act in a world that outstrips the one most concretely present to them, and … avoid dismissing their ideals as unimportant or, worse, bad-faith alibis for the worlds they actually create" (457). Following Robbins's suggestion to focus on strivings for the good, Cheryl Mattingly (2014a) discusses the struggles of African American parents in Los Angeles to provide good lives for their children under circumstances of poverty and inequality. Mattingly focuses on "moments of action" that are "experiments in how life might or should be lived" (14–15). She discusses how activities in such settings as parks, clinic waiting rooms, soccer fields, and churches "provide vantage points on familiar or prior ways of seeing, acting, [and] believing that are actively brought into question" (15). This approach, argues Mattingly, reveals the usefulness of a "first-person" as opposed to a "third-person" approach to Aristotelian virtue ethics. In effect, Mattingly asks whether in making everyday judgments, people wonder "How should I act in this situation given the ongoing relationships in which I'm embedded?" or alternatively "How should I act given my characteristics as seen by an observer?" She resolves the issue in favor of the former.[6] For example, a mother wondering whether her disabled son should play soccer does not adopt

> a universalizing third person perspective, as one might imagine a health researcher doing. Rather, she asks from "inside," as an engaged actor who finds herself embedded within … a situation in which the results of her actions are deeply consequential for her and those she cares about. Her stance of "care" is a manifestation of something very basic to human experience … Existence just *is* care, Heidegger said. It is this feature of our existence that makes it impossible to adequately characterize humans without adopting a first person starting point. We simply are not the sort of beings who can be summed up by the categories into which we can be placed or the properties we have, in a third person sort of way … We do not experience ourselves, ontologically, merely as a type of being, a member of a species. We are not simply determined by these categories, properties, and practices but also in orienting to them and experiencing our lives in light of them, we are able to put them into question. (12, 14)

This approach has much to recommend it, in particular its situational focus on open-ended trajectories of care, a subject to which I return below. However, "we" are not all equally able to effectively put into question "the categories into which we can be placed." Some of the most powerful passages in the history of

American letters attest to this point, for instance the opening of Ralph Ellison's *Invisible Man* (1995):

I am an invisible man. No, I am not a spook like those that haunted Edgar Allan Poe; nor am I one of your Hollywood-movie ectoplasms. I am a man of substance, of flesh and bone, fiber and liquids—and I might even be said to possess a mind. I am invisible, understand, simply because other people refuse to see me. Like the bodiless heads you sometimes see in circus sideshows, it is as though I have been surrounded by mirrors of hard, distorting glass. When they approach me they see only my surroundings, themselves, or figments of their imagination—indeed, everything and anything except me. (3)

If nothing else, this and similar accounts by W. E. B. Du Bois (1990), James Baldwin (1963), and Ta-Nehisi Coates (2015) make clear that what Robbins calls an "anthropology of the good" would need to come to terms with the structuring power of "bad-faith alibis," in this case those springing from the possessive investment in whiteness in the United States (Lipsitz 2006; see Hodges 2020; S. Sullivan 2014).

Specifically, Ellison draws attention to the uncanniness of being systematically misrecognized by others, to the extent that disturbing distortions of what is most familiar—one's very body—become inextricable components of one's sense of self.[7] How, then, does knowing God as a presence located outside the self, yet within it as well, reframe one's sense of the familiar, the alien, and the alien-in-the-familiar? To adapt Mattingly's remarks on third-person stances, Pentecostal insight hinges on believers' willingness to assess who they are, how they should act, and how they should hope *given their characteristics in God's eyes*. For example, James Cone points out in *The Cross and the Lynching Tree* (2011) that "Christ crucified manifested God's … transcendent presence in the lives of black Christians that empowered them to believe that *ultimately*, in God's eschatological future, they would not be defeated by the 'troubles of this world' " (2).[8] How and why might the insights that God provides into what Robbins calls "a world that outstrips the one most concretely present" contribute to forms of recognition of oneself and others that are in various ways true or—to continue with Ellison's visual metaphor—distorted?

As a Christian problematic, God's ability to provide true as opposed to distorted reflections of one's self is a common North American preoccupation. Describing healing prayer in a Catholic Charismatic movement, Thomas Csordas (2004) argues that "the capacity for intimacy begins with an existential coming to terms with the alterity of the self and that the presence of Jesus is an embodied metaphor for that condition of selfhood" (169). R. Marie Griffith (1997) makes a similar argument about ambitions for self-knowledge and intimacy with God among members of the evangelical Women's Aglow Fellowship. These women "attempt to be transparent to one another, to conform surface appearances with inward emotional and spiritual states rather than make the one a mask for the other" (122; cf. Pfeil 2011). A passage from a popular Aglow publication reads: "The heart cry in every truly honest person is 'Please understand me. Please help me discover who I am'" (123). In her study of right-wing Tea Party members in Louisiana, Arlie Russell Hochschild (2016) relates the narrative of a woman named Jackie Tabor who asked Jesus to save her following an abusive childhood: "I walked into the bathroom and looked into the mirror at a completely different girl ... Clean, beautiful. I believe that, for the first time, I saw in the mirror how He saw me. He showed me *who I am to Him*" (172).[9] In keeping with all this material derived from majority white faith communities, Luhrmann (2012) concludes that for members of the Vineyard movement, God assumes the role of an "empathetic therapist ... an internal 'object' [Kohut 1971] that is loving, caring, and concerned with what is best for them" (297)—and that, clearly, knows them perfectly.

That questions of recognition may be profoundly felt concerns for believers is likewise suggested by a passage in Connie Porter's novel *Imani All Mine* (1999), narrated by a young African American woman named Tasha growing up in Buffalo:

> The preacher say, Won't you come this morning?
>
> Looking right straight at me. I can feel his eyes on me, and my feet stand still while the music roll up hard against me ... That music in my legs making me think that it's all right to take a step. Even if I don't believe what it's saying. I don't think it's lying to me. Like some boy lying to me. (92)

Tasha feels that the music encouraging her to move is not "lying" to her, unlike the boy who raped her. But why should God be represented specifically as *not lying*? For Tasha, the moral peril is less that she might fail to recognize herself as an empathetic therapist would wish than that she might fail to discern others' misrepresentations of themselves, and consequently be made to serve their desires.

While I pursue this comparison in later chapters, for now I wish to note that certain forms of distorted recognition have been extensively discussed at an analytical level in literature on Christianity in the United States, namely those that serve to entrench white privilege (for overviews, see Butler 2021; Jones

2020; Tisby 2019). On the basis of research conducted in the 1990s, Michael Emerson and Christian Smith (2000) show that most white evangelicals do not recognize the existence of systemic racism because they emphasize the overriding importance of individual sin, repentance, and personal relationships with God. Carolyn Renée Dupont (2013) demonstrates that during the 1960s the Christian faith of the majority of white southerners led them to believe that God had ordained segregation and racial hierarchy. Dupont's treatment dovetails with Iain MacRobert's study (1988) of how the multiracial and ecumenical qualities of the Azusa Street revival of 1906 were subverted in subsequent decades as Pentecostal denominations separated along racial lines (see also Anderson 1979). Marla Frederick (2016) shows how contemporary evangelical tropes that sustain white supremacy—concerning, for instance, the value of individual work—are cast as universally applicable, whereas appeals to collective action against injustice are usually framed in parochial terms as "Black social gospel" (see Curtis 2021; Tranby and Hartmann 2008). George Yancy (2012) imagines "how daring and *dangerous*" it would be for any of the members of a predominantly white liberal church he attends to say in public prayer: "I have been thinking about how, despite the fact that I consider myself a white anti-racist, I continue to incur white privilege, I continue to carry the weight of racist training in my body" (3–4). As it is, Yancy implies, they are going about with distorted images of their own righteousness (see Harvey 2014).

In an ethnography demonstrating how faith in God can contribute to such distortions and legitimize possessive investments in whiteness, Omri Elisha (2011) shows how white evangelical Christians in Tennessee aim to exercise "compassion" by assisting poor African American residents of Knoxville. These suburban donors are frustrated when recipients do not recompense the gifts of the Holy Spirit by giving up bad habits and sinful lifestyles. Much of the poignancy of Elisha's account derives from his portrayal of how the efforts of suburban evangelicals to practice "compassionate giving" stem from their own critical awareness of "the individuating norms of a commodity-based economy" (2008: 180). In effect, they aspire through their giving to flee the Weberian iron cage, yet they hold recipients to standards of "accountability" whereby, ironically, the poor are supposed to alter their habits so as to abide by those very norms. Donors are particularly troubled by recipients who fail to respond with proper gratitude, since "true compassion is understood as a gift of such extraordinarily evocative power for both giver and recipient that the latter will inevitably experience it as transformative" (171). In the upshot, donors reaffirm rather than interrogate their ideals of "accountability." Yet however distorting its effects, suburban evangelicals' charity represents an effort to gain insight into the operations of "a world that outstrips the one most concretely present."[10] In the terms provided by the world they envision, relations of care and understandings of personal value are supposed to be transfigured through the rupture in time brought about by the gift of salvation.

## Time and God's Care

To understand how believers legitimize or call into question the ways privilege and suffering are distributed, we need to consider in broad terms the various kinds of connections they make between the ethical (which has to do with evaluation) and the vital (which pertains to human flourishing or affliction). To begin exploring these connections, I wish to extend Elisha's argument about believers' understandings of time. A good reason to compare different kinds of Christian insights into the nature of time, care, and value is that those insights engage in multiple and sometimes contradictory ways with what Elizabeth Povinelli (2011) calls the "various forms of eventfulness" that "distribute the texture of enervation and endurance in late liberalism" (133). By "late liberalism," Povinelli refers to the ways that forms of governmentality have configured possibilities of abandonment and belonging in response to anti-colonial, civil rights, and Islamic revival movements. Under conditions of late liberalism, she argues, a certain distribution of "life and death, endurance and exhaustion, and hope and harm … is made ethically and politically sensible and compelling" (132). In particular, late liberal governmentality renders the suffering of the poor ethically sensible in the future perfect tense, as in such statements as "Once they manage to work hard enough, their struggles will have been worth it." This move discounts the present durative time, in which bodies are exhausted. What interests me in Povinelli's account of how suffering becomes ethically intelligible are the linkages she draws between temporality on the one hand and bodily enervation and—implicitly but for my purposes crucially—vitality and care on the other.

The subject of "what time is and what it should be used for" (Bear 2016: 494) has been a major preoccupation for anthropologists studying Christianity, who have made clear how dominant are tropes of rupture with "the past" of the kind discussed by Elisha (see Meyer 1999; Robbins 2004, 2010). They have enriched this point by describing the broad range of insights that believers gain into the nature of eventfulness: the continuities they draw between their own lives and those of biblical personages (Engelke 2004; Harding 2000); their occupancy of an "expansive present" in which they repeatedly relive scriptural narratives (Haynes 2020); their practices of narrating future events proleptically, as though they have already taken place (Coleman 2015); and their understandings of how Jesus has "already" triumphed but "not yet" returned to redeem the world, so that the devil is "still" permitted to kill, steal, and destroy (Bialecki 2017). Recently, scholars have devoted attention as well to how such temporal frameworks operate in ways that make forms of vitality and care ethically sensible.[11]

One such approach to what believers do with time involves the significance of labor. In *The Labor of Faith* (2017), Judith Casselberry describes women's spiritual authority in the Church of Our Lord Jesus Christ of the Apostolic Faith, Inc. (COOLJC), one of the largest African American Pentecostal denominations in the United States. Casselberry draws on scholarship showing how African American women have advanced communal agendas within churches officially headed by men (Abrums 2010; Alexander 2011; Best 2005; Butler 2007; Collier-Thomas 2010; Crumbley 2012; Frederick 2003; Gilkes 2001; Higginbotham 1993; Kostarelos 1995; Lincoln and Mamiya 1990; Sanders 1996), yet she focuses primarily on how "living in holiness is a process that requires religious labor" (21). Casselberry documents the very substantial amount of time that women in the COOLJC commit to working for God, for instance by operating church auxiliaries and winning converts for Jesus by praying with them at altar calls. This labor provides them with an understanding of their own value as persons that does not derive from the capitalist market. In 1912, pioneering African American businesswoman Maggie Lena Walker "queried, 'How many occupations have Negro Women? Let us count them: Negro women are domestic menials, teachers and church builders'" (6). Casselberry remarks: "To my mind, in identifying the church work of Black women as an occupation, Walker places the effort and outcome of women's religious labor in its proper context" (6), namely as caring labor of a kind that has long undergirded the social reproduction of their families and communities. While women intend their work to benefit many people, they are especially committed to recognizing how the labor they dedicate to the church appears from God's perspective. The labor time of working "heartily, as to the Lord" (Col. 3:23) is not an abstract number of hours but is instead materialized in the concrete and aesthetic forms, such as holy dress, by which God works on and through them.

Another approach to the connections between temporality, vitality, and care is taken by Bruno Reinhardt (2018) in his sensitive discussion of "existence-as-waiting" on a Ghanaian prayer mountain. Reinhardt shows how prayer involves "a temporal and pedagogical journey" (133) across a set of chronotopes, including messianic end-times, breakthroughs in the here and now, and preemption of the devil via spiritual counterattack—all of which together constitute "an equipment of endurance" (131). Believers on the prayer mountain, Reinhardt writes, "build their own temporal chemistries to endure, and inhabit [a range of] times at diverse intensities" (133). The key point, which can be readily extended to premillennial varieties of Christian faith in general (Harding 2000; Webster 2013), is that believers regard time as ultimately in God's control rather than their own. As a result, the time in which God works on his people is a trajectory of care. Further, an important way in which God cares for believers is by giving them insight into the patterning of events in time.

Here we return to design. To be a Pentecostal believer is to know that as one exists only as a created being, God and his designs for one's life are not generated by oneself (which is why Reinhardt's "build their own" formulation is perhaps misleading). God has a character and operates according to a time of his own with which believers must come to terms if they are to flourish while enduring their hardships. However, the trajectories of God's care differ in important respects among the churches I describe, as do the ways in which God's care intersects with the trajectories taken by familial, therapeutic, or social welfare varieties of care. To illustrate the former—briefly, and without yet delving into the relevant semantic fields—I devote the remainder of this section to describing two divergent sets of ways in which members of the majority white and African American churches gain insight into God's designs.

At the conclusion of most services at the suburban church of Eternal Hope, believers come to pray at the altar, a raised platform running across the front of the worship space, while soothing music is played on keyboard, brass, and percussion. Impromptu groups congregate to "intercede" for these people by laying hands on them, whispering encouragement, and speaking in tongues.[12] Men usually lay hands on men, women on women. Intercession powerfully expresses the sentiment "WE CARE"—words printed in large capitals as a heading on one of the church's publicity fliers. This is a time and place set apart for recognizing one's own and others' vulnerabilities, weaknesses, and needs for guidance. During intercession, the spirit of God inhabits the bodies of believers in ways that reconfigure their relations to the divine. Touching and hearing, in both literal and figurative senses, build up their vitality. "I have very low faith when it comes to praying for myself, but I have a lot of faith when praying for others," explained a young woman named Kathy in an interview. "Something really powerful happens when I lay hands on them. I don't want to be namby-pamby about it [i.e., merely go through the motions of praying]. I want to really be, like, a human antenna, increasing the faith, really getting hold of God for this person, really turn their situation around." In grasping God and acting as an antenna, Kathy's body becomes an extension, a prosthesis of the divine. Likewise, Arlene told me, "The power of touch is—powerful. If we have the spirit of God in us, we are a vessel of God working through us." Kathy figured herself as a vicarious speaker: "We're like an oracle of the Holy Spirit, somebody who is used by God" to speak words of comfort during intercession. This ability to become permeable to God is available not only to ritual experts but to anyone who has been born again. They draw explicit contrasts in this respect to the practices of Catholics, who Arlene argued "pray to the saints, bypassing God."

Intercession is a time when God gives believers insight into the ways he inhabits their bodies, into their own and others' affective states, and into their embodied connections to the recipients of prayer. Soon after her own conversion from Catholicism, Arlene recalled, she had an early occasion to intercede for someone in a Pentecostal church:

> A girl, ten years younger than me, was going to have a child out of wedlock. She was sad, it wasn't the greatest situation. I could feel that draw to her, felt it in my chest, the Spirit of God moved on me, and I wept and wept and wept. And then when service was done, an older woman came up to me and said, "You were feeling the emotion of it, you felt sad for her." Sadness drew me to her, but when I was praying I knew it was more than that. I've learned since that it was more than my sadness, I've come to understand that it was the Spirit of God using me. I was touched in my emotions, and I went to pray, but it was God praying through me.

Arlene linked her proclivity toward vicarious suffering to her Catholic upbringing, which led her during her youth to "pray for the dead in the cemetery. It would move on my heart to see all the flags on the graves, I would pray for the dead people who had made a sacrifice." The insight that God provided Arlene through this intercession event, though, entailed a shift in her understanding of motivation. She might have been drawn to pray by what she called her "emotion" of sadness about another woman's suffering, but she subsequently realized that the spirit of God was operating through her. Specifically, by "praying through" and "mov[ing] on" Arlene—again using her body as a prosthesis—God was loving the recipient of her prayer in a manner that Arlene in-and-of herself could not. As these believers gain insight into what is transpiring during intercession, they come to know what it is to love and be comforted by God, which is for them a key moral ambition. At a revival held for members of Eternal Hope's denomination, a preacher asked the audience, "How many of you enjoy receiving negative criticism?" No one raised a hand, nor was anyone expected to do so; the preacher's message was that God does not provide any such.

Members of the African American congregations of Victory Gospel and Heaven's Tabernacle have their own approaches to touching, hearing, and what they call "emotions" that I describe later on. Some differences stem from the fact that whereas charisma and authority are dispersed throughout the congregation of Eternal Hope during intercession, in the African American churches they are consistently concentrated in the persons of Pastor John and Pastor Hadley, who together with subordinate ministers and some musicians are known as "leaders" (on concentrated and dispersed charisma, see P. Werbner and R. Werbner, forthcoming). As is the case in Eternal Hope as well, knowledge about the content and significance of God's message for his people is not equally distributed. Pastors possess authority in their sermons to elaborate God's *logos* word written in the Bible into an inspired *rhema* word that addresses believers' specific circumstances. Pastor John and Pastor Hadley elicit participation from their congregations in accordance with the special insight God gives them into what their audiences need to hear, whereas only other leaders are expected to be able to discern what pastors need from God and "cover" them in prayer. When members of the African American churches speak of "intercessory prayer," they usually refer to interventions by leaders whose expertise in discernment lends power to their sympathetic words and acts, including fasting and "laying out" in intense supplication on others' behalf. By contrast, intercession as practiced in Eternal Hope is an occasion when charismatic responsiveness to the needs of others is exceptionally dispersed.

For now, though, I wish to carry forward the theme of time and vitality in relation to God's care. Members of Heaven's Tabernacle and Victory Gospel are often keenly aware of the disjunctures between the rhythms of what they call "God's time" and the time over which their own actions and intentions unfold.[13] As was the case when God told Pastor Hadley that "you never get it back the way you planted it," when God talks back (Luhrmann 2012) to these believers he often really *talks back*, reminding them sharply of what they have said and done. For them, being willing to receive what they call "correction" from God is key to developing a sense of how he cares for them as they "go through" difficulties. As in mainstream North American usage, when these believers say that a person is "going through" something, they mean that he or she is having severe problems. Yet they maintain that "after you have suffered, after you go through, then you will be established" in your faith in God, and they encourage each other to specify how God has helped them to "go through" trouble successfully. They commonly speak in these terms about encounters with the social welfare and criminal justice systems, which together with the exigencies of rent and debt impose punitive temporal frameworks on the racialized poor. Testimonies abound of the miraculous ways in which God supersedes "the world's system," for instance by supplying those who have faithfully rendered tithes with ways to pay off bills at the last minute. By means of such retemporalizing moves, afflictions are cast as tests of moral fortitude. Importantly, though, believers say that they often misconstrue and consequently fail these tests. "The reason that you're going through," Pastor John commonly preaches, "is that you keep falling for the same tricks of the devil, and it's like a revolving door—the same things are coming up on you over and over again."

As I hinted earlier, such messages resonate with the blues. Jon Michael Spencer (1989) argues that African American blues musicians of the early twentieth century were skeptical of Christian preachers' adage "no cross, no crown," which expressed certainty about eternal rewards for present-day afflictions. Notwithstanding their oppositions, preachers and blues players shared common concerns about how to account for suffering. In particular, blues performers drew on the biblical passage "whatsoever a man soweth, that shall he also reap" (Gal. 6:7) in order to explain their misfortunes "as resulting essentially from the very sins the church accuse[d] them of: drinking, gambling, and in general living a life of reckless abandon" (26). Spencer describes this sensibility as a "theodicy," which I find an unfortunate distortion in that blues players were reflecting on why their sufferings were justified, not on how God can be justified. Still, the mutual shaping of blues and Christian imagery is clear. In "Dirty Deal Blues," recorded in 1935,

> Robert Wilkins (who later became a preacher) identifies the "reap" theodicy as a universal law inherent to God's creation:
>
> > Oh baby I'm so glad that this whole round world do know
> >
> > That every living creature reap just what they sow.[14]
>
> Tommy Johnson, in "Bye-Bye Blues," [recorded in 1928] confidently exhorts that those who do not reap what they sow at present will eventually pay the price for their transgressions:
>
> > Says Good Book tell you reap just what you sow
> >
> > Going to reap it now or baby reap it by-and-by.[15] (27)

...

> Perhaps the most riveting statement of the "reap" theodicy is found in the last
> verse of Bertha Henderson's "Lead Hearted Blues," [recorded in 1927–8] where
> she hints that having the blues is itself a "reaping":
>
> Lord, Lord, can't rest no place I go
>
> Blues is driving me crazy, must be reaping what I sow.[16] (29)

These blues musicians present "you reap what you sow" as a vital (both important and life-giving) insight that renders critical clues to present circumstances and future likelihoods. Kelly Brown Douglas (2012) points out that the blues are a kind of playful "signifyin' knowledge" (Gates 1988) imbued with coded meanings. A song about the trauma of a bad relationship can also be "a poignant commentary concerning the inherent difficulty of maintaining black relationships in a world hostile to black life" (Douglas 2012: 15). Such knowledge is "profoundly wise as it provides valuable insight into a given situation or predicament. ... Moreover, because it does not pretend to be objective or universal, signifyin' provides a passionate analysis of any given black condition" (13).[17] In Mattingly's terms, the blues provide "vantage points on familiar or prior ways of seeing, acting, [and] believing that are actively brought into question" (2014a: 15).

For all the Pentecostal believers I am discussing, recognizing God's care depends on gaining insight into forms of enervation or moral peril. However, *they are doing different things with time*, and consequently (as Povinelli would lead us to expect) with expressions of vitality. In speaking about why they are "going through," members of the African American churches attach ethical significance, as did blues players, to discerning the rhythms in which afflictions and (for them) miracles unfold. As Mother Smith, the church mother at Victory Gospel,[18] often comments during Sunday school, "You always reap what you sow. It's a spiritual law that can never and will never be broken." By contrast, members of the majority white church give ethical weight to the specific occasions, ritual or otherwise, when the self is exposed before God, calling forth expressions of sympathy, vicarious suffering, or joyful praise that enhance their ongoing relationship with Jesus and their understanding of his purposes for their lives. These instances of exposure and intimacy arguably represent counterpoints to the empty time that Arlene conjured with her image of an endless road—they are, as it were, landmarks on the journey of faith. Men in Eternal Hope told me that the nearest secular equivalent to "getting the Holy Ghost" is a sporting event. You can cheer for a great play at a game, they said, but five minutes later you will have lost the excitement. Getting the Holy Ghost, by contrast, gives you an emotional boost that will last the entire week.[19]

While members of Eternal Hope frequently relate how God has helped them "go through" difficulties, they are less inclined than members of the African American churches to speak of "going through" as intrinsic to God's designs for their lives. They are much less disposed to attribute suffering to the divergence of their own actions from God's timing, so that I rarely heard them use metaphors of sowing and reaping to account for their misfortunes. Rather, they speak of "going through" as an unavoidable aspect of existence that they endure with the help of God and one another. "Even though you know you have to go through whatever you're dealing with," a middle-aged woman named Lynne at Eternal Hope explained to me, "like marital problems, or a child on drugs like I did, you've got to trust the Holy Ghost, and He will give you the wisdom, knowledge, strength, and courage to get through it." Members of Eternal Hope often narrate such difficulties as preludes to revelatory moments when they have come to appreciate Jesus' love all the more, so that they may serve as witnesses and intercessors. Kathy remarked, "We get trials—but as long as we hold onto God we're made into better people through those trials, and we become more and more like Jesus with everything we go through if our heart's right and we're trying to do the right thing."

These different connotations of "going through" signal some important distinctions concerning the significance of belief. All of these church members refer to themselves as "believers," and I employ the term as an identifier for the sake of simplicity. Yet as many scholars have pointed out (e.g., Premawardhana 2018), such a move runs the risk of reifying Christians and Christianity, foreclosing analysis of the broader relations in which people who call themselves Christians are engaged. In reference to African American Christian traditions, Sascha Goluboff (2011) points out that scholarly narratives of conversion as a rupture with "the past" do not adequately reflect the common trajectory of being raised with exposure to church, falling away, and subsequently returning (see also Nelson 2005: 78–80). A trope that does readily convey such experiences, however, is the necessity to have "gone through" in order to have faith. Even as ministers and teachers in Victory Gospel and Heaven's Tabernacle encourage their congregations to "be in the world but not of it," they model the content of belief by speaking during church services of how they used to act when they were "in the world." For example:

I was never a punk [a coward] when I was in the streets, so do you think I'm going to be a punk now that I'm walking with God?

I used to teach my daughters how to manipulate people in the streets and how to dress to get what they wanted, but now I'm teaching people how to go through [i.e., how to trust God to provide].

I used to be a great soldier for the devil, so do you think he'd let me live if I backslid out from under God's covering? No, he'd take me right out [i.e., kill me, as would gang members under analogous circumstances].

In a sense, such statements reverse the tropes of the blues. Rather than using Christian language to account for experiences "in the world," they deploy the language of "the world" not only to encourage but to conceptualize Christian commitment. They come close to suggesting that you need to have been a sinner in order to be a saint.

In Eternal Hope, by contrast, trajectories of prior falling away are not presented as intrinsic to faith. Eternal Hope members speak of how the process of "going through" trouble renders their relationships with God and other people relatively close or distant, so that the significance of belief hinges on understandings of intimacy. Kathy's father Benny, who has been attending Eternal Hope for thirty years, spoke of group worship as an intimate act not of "going" but of "bringing through": "With God, you're helping people, you're helping yourself, you're bringing people through things. You see someone on the street, and you can bring God into their life. You can see him go from homeless, to a shelter, to an apartment, to getting a job and turning his whole life around." Combining the two metaphors, Pastor Hadley often comments: "There's nothing you've gone through that He hasn't brought you through." Unlike Benny, though, she also says, "Either you're going through now, you're about to go through, or you've just come out of something"—a bracing counterpoint to the maxim "Trouble don't last always."

## Discernment as a Form of Vitality

In deploying these metaphors of "going through" and "bringing through," believers configure their sense of their being over time. Even as these expressions refer to suffering, then, they signify certain kinds of vitality. My core argument in this book is that Pentecostal insights render particular forms of vitality ethically and politically sensible. Again, such forms of vitality are liable to transcend as well as to incorporate ableness, health, or well-being. A common saying in Victory Gospel and Heaven's Tabernacle is that "the olive has to be squeezed before it releases the oil" or "the anointing." The term "anointing" refers to inspired words and to the pattern of their transmission from God to his prophets and from senior prophets to more junior ones, while the image of "squeezing" connotes "going through" troubles. Mother Smith described vitality in similar terms to the congregation of Victory Gospel: "Jesus modeled *the life of God* [my emphasis] for the rest of us. He says to us: 'I was born, I was under the authority of My parents, I had people coming against Me and killing Me, and now you go through that so you can show people in the world that they don't have to lie, steal, and kill.' "[20] While Eternal Hope members likewise identify divinely inspired words as "anointed," I did not hear them speak of anointing as contingent upon prior "squeezing."

For members of the urban churches in particular, then, vitality involves a set of intersections and tensions between "life more abundantly" and "going through." That God has designed "going through" as both a form of vitality and a precondition for salvation is a prominent and I think distinctive theme in African American Pentecostal communities (though of course the degree of prominence varies).[21] While this is not the case in the suburban church of Eternal Hope, understanding God's designs for vitality requires discernment there as well, especially in practices of intercession. Yet to reframe the initial question of why it is important to receive insights from God, why should it be necessary to grasp such designs in order to have "a relationship with God," or to envision how one's conduct appears in God's eyes? Here it is crucial to bear in mind a key connection between the ethical and the vital, namely that *God has designed discernment to be not only a source but a form of vitality*. In other words, to discern God's activity in the world does not mean merely to acknowledge the presence of God or even, at base, to have a communicative relationship with the deity. Rather, it is to know and abide by God's designs for being alive, ultimately past death.

In all the churches I am discussing, critical practices of discernment are key to salvation, in that the Holy Spirit "convicts" new converts, compelling them to understand that they are sinners who need to be saved. Thus, the devil is presented not only as a destroyer but even more fundamentally as a deceiver (see Nelson 2005: 107–10). To carry out his destructive plans, the devil instills doubt in humans about God's word and presence, paradigmatically by asking Eve, "Did God really say, 'You must not eat from any tree in the garden'?" (Gen. 3:1 NIV). The devil's design is to keep people ignorant of God and isolated from believers, making them feel (in the words of Pastor John and

Pastor Hadley) first "oppressed" then "depressed" and finally causing them to be "possessed" by an evil spirit.

While the devil's deceptions are experienced corporeally, the same is true of the kinds of discernment that God affords. Discernment has a transfiguring effect upon the person by virtue of the "indwelling" power of the Holy Spirit. "If you're saved," Pastor Hadley often remarks to her congregation, "people should say there's something different about you." Having a relationship with God means that you know that God has a plan and purpose for your life, and that you need to "repent on a daily" for your "sins of omission and commission." Such knowledge should so transform your demeanor that you will show "the fruits of the Spirit" (Gal. 5:22–23) in your appearance and actions. Pastor Hadley compares getting to know God to inviting him into one's house, which is a metaphor for the body and personality: "The Holy Ghost is a gentleman. He's not going to go anywhere He's not invited, but anywhere He goes He cleans. If you only invite Him into your living room, He won't enter your kitchen or your bedroom, and it will stay dirty in there." Likewise for former Catholics in Eternal Hope, the process of becoming saints provides new kinds of bodily access to divine presence, including the ability to act as "oracles" of his word. As I discuss in Chapters 3 and 4, God's presence fosters expressions of intimacy and openness that lead them to understand the sources of their vitality in novel ways, for instance by providing alternative grounds for kinship. Further, members of Eternal Hope devote great emotional and physical energy to bringing other people through their troubles, so that their prayers constitute a form of corporeal labor that they feel is unrecognized and devalued by secular elites.

In other words, discernment itself is a kind of flourishing, a fact that helps to account for the repeated insistence during services that *we know* Jesus is a healer, *we know* God is provider, and *we know* no weapon formed against us shall prosper. When the saints of Heaven's Tabernacle sing, "Let all the other names fade away, / Till there's only You,"[22] Pastor Hadley makes clear that the "other names" are medical diagnoses, anxiety, weariness, and grief—all of which the devil uses to try to make believers forget that "God knows your name, because it's written in the Lamb's book of life." As a form of vitality, discernment thus counteracts oppression. Yet by the same token, because discernment is not self-generated but rather an aspect of the indwelling of the Holy Ghost, failure to demonstrate awareness of God's activity may render believers vulnerable to demonic attack. This concern is made explicit in the African American churches, in keeping with their emphasis on "tests" that might not be passed. For example, if members of Pastor Hadley's congregation do not show proper attention or enthusiasm while she is praying for a person's healing, she may admonish them that "something might come up" on them as a result, so that they would have to "go through." Consistently, then, God both provides and enjoins insight into possibilities for vitality.

In short, Pentecostal believers need to exercise discernment because their insights play an important part in bringing God's designs to fruition. Even so, they insist that those designs operate in ways ultimately not under human control. As Glenn Hinson (2000) has eloquently described in regard to African American churches, while believers must "set the atmosphere" by praying aloud at the beginning of a service in order to receive the word God will use to transform their hearts, it is God who calls the preacher to deliver the divine word, and God who drives the motion of the service to suit his own purposes. During ritual time, participants must come to terms with the ways the Spirit may override human intention. I have had to do so as well. Both during my time in Pentecostal churches in Buffalo and during my previous fieldwork in Botswana, I have experienced numerous charisms for which my agnostic Jewish upbringing did not prepare me. In the Pentecostal churches, I am routinely "slain in the Spirit" (that is, I fall to the ground as a pastor lays hands on me) and have sometimes been so forcefully caused to dance by the Spirit that I am unable to stop. Although I cannot say that I realize my truest self through encounters with God, or that I allow God to organize my sense of time—circumstances that certainly do set me apart from these believers—the exteriority of the Spirit is as real to me at this point as that of any other aspect of my experience.

I have decided to write intermittently here about my engagements with God notwithstanding the obvious risks (for one, I don't want this book to be about myself) because they have provided important grounds for my involvement with believers. Historian Ann Taves (1999) has shown that "experiencing religion" and "explaining experience" were intertwined endeavors from the time of John Wesley (1703–1791) to that of William James (1842–1910). As Robert Orsi (2016) points out, the academic (non-theological) study of religion has since been largely devoted to separating the two, with some important exceptions (e.g., Hinson 2000; Turner 1992). Yet Orsi argues that there is no reason not to try to experience and explain alongside believers what transcendent beings, whom he calls "gods," have designed as historical actors. To do so is to ask what the pragmatic and ethical implications might be of the efforts believers make to engage with godly designs.

## "Taking Correction": Ethnographic and Religious Knowledge and Authority

A similar question may be posed about the ethnographer's engagements. If as Pastor Hadley says, "God is the friend who doesn't tell your business," what does that make me? One source of the complex tensions between my ethnographic "revelation of concealed realities" (Jones 2014: 53) and believers' efforts to generate religious insight is that the latter often entail specifying areas of necessary ignorance. As Mother Smith commented during a session of Sunday school, "God will put someone on your heart for prayer but might not tell you what that person's situation is, because you're not ready for that kind of knowledge. You might go running around telling everyone in the church about it." In other words, insight into other people's circumstances is problematized in religious terms, especially when those people occupy precarious positions that make them vulnerable to what others say and write about them.

This is less the case for members of the suburban church of Eternal Hope, a circumstance that rendered the terms of my engagements there comparatively straightforward. I attended services at Eternal Hope and recorded a series of wide-ranging life history interviews with individual members over a period of about a year and a half from 2012 to 2014, and have kept in touch since with Kathy, my principal contact.[23] In response to their questions about why I was interested in speaking to them about their faith, I told them of my previous work in Apostolic Christian churches in Botswana (Klaits 2010), about which they expressed frank curiosity. My recollections of the relationships I established there helped to reassure them that I did not intend to disparage their faith. (This is a greater concern for believers in the Buffalo area white community, where Pentecostalism is not mainstream, than it is in the African American community where it is much more so.) Having made initial introductions through Kathy, a friend of one of my students, I was invited by her parents Benny, a postal worker, and Janet, a homemaker, to study the Bible at their home. Church members embraced the opportunity to combine ethnographic interviewing with witnessing about their knowledge of God, and I was receptive to their efforts. In particular, the three hour-long conversations I had with Arlene gave me a wish to be baptized. Generally suspicious of secular liberal arts education and the class biases of many bourgeois academics like myself, believers were overjoyed when I emerged from the water shouting and convulsing so powerfully that the baptizer almost dropped me back in the pool.

All the same, I was set apart by my ethnographic enterprise, by various signals of class standing and political outlook, and most conspicuously by the absence of my own family, about whom members of all these churches continually inquired. My wife Laura, a committed rationalist, quite understandably had her fill of Christianity during our time together in Botswana and did not wish to become involved in the churches in Buffalo. This was especially problematic from the perspective of Eternal Hope members, who hope for the salvation of as many of their kin as possible, though less so in the eyes of African American saints who often regard their prayers as extending protection to unbelieving kin. Members of Eternal Hope expressed concerns that I was "unequally yoked" in my marriage, a circumstance that for many of them has contributed to divorce.

One reason Eternal Hope members find it important to ensure the salvation of their families involves the intimacies of Pentecostal kinship. "What would heaven be like without my family?" a minister asked, referring both to his kin and his nonbiologically related church family. The promise of spending eternity in heaven with their families is a powerful vision for these believers, who worry that their nonbelieving kin will be damned (and, as this preacher suggested, that their own joy in heaven would be diminished in consequence). As Janet said to me, "It will be that much better to be in heaven with all the people we've struggled with! It will be more jubilant rejoicing in heaven to be with all the people we rejoiced with. We held each other's hands up when we were tired, we prayed for them, we visited each other in the hospital." While most adult members of Eternal Hope were not raised in the faith, the married couple who began the ministry were. During the period of my involvement, the founding bishop was in declining health and no longer led services, but his wife had a prominent organizational role both within the church and within its denominational network. Underscoring the ancestral depth and multiracial heritage of the Pentecostal movement in the United States—and hinting at the existence of a Pentecostal elite—she told me proudly that her own parents had been baptized by no less prominent an African American minister than G. T. Haywood, the presiding bishop of the PAW who endured its schism when white southerners separated in 1924 (see MacRobert 1988).

Many messages in Eternal Hope convey that God desires gender complementarity rather than equality. For example, women do not usually preach and cannot serve as pastors in its denomination. On the other hand, many women who attend Eternal Hope have independent careers, a circumstance that likely tends to mitigate the kinds of male microaggressions that Elaine Lawless (1988) encountered in a Pentecostal church in rural Indiana. They play important roles as church administrators, musicians, choir leaders, and teachers, and some occupy prominent positions within Pentecostal genealogies. For instance, Pastor Charles, the current leader of Eternal Hope, was raised Catholic but arrived at his ministerial position after marrying the founding couple's daughter. Unfortunately, I was not able to establish a close relationship with Pastor Charles, whose many duties allowed him time for only one formal interview with me.

While in the process of concluding my work at Eternal Hope, I carried out a series of interviews together with Shay-Akil (formerly Shenita) McLean, my research assistant at the time, with African American residents on the East Side of Buffalo about caring for kin who are ill or disabled. These interviews, which did not focus on religion, provided points of initial entry into Victory Gospel and Heaven's Tabernacle, where McLean and I carried out a phase of the project focused on tithing in Black churches (Klaits and McLean 2015).[24] It was at this point that my activities started to become something of a burden, I'm afraid, to Pastor John in particular. Issues of practical and representational power have lain closer to the surface of my relationship with him than they have with most others. After attending services at Victory Gospel for several months and rendering tithes as was expected of me, I asked Pastor John's permission to carry out interviews with individual members, who would receive gift cards to supermarkets as thanks for their participation. He expressed concern about my plans, telling me that I was asking to be placed in a "position of confidence" with the saints. I did not understand this phrase at the time. Much later, I realized that in Pastor John's view, I was asking to be given authority of a kind that would entitle me to make sensitive inquiries. He himself occupies such a position in relation to the saints of Victory Gospel, and he has spiritual mentors who have comparable authority over him. At one point, Pastor John explained the nature of this relationship to a group of members whom he was training for leadership positions:

> Part of having character is being accountable to leadership. You don't belong in your career if you can't be accountable. I'm totally submitted to my apostle, my Bishop [who is based in another US state]. My Bishop knows everything about me, good, bad, and ugly. It's my duty to make sure that I submit myself, and that I'm accountable. Bishop X knows me, not just superficially. In order to grow, you have to reveal. If you believe that God is in control, what do you have to lose by being open and honest [with your leader]? How can you get wisdom if you can't be open? I'm talking about things deep down in your heart that you should be getting wisdom on, but you're afraid because you don't want anyone to know

what you're up to. Bishop X is not just anyone, I'm accountable to him. If he breaks that oath [of secrecy], God have mercy on him.

From this point of view, my own request to be allowed to ask the saints to be "open and honest" with me so that I could retail their secrets to the world must have appeared the very height of intrusiveness. Nonetheless, Pastor John gave me permission to solicit and conduct individual interviews. As a result of these interviews, I established a long-term acquaintance with a young woman called Christine whose circumstances I describe in Chapters 2 and 4.

As Simon Coleman and John Dulin (2020) note, "*ongoing* decisions over what and how much to reveal/conceal are at the beating heart of everyday ethical constructions of both morally charged situations and moral selves" (10). A turning point in my relationship with Pastor John occurred several months after I began the interviews, when I made the mistake of asking his wife, the First Lady of the church, whether she would be willing to divulge how much money she earned. She said no, and I found out from a third party that I had offended Pastor John. I sat down with Pastor John and spoke as follows:

> Let me tell you a story. As you know, when I lived in Botswana I had a spiritual mother.[25] One day early in my time there, I was in her neighborhood but was on my way to visit someone else. I passed by her yard and waved to the people sitting in front of the house, and continued on.
>
> Pastor John nodded, but I shook my head.
>
> The next day when I went to see her, she scolded me very sharply. She told me, "You do *not* walk by your mother's yard without coming inside the house to greet her!" I felt bad about what I'd done, but soon I realized that I had actually been given a great honor: She loved me enough to rebuke me to my face. I hope that you and I can get to the point that when I make mistakes, you'll tell me straight out

—as has in fact happened several times since. Pastor John replied, "Well, it would have been more appropriate to ask *me* how much money we make." I said, "I know, and I'm sorry." He told me, and we left it at that.

The reason I recount this exchange here is that a few days later, Pastor John repeated our conversation to the entire congregation of Victory Gospel, without mentioning the particulars of my offense against himself and First Lady. "Now I understand that Brother Fred can take correction," he remarked, and went on to tell the saints of the importance of being willing to "take correction" from their leader, stressing that some of them have a hard time doing so. This was one of the steps Pastor John has taken to legitimize my presence and my activities in the eyes of the saints. (Once during a Sunday service, Pastor John put his hand on my shoulder and called out, "What I like about this brother is that he refuses to be intimidated. People might say, 'What's this white guy doing in a Black church?' but he's still here." Indeed, I continued to be involved in both his and Pastor Hadley's congregations through 2019, and kept in touch over the phone while preparing this book during the state-mandated church closures caused by the Covid-19 pandemic in 2020.) In effect, Pastor John was telling the congregation that in "taking correction" I was willing to "submit myself" to his authority. Of course, this was only very partially the case: a truly "submitted" person would not compose an ethnographic text but a religious one instead.

In an effort to acquaint Pastor John with the kind of knowledge I was trying to generate and show him how it might circulate, I invited him to attend a panel at a meeting of the American Anthropological Association in 2016 where I presented a paper about his church.[26] Afterward, I asked him whether he considered the endeavor of anthropology to be worthwhile. In reply, he compared me to one of the Magi: "The Magi were not people of God, they were stargazers. These were not Bible scholars. But they found the Savior. I believe there were other Magi in the land, but these particular Magi recognized and knew what had happened." In one sense he was giving me a gracious compliment, yet in another he was suggesting that while I might have the representational power of a certain version of anthropology on my side—since I am an academic insider if ever there was one (cf. Harrison 2008)—he had God's on his own.

On a practical level, shortly after the above incident with First Lady I confined myself at Victory Gospel largely to participating in services, where I was welcome to take notes and make audio recordings. Around this time, I began working at Heaven's Tabernacle as well. After a few informal visits, Pastor Hadley gave me permission to announce that I was conducting a research project, but after carrying out a few interviews I concentrated on taking part in services and Bible studies. Much later, I obtained both pastors' permission to carry out individual interviews focused on "God's timing," a concern prominent in both congregations. I have informed Pastor John and Pastor Hadley of my involvement in the other's church, but we do not talk much about this. It is transgressive in the African American community to "church hop" because ministries implicitly compete with one another over members and resources, and also because one might be exposed to negative spiritual influences outside one's "church home."

Whereas much of Pastor John's preaching is geared to buttressing patriarchal authority in the face of state-led assaults on Black men, Pastor Hadley focuses her attention largely on relations among women, or on the ways women relate to one another through men. She is less concerned than Pastor John with establishing bounds of "confidence" among members of Heaven's Tabernacle. Yet she too insists on the importance of "submitting" to authority in carrying out assigned duties, since the source of "elevation" to more prominent roles consists of "obedience" to people whom "God has placed over your life." Spiritual authority of this kind may operate outside the boundaries of a congregation. Several women unaffiliated with Heaven's Tabernacle have over the years asked Pastor Hadley to become their "spiritual mom" so that she would provide them guidance. She told me that she has been "overwhelmed" by such requests: "You just never know who's looking at you close enough to be a part of their life. To govern it, you know to govern it? And help them. Because that's a very significant part—it's very serious. I don't take it lightly." Pastor Hadley's spiritual network is very wide-ranging, spanning women residing in multiple US states including other pastors who often provide material as well as emotional support to one another. Connections among praying women may take other genealogical forms as well. Pastor Hadley told her congregation that the "anointing" in her family to preach came from her mother's mother's mother, that she gave her life to the Lord on the encouragement of an aunt, and that as a leader of a women's prayer group she was under the supervision of a godmother who supplied guidance and discernment.[27] In addition, Pastor Hadley's daughter Cheryl receives many prophetic insights in visions and dreams that she frequently shares with the congregation.

Pastor Hadley described to me how her own "elevation" from Evangelist or prayer group leader to the office of Pastor occurred through an encounter with Apostle Cooper, a male pastor based in another US city who currently serves as her Overseer, a relationship that helps to legitimize her as a female pastor in the eyes of some men.[28] The tie between Pastor Hadley and Apostle Cooper developed through insights shared among women. She met Apostle Cooper after inviting him on her godmother's advice to fill in at a revival for another pastor. At this revival, Pastor Hadley recalled in a conversation with me, Apostle Cooper remarked that he had been "mandated" to attend, thereby signaling that God had a special purpose in sending him there. A short time later, the women's prayer group was traveling to another revival. Pastor Hadley remembered that

I had a car full of women following me, and the Lord talked to me and told me to come from up under my godmother. As I'm thinking it, He's speaking to me about it. My daughter was in the car behind me, she called me, she said, "Mom, the Lord said come up under [your godmother] and go up under Apostle Cooper."

This was an instance of "confirmation," whereby God communicates to a believer about a matter that was already in her awareness. At a subsequent revival, Apostle Cooper asked, "Who is the leader of these women?" Pastor Hadley recalled, "I felt that when I took a step forward to the Apostle, that I would be accepting a pastorial role."

While Pastor Hadley's congregation was almost entirely female during most of the time I spent with them, she wishes to minister to men as well as women and was happy to have me participating as "a cube of sugar in the middle of the hot chocolate," as she put it to the group. She asked me to take turns leading weekly evening Bible study sessions, which she frames as "practical lessons for practical living." I learned a great deal from struggling to imitate (with very limited success) the ways Pastor Hadley brings the scripture to bear on the experiences of the saints, and from their own generous efforts to help me along in my role as an instructor. In Victory Gospel as well, Pastor John and ministers who serve under his leadership take Bible study sessions as opportunities to apply scripture to everyday situations, though there is somewhat less interplay between instructor and audience. Pastor John often concludes Bible studies in a prophetic vein, receiving words and visions from the Holy Ghost about the situations of people in attendance or others whom they may know. He announces these communications, which are addressed to individuals, to the group at large as they remain in their seats, or alternatively asks the saints to line up in front of him as he speaks to each in turn, causing them to fall in the Spirit as he subsequently lays hands on them.

All of these believers' methods of generating knowledge and authority are premised on their ability to recognize the voice of God, who is the ultimate source of guidance and vitality. In the African American churches, more attention is paid than in Eternal Hope to learning to recognize and counter the voice of the devil as well. Pastor John tells the saints that they should learn to distinguish four internal voices: their thoughts, the voice of their bodies communicating that they are hungry or tired, God's voice, and the devil's voice. Pastor Hadley often speaks of the activities of imps whose task is to prevent the word of God from coming forth or being heard: they cause her to feel sick the night before she is to preach, and they tell saints to make excuses to avoid coming to church. This emphasis is in keeping with an important difference between the orientations of Eternal Hope and the two African American churches, namely that the latter are "deliverance ministries" in which pastors cast out demons from the bodies of sufferers while Eternal Hope is not. Curious about how a majority white deliverance ministry might be compared with Heaven's Tabernacle or Victory Gospel, I visited such a congregation informally but was unable to carry out research there. To address this inconsistency, in Chapter 3 I compare the designs for communication and care that underlie Pastor John's and Pastor Hadley's deliverance practices to those described in Frank and Ida Mae Hammond's influential exorcism manual *Pigs in the Parlor* (2010).

I wish to conclude this discussion of how knowledge is authorized with a few words about privacy. In addition to changing the names of research participants and their churches, I have deliberately obscured certain biographical and institutional particulars that, however important in their own right, would in my judgment compromise participants' privacy if divulged. Privacy is especially important given that some have entrusted me with knowledge of their past involvement in illegal activities. In the course of writing, I have read or shown potentially sensitive passages to relevant parties and obtained their permission to publish. Accordingly, I ask all readers who are in a position to identify the people or institutions mentioned in this book to refrain from doing so in any public forum.

## A Look Ahead

Insights from God shape trajectories of care by fostering believers' critical insights into designs for vitality, a theme I trace over the remainder of the book. In Chapter 2, I consider how insights spring from activities occurring within particular places in Buffalo and its suburbs, and I describe the designs for racial segregation that have exerted powerful influence over residents' life chances. In each of the churches I discuss, the moral and physical perils of "the world" are counteracted in the main worship area known as the sanctuary, a place of holiness where believers ideally find protection and reassurance. Chapter 3 turns to the kinds of communications among bodies and spirits that occur within the sanctuary and elsewhere. I explore the complex idioms believers use to elicit or repudiate certain kinds of spiritual and intercorporeal connections. While believers at Eternal Hope promote imageries of openness to God that help them strike balances between autonomy and dependence, members of the African American churches rely to a greater extent on forms of enclosure that elicit divine care and protection. As believers reflect on how varieties of enclosure and openness have shaped lived relations of care, they remake kinship ties by applying God's designs for communication and connection to them.

In Chapter 4, I build on this treatment of kinship by exploring how the meanings that believers attach to their dependence on God shape their sense of how and whether to depend on other people. Here my treatment of vitality centers on understandings of personal capacity, which are key to the different kinds of critical stances these believers take in regard to practices of giving and asking. In asking God for assistance, Eternal Hope members find it crucial to admit their lack of individual self-sufficiency, while those in the urban churches are more concerned with identifying ways of getting by that are not contrary to God's will. Chapter 5 considers linkages between vitality and time, focusing on how believers make efforts to "seek confirmation" about the significance of events by listening for the word of God in music, preaching, and daily conversations. As they "seek confirmation," believers come to inhabit time in ways that direct their critical attention to what they perceive as vital elements within themselves. Specifically, suburban church members articulate ambitions to ensure peace of mind in the midst of difficulties, while those in the urban churches reflect on how they use or misuse their creative powers to shape their circumstances. In the conclusion, I draw together these themes by considering some analytical and political implications of the divergent ways these believers articulate the place of suffering in God's designs.

Finally, in order to dispel any illusion that mine is the final word on these subjects, I have invited a current and a former student, LaShekia Chatman and Michael Richbart respectively, to offer commentaries on the text in an Appendix, which also contains transcriptions of conversations between myself and each of them.

# Being in the World but Not of It in Buffalo: Insights Derived from Places

Speaking to the congregation at Victory Gospel about the main worship space known as the sanctuary, Pastor John often remarks "You are safe here" from dangers faced outside. "If the devil dares to come" into the sanctuary, Pastor Hadley often says at Heaven's Tabernacle, "he will be exposed and dealt with." Inhabiting the space of the sanctuary makes Pastor Hadley particularly sensitive to the presence of both the Holy Ghost and demonic spirits. There have been occasions, she recalls, when God has revealed to her the presence of evil forces within the sanctuary by causing pain in particular parts of her body. One of her mentors, another female pastor, taught her that a headache signals the presence of a spirit of witchcraft, while a pain in the back shows that "the enemy is fighting the backbone of the church," namely pastors or other leaders.

In all the Pentecostal churches I am considering, the sanctuary is the site of greatest protection and holiness. For most of the period when I worked at Heaven's Tabernacle, the sanctuary consisted of the first floor of a house in poor repair owned by a retired pastor, now deceased, who lived upstairs. Opening directly onto the street, the first level of the house had been converted into a worship space by the removal of all the walls except for the ones separating it from a kitchen and a back room used for Sunday school. For most of my time at Victory Gospel, the church was housed in a former club building with a spacious hall, while Eternal Hope's sanctuary is part of a larger complex including rooms for rehearsals and gatherings for meals. In all three churches, there is a raised platform known as the altar where the preacher stands to deliver the word from God. In both Eternal Hope and Victory Gospel, the altar is a stage running across one end of the sanctuary, while in Heaven's Tabernacle it consisted of a rectangular platform a few meters square. No one is allowed onto the altar without the pastor's permission. Pastor Hadley identifies this space as the pulpit—an elevated place where she stands to "pull" people out of a "pit."

At Eternal Hope, believers compare the altar to a "radio tower," saying that the closer they approach it during intercession the more spiritual power they feel. As one man told me, "By the time I get to the fourth row" while moving forward to pray and intercede, "I can feel the thickness. I forget about the problems, the debts, whatever. The closer you get to the altar, the peace is overwhelming."

In addition to being safe and sacred, the sanctuary is a place where believers receive insights from God about a range of moral and physical perils, and where they consider how God wishes them to confront those perils. A visiting preacher at Victory Gospel once compared the sanctuary to a "locker room" where members of a team receive coaching before meeting opponents. For instance, toward the end of a weekday evening Bible study during which Pastor John preached that God will "allow people to take advantage of you just to see how you will respond," he related to the congregation that he had just been "through a test." He had been pulled over by traffic officers some time previously, ostensibly for a driving violation but likely because someone who did not like his appearance called the police. He had protested. "I was about to get crazy, but I would have got beat up, so I gave them what they wanted," namely his driver's license. Two weeks later, he was pulled over again. The officer told him that he didn't have proper insurance, and then five other officers arrived, put him in handcuffs, and took him to the station. He started praying in the cell. At that point, a young African American man was led in crying while the officers laughed. Pastor John ministered to him and behaved very politely to the police. "I was so embarrassed, but embarrassment will find you sometimes," he remarked to the congregation. "The sergeant promised to wipe my record, and I saw the lady at the station write on her report: 'The man was very cooperative.'" The police told him that it was a case of mistaken identity. In fact, Pastor John commented to me later, they had probably used the insurance issue as an excuse to pull over someone who fit a description of "a big Black guy wearing a hood."

Pastor John continued in the sanctuary:

> Even if they're in the wrong, that don't give you a reason to get out of control. You see, I failed the first test [when he was pulled over the first time]. I shouldn't have said anything to those individuals [the traffic officers]. I'm proud of myself because they wrote "cooperative," because I don't like the police. I didn't allow my feelings to get in the way. When I told God, "Don't take me through that embarrassment," I was blocking my own blessing. If I hadn't been taken to the station, I would never have been able to minister to that young man.

He began singing, " 'God is intentional, He's intentional'. All things are working for my good," he concluded, "it works in your favor, the good and the bad. If Joseph had not gone to prison, he would not have received favor from Pharaoh, who made him the second most important man in the kingdom."

"Honestly, I was afraid," Pastor John told me later on, when I asked his permission to write about this incident. He is all too familiar with and outraged by the police murders of George Floyd, Rayshard Brooks, Breonna Taylor, Tamir Rice, Eric Garner, Michael Brown, and so many other people of color in the United States in recent years. At the same time, Pastor John takes God's designs for vitality extremely seriously. While those designs include "tests," God's intent is to bring life and ultimately salvation, countering the devil's plans to kill, steal, and destroy. According to all the believers whom I describe, to abide by God's designs is "to be in the world, but not of it," a phrase that lends itself to multiple framings (see McRoberts 2003; Sanders 1996) but in general signifies the need for insight into the differences between those designs and those of "the world" and "the flesh." In Pastor John's narrative of the above incident, it was this kind of insight that enabled him to overcome the schemes of the police as well as his own fear and anger, so that the strategy of "the world's system" to bring down Black men was subverted. He frequently says that if he had not given his life to the Lord, he would not now be alive. In the approximately twenty years since he graduated from high school, over forty of his classmates have died.

For Pastor John, the ways "the world's system" operates are clear. He has organized a group of pastors from urban and suburban Protestant churches to help carry out assistance projects on the East Side of Buffalo, for instance cleanups and property improvement. He told me that during the mass protests over the police murder of George Floyd in 2020, one of the suburban pastors asked him whether African Americans hate whites. He replied patiently, "No, we don't hate you, but you owe us." He elaborated to me:

> We own nothing, and I'm just sick of that. There was slavery, now you're sending us to prisons for non-violent offenses, and then giving us no opportunities once we get out. We didn't get the drugs, you brought the drugs to our community. Developers are building Family Dollars [a discount chain] everywhere, Arabs are buying properties everywhere. Corner stores are selling expired milk. We need to be the majority owner [of property and businesses], we need to hire our people, we want to keep the generational wealth in the community. That's the whole point: to create our own generational wealth.

At the same time, Pastor John understands that "the love of money is the root of all evil" (1 Tim. 6:10). He went on:

> I told some of our Black neighbors, "I don't see you protesting about having [known killers] in the neighborhood." We're scared of [them]. Why are we killing our own people? Money! My nephew got knocked off for some weed or cocaine by his own buddy for $1500, he was set up, he took nine shots to the body. We got to keep encouraging our people to live, not to die.

In this chapter, I present such critical commentaries on life possibilities in and around Buffalo together with broader contextual material so as to grasp how "the world(s)" that believers inhabit shape the content of their faith. I concentrate here on how believers' experiences of urban and suburban spaces shape their understandings of "the world" and God's activity within it. Pastor John understands that many aspects of urban space in Buffalo, as in other US cities (Carter 2019; Ralph 2014; Rios 2011; Shabazz 2015; Summers 2019), have been so designed as to impoverish, isolate, contain, punish, capitalize on, sicken, maim, and kill people of color. Ultimately, Pastor John insists, these designs are outcomes of the operations of the devil, who wishes to "kill the seed" in Black men, because he knows that he can destroy the people if he kills the seed. God's designs, by contrast, foster vitality. Some aspects of God's spatial designs, such as worship gatherings, are visible to all who care to look, while others—such as the transformation of a cell in a police station into a place of witnessing—are apparent only to those with discernment. For members of the suburban church of Eternal Hope as well, God's designs for vitality have spatial dimensions, as those designs encourage forms of emotional openness that counteract the kinds of isolation that commonly spring from working-class experiences of anger and bitterness.

Together with describing how these churches are situated within wider environments and providing some biographical backgrounds, I explore in this chapter the relations between insight and place. Broadly speaking, insights derived from God or other sources provide people with knowledge about the characteristics of places (such as, in Pastor John's narrative, Buffalo or the United States); they acquire insight as a consequence of being in or moving among particular places (such as the sanctuary); and their insights affect what happens in specific places (such as the police station). As a result, they come to appreciate how vitality, enervation, and violence stem in part from various kinds of spatial design.

Especially under the precarious circumstances of residents of the inner city, personal vitality in both senses of "life more abundantly" and "going through" hinges on developing critical insights into the moral contours of one's dependence on family members, social welfare institutions, and participants in informal economies such as drug dealing. Pastor John and Pastor Hadley invite believers to build on these insights but also to consider them inadequate or morally suspect to the extent that they detract from their sense of dependence on God, an issue I revisit more fully in Chapter 4. To begin, I discuss the history of discriminatory housing practices in Buffalo that have made the metropolitan area one of the most racially segregated in the country. I then turn to the ways the precarious lifeworlds of the urban poor compel them to acquire insights into dynamics of exploitation and dependence in particular locales, and I describe how the insights pastors receive from God enable them to extend the holiness of the sanctuary into other urban spaces. Next, I concentrate on the ways members of the suburban church of Eternal Hope construct geographies of faith and moral peril as they gain insight into the importance of sincere self-presentation. I finish by discussing the feelings of injury and grievance that are liable to arise when people depart from church, rejecting it as a locale of care.

## Designs for Segregation in Buffalo

The landscape in and around Buffalo is replete with evidence of stark wealth differences. The East Side of the city (east of Main Street) contains predominantly single- or double-family housing dating from the early twentieth century, often in poor repair. It is some of the oldest housing stock in the nation, contributing to high levels of asthma and lead poisoning.[1] There are many empty lots, corner shops, and discount chains but few supermarkets (Lee and Lim 2009). The neighborhood where Eternal Hope is located, in one of the so-called inner-ring working-class suburbs of Buffalo, consists of modest bungalows constructed in the mid-twentieth century where residents have been exposed to high levels of industrial pollution. A brief online survey of property values reveals that home prices in the neighborhoods around Eternal Hope are approximately twice as high as those on the East Side. (To be clear about my own positioning, the house prices in the neighborhood where I currently live are about five times as high.)

To cross Main Street from the East Side into the trendy shopping districts of Allentown and Elmwood Village, or to leave the East Side in the other direction by crossing the city line at Eggert Road into Snyder, is to be sharply reminded of the legacy of racially discriminatory housing practices in Buffalo dating to the first half of the twentieth century, since some of the wealthiest parts of the metropolitan area lie just across these boundaries. The oldest wealth derives from the city's development as a port at the western end of the Erie Canal, opened in 1825 to facilitate the colonization of North America. In 1900, Buffalo was the eighth largest city in the nation.[2] It attracted Irish, German, Italian, Polish, and other Eastern European immigrants who were predominantly Catholic. This Catholic heritage is visible in several large and now boarded-up churches on the East Side. According to the decennial US census, the population of the city peaked in 1950 at 580,132, when the steel industry was a major employer, but declined in every subsequent census until that of 2020, when it was 6.5 percent higher than in 2010.[3] The 2020 census records the population of Buffalo proper as 278,349 and that of the remainder of Erie County, within which the city is located, as 675,887.[4]

The proportion of the population classified as White in the Buffalo metropolitan area in 2010 was 79.5 percent, much higher than that in the country as a whole (63.7 percent), a difference mainly attributable to the region's relatively small Hispanic population (4.1 percent as opposed to 16.3 percent in the United States). In the Buffalo suburbs (the portion of Erie County outside the city proper), a heavily lopsided 90.4 percent of residents were White, 3.5 percent were Black, 2.3 percent were Asian, 2.2 percent were Hispanic, and 2.1 percent were classified as Other.[5] Accordingly, the census ranked the Buffalo-Niagara Falls metropolitan area as the eighth most segregated in the country by the White/Black Dissimilarity Index.[6] In Buffalo city (especially the West Side), there is a large Puerto Rican community, together with many immigrants from Bangladesh, Somalia, Myanmar, Yemen, and elsewhere who have contributed to the recent increase in the city's population. There is also a sizeable, predominantly white professional population and a number of largely white working-class neighborhoods in the city, including South Buffalo and Black Rock. Census estimates issued in 2019 for the city of Buffalo list 43.1 percent of the population as White alone (not Hispanic or Latino), 36.5 percent as Black or African American alone, 12.3 percent as Hispanic or Latino, 5.9 percent as Asian alone, 0.5 percent as American Indian alone, and 4.0 percent as Two or More Races.[7]

Key legislative steps taken on the national level, including the racially discriminatory design of the Federal Housing Administration in 1934 and the passage of the 1944 G.I. Bill, have historically enabled white households to build up wealth and have helped to expand the boundaries of whiteness to incorporate previously marginalized groups such as Catholics (Katznelson 2005; Orsi 2005; Roediger 2005; Rothstein 2017). At the same time, the efforts African American families have made since the abolition of slavery to accumulate and pass down wealth to their descendants have been impeded in a host of ways (Hannah-Jones

2020). For instance, "the condemnation of Blackness" (Muhammad 2010) as linked to deviance and criminality has been central to the real estate industry's profit-making strategies (Taylor 2019), which in turn perpetuate discriminatory zoning practices and educational inequities. Such inequities operate within the Buffalo suburbs as well, where the public schools in the working-class neighborhoods surrounding Eternal Hope have fewer resources than those in the wealthier suburbs, since public schools are funded by local property taxes. In the United States as a whole, the median white household currently owns nearly ten times more wealth than the median Black household (McIntosh et al. 2020), and white men earn on average about twice as much as Black men, due in large part to the effects of mass incarceration based on the criminalization of drug possession by people of color (Pettit 2012; see Alexander 2010; Forman 2017; Wacquant 2009).[8]

In a historical study of racial segregation in Buffalo, political scientist Neil Kraus (2000) makes a case for focusing on local decisions about land use, as distinct from shifting employment patterns brought about by deindustrialization (Wilson 1987), as explanations for the durability of concentrated urban poverty (see also Goldman 2007).[9] Ethnic enclaving has a long history in Buffalo; Ferry Street was a dividing line between German and Italian neighborhoods during the mid-twentieth century. Yet as in many US cities, discrimination faced by African Americans has operated at far more systematic levels since large-scale Black migration to the city began in the years following the First World War (Williams 1999). Kraus highlights continuities between local officials' opposition to federal efforts to provide African Americans access to public housing in Buffalo during the 1930s and 1940s, the consequent overcrowding of many Black residents in slum conditions, "urban renewal" projects in the 1950s and 1960s that displaced many of those residents into neighborhoods where real estate agents used blockbusting techniques to encourage white property owners to leave for the suburbs, and the construction of highways during the 1960s that contributed to the isolation of neighborhoods on the East Side by enabling "local and regional residents to completely avoid this section of the city" (2000: 125).

Fair housing ordinances designed to ensure that African Americans would not be discriminated against when trying to rent or buy property outside certain districts of the East Side were debated in the Buffalo city council during 1967–8, but "white neighborhood opposition was simply too strong" to attract a majority of votes (132). Title VIII of the 1968 US Civil Rights Act promised to reduce housing discrimination, yet it exempted owner-occupied one- or two-family houses from its coverage, as had the 1961 New York State antidiscrimination housing law. In Buffalo, the abundance of such homes and the relative scarcity of apartment buildings "meant that blacks or other ethnic groups could still be legally kept out of a majority of the city" (131). New lower-income housing was built at a very slow rate during the 1960s and 1970s. As a result, the demolition of older homes for urban renewal and highway construction led to a proliferation of vacant lots and to overcrowding in remaining properties on much of the East Side, where "housing loss actually surpassed population loss" (141). These forms of disinvestment were exacerbated by mortgage loan discrimination against both white and African American owners of older housing stock in the city during the 1970s (191–2), a practice in keeping with real estate industry interests in elevating suburban home prices by depressing urban ones (Taylor 2019). The reverse problem occurred in the years preceding the recession of 2008, when predatory lenders encouraged poorer borrowers to take out loans on so-called subprime properties. On a national level, African Americans lost about half their wealth due to predatory lending and job losses in the subsequent years.[10]

Designs to isolate African American neighborhoods remain in force in the United States as a whole (Bullard, Johnson, and Torres 2004). In Buffalo, the city subway line does not currently extend to the suburbs. Bus service from the city to suburban commercial areas is inconvenient, and municipal buses do not service most suburban residential districts at all. Recently, real estate and university interests in "revitalizing" (a telling metaphor) predominantly African American neighborhoods near downtown Buffalo have caused residents to fear displacement caused by higher rents. Residents have voiced concerns that refurbished housing will attract young professionals who would not remain in the city once they had children. Rather than sending children to the underfunded Buffalo city schools, residents worry, newcomers are likely to move to the suburbs and exacerbate current problems of eviction and involuntary mobility by becoming absentee landlords (Silverman et al. 2018, 2019). The eviction filing rate (that is, eviction court cases per number of rentals) in Buffalo is higher than in Milwaukee, Cleveland, Cincinnati, and Philadelphia, and the impact of involuntary mobility falls disproportionately on women, people of color, and people with disabilities (Magavern 2018; see Desmond 2016). On the subject of gentrification, Pastor John remarked to me, "If we're forced out of Buffalo, we'll have to go to Cheektowaga," an adjacent working-class suburb, "where they're really racist." These issues provided impetus for community and political organizing efforts that culminated in the 2021 mayoral nomination of democratic socialist candidate India Walton (Taylor 2021), who was subsequently defeated by a write-in campaign in the general election by incumbent Byron Brown.

## Insights into Exploitation and Dependence

The precarious lifeworlds arising from these discriminatory arrangements compel poor urban residents to develop insight into the ways people exploit and/or depend on one another in particular locales. The kinds of discernment practiced in Victory Gospel and Heaven's Tabernacle derive form and significance in part from each of these locales—homes, welfare offices, courts, "the street"—where city dwellers assess the ambiguities of exploitation, dependence, vitality, and danger even as they become subject to the assessments of others in turn.

Clary, a man who attends Victory Gospel, recalled growing up as an African American child during the 1980s in what was then a predominantly white neighborhood on the East Side. His early years were shaped by the effects of housing controversies, which forced him to understand that many white people found his presence unwelcome. In 1980 and 1989, efforts to pass a comprehensive municipal fair housing ordinance were supported by African American representatives on the Buffalo city council but were frustrated by vetoes by Mayor Jimmy Griffin.[11] Debates during the late 1980s were particularly strident: "white neighborhood opposition remained staunch, making prospects for passage challenging and shaping a public debate which became bitterly divisive" (Kraus 2000: 198). Clary and I spoke in the house where he had lived at the time with his late mother.

> I was six years old, trying to walk to school, you got people out here trying to run us over, screaming out of their car at us, letting their dogs out on us. This is a part of my immediate understanding of life. … There was this white guy who saw us coming from school, he set a German shepherd on us. Most of us got away, but there was this girl who couldn't get away, and the dog grabbed her and clamped onto her chest. He was sitting there screaming, "Yeah, get her! Get her!" … There was a white guy who came out of a store with a bat and clocked the dog over the head, and actually killed the dog … I don't hold it against people, because I know that arrogance and ignorance is an individual thing, it's not a race thing.

When he was around eight years old, Clary and some friends were picked up by the police for throwing rocks, released at the station in the heavily white enclave of South Buffalo, and told, "See if you make it home."

In relating how he had become a member of Victory Gospel, Clary described the respect he had acquired as a drug dealer with many subordinates but explained that he had subsequently become dependent on Pastor John's insights from God. Pastor John knew Clary, who is seven years his senior, by reputation during his youth; they had gone to rival schools and would sometimes get into fights to prove their toughness. They both turned to drug dealing during their teenage years, Pastor John after he had been expelled from both of his divorced parents' homes following a series of wayward incidents and Clary out of what he called "infatuation" with sneakers and gold chains. "I was a spoiled kid, I didn't need to be in the streets," Clary said, because his mother was able to buy him new sets of clothes at the beginning of each school year, as well as at Christmas and over the summer. "I knew my mother was sacrificing to buy me a pair of sneakers, but I wanted a new pair every week, not every month." By simply stepping off his porch, he learned that he could easily make a great deal of money. "I just liked the life. The crack epidemic hit in the early 1980s, I would walk out the door and it was right here." Playing video games at arcades at age eleven, he received quarters from dealers in exchange for holding bags of drugs when the police came. Over subsequent years, he rose to prominence in the informal economy while also engaging in wage work. Clary reflected ruefully on the respect he had gained as someone with knowledge of how to make it on "the street," pointing out that young people are entranced by shows of prosperity but lack insight into the ways his own vitality has been sapped because he has not been able to care properly for his family at their homes:

> I blame myself a lot for not teaching the youth as much as I should have. These kids, they look up to me for being the big homey. They flatter me a little bit, but I'm the cause of a lot of these people being on the street. I've been on the heights, and I've had so many generations praise me for how good I made it. They tell me, "You're one of the reasons I wanted to hustle." ... It started to discourage me because they didn't see the grit of it, the blood, sweat, and tears of what you got to go through. They don't see that I neglected my grandmother. She died when I was in prison ... Even though I wasn't no deadbeat dad, the fact that I was gone, in jail, because of the street life [hurt my family]. When I went to jail, [my son] didn't have nobody but my mother, and she [was too elderly to] chase him when he disrespected the neighbors. My being gone allowed him to go into the streets, find substitute fathers, substitute mentors. A lot of these kids don't understand that this life drains the life out of you. Then the violence. A lot of people have tried to break into my house. They try to follow my lady, my sons home. This world is really sucking the life out of me and my loved ones.

Soon after he started Victory Gospel, Pastor John resumed his acquaintance with Clary by playing basketball, without telling him that he was a pastor.[12] A short time later, Clary was involved in an incident that led to his incarceration on a parole violation. Released on bail, Clary got out of the car that had taken him from jail to find Pastor John driving up the street: "and it was not even a street where he usually goes." It was then, Clary recalled, that Pastor John revealed that he was a pastor, explaining to Clary that he was looking for him because God had made him "heavy on his heart" by means of a dream. Over the following weeks, Pastor John testified in court as a character witness to help him get released. Impressed by the insight that had led Pastor John to find him when and where he did, Clary began attending Victory Gospel, though with some skepticism derived from experiences on the street that had taught him to distinguish between people who have his own interests at heart and those who wish to manipulate him for their own purposes: "I've known pastors who sell drugs, do pimping. When you're a prostitute, you pick your pimp on how good a game he can talk. That's how I used to perceive pastors: they're like a pimp, they talk good, they get people to give you money." As time passed, though, Clary came to feel that Pastor John was the only person keeping him in Buffalo.

> All my elders are dead except my father, and he wasn't vital in my upbringing, unlike my mother, grandmother, uncle, aunt, great-aunts. All the other people around me are part of the underworld. The only other person that I have is John. In my mind, I'm putting all the weight of me on him. I think he knows that. He ain't give me finances, but he gave me hope. I don't know what I would have did without God when my mother died. And on the flip side of that, I want to help John succeed. We're a pretty poor congregation … I want to be there to help that church grow.

Clary's suspicions of pastors who "talk a good game" reflect broadly shared concerns among the urban poor both about the need to discern forms of interpersonal exploitation concealed by deceptive appearances and about the often violent consequences apt to ensue when these are discovered. Christine, a woman currently in her early thirties who joined Victory Gospel on the encouragement of a cousin about two years before I met her, recalled having been an angry child and teenager who reacted forcefully to any perceived disrespect: "I would go from zero to a hundred if I thought I was being played." She and her then-husband Tony, also a member of Victory Gospel, explained that "being played" means that someone is not only trying to manipulate you but "insulting your intelligence— they think they can do anything to you, say anything they want, and there won't be any consequences." Clearly, the insult lies not only in being cheated of resources but in being outcompeted in discernment. Christine identified her personal transformation as stemming from her involvement with Victory Gospel, where she encountered forms of discernment that affirmed rather than degraded her. She had had some exposure as a child to Christianity through her grandmother, who attended a Baptist church, but was not a committed believer during her youth. "People can be cruel out in the world," she told me.

> But in the church, Pastor [John] don't see what you are now, he sees what you're going to be. When I first came to church, I had a hard exterior, so rough and hard and angry, but Pastor seen beyond that. The Lord spoke it to me first. One day in Bible study I'm just writing, taking notes and He spoke to me: "You're going to be an evangelist, you're going to preach this Gospel." Right after that, Pastor said the same thing, so it was like confirmation. The Lord was speaking to me and speaking to him too about what I was going to be. Pastor sees that when he's looking at me. He sees what I'm going to be, what I'm going to be doing instead of what I am now.

While Christine had learned to recognize the voice of God at a young age, Pastor John's words of insight into what lay beneath her "hard exterior" have been a key point of reference for her. She alluded to her continued belief that "God has a call on my life" even after she left Victory Gospel a few years later, following a friend to another church.

Tony recalled that in his first year of high school, a teacher had given the class an assignment to write about something they wished they could change about their life or had done differently in retrospect. He had raised his hand and said, "I can't do this assignment, because I wouldn't change anything." Describing "going through" as a source of both vitality and discernment, he elaborated to me:

> I wouldn't be the person I am now. I wouldn't know what I know now. I wouldn't be able to handle things the way I do now. I wouldn't be able to avoid certain things that may come against me the way I do now. If I hadn't broken into a house [an act that led to his arrest at age sixteen], I wouldn't really know the consequence of breaking into a house. I knew that was wrong, but I wouldn't know that I would go to jail—and I didn't like that place. If I had been eighteen then, and they found [the drugs and weapons] they found in my house, I would probably still be in jail today, I wouldn't have the kids I have today.

As things stand, he went on, "there are very few situations I can't give people advice about," alluding to gang life and entanglements with the judicial system.

One of his younger cousins Tyrell had recently been released from jail and was worried about finding a lawyer. Encouraging Tyrell to come to Victory Gospel, Tony told him that the Lord had already handled the situation, and they subsequently discovered that no further charges were being pressed. Tony remarked that he had learned from Pastor John that "signs are for unbelievers," to whom God will dramatically demonstrate his power in order to encourage them to be saved.

At one point, Christine and Tony moved from a second-floor apartment into a house on the East Side where Tony had lived for a couple years when he was about eight to ten years old, and he reminisced with me about his childhood there. Back then, the house had belonged to his paternal grandmother, whom Tony had been visiting regularly while staying with his mother and stepfather, whose discipline he did not appreciate. At a certain point, Tony told his mother that he wanted to live permanently with his grandmother. She told him, "All right, you go over there if you think you like it better, and see what you learn." Tony recalled that his grandmother was out of the house most days playing bingo, while his father was mostly absent. As a result, he lived largely unsupervised with some younger cousins including Tyrell, who has thus relied on Tony from an early age. Tony stressed that this experience had taught him to become a provider at a young age. He would ask neighbors for food and steal some from stores, following his grandmother's instructions delivered over the phone on how to prepare it. He also remembered an enjoyable time when his grandmother told the children to clean the hardwood floor, and they had slid around after dumping water all over it.

In other ways as well, Tony and Christine spoke of their homes as places where valuable knowledge about relationships is generated and acted upon. Tony remarked that the tub in the house into which they had just moved was plugged up, as was the tub in their previous apartment. This showed, he said, that there was a spiritual "blockage" in their marriage, and that once "that little hairball" was cleared "so many blessings would flow that we wouldn't have room enough to receive them." He recalled that a few months earlier, the pipes in Mother Smith's house had frozen and the estimate for repairs came to $3,000, which she found far too high and refused to pay. Pastor John prophesied in church that her water would soon start flowing again, and it soon did without any problems—a series of events taken to demonstrate the blessings that flow as a consequence of maintaining faith.

Speaking in a different vein about how domestic arrangements provide insights into dependence and exploitation, Christine recalled that in the early years of her marriage to a previous husband, the couple had lived with his mother. When Christine's first son was born with a congenital illness that qualified him to receive monthly SSI (Supplementary Security Income) payments, her mother-in-law asked her for $350 per month in addition to another $350 from her then-husband's wages from his job at a car wash. Christine refused because the couple were trying to save money for a home of their own. She moved back in with her own mother, whereupon her mother-in-law filed a complaint with Child Protective Services (CPS) against her, claiming falsely that the baby had no crib.

In telling me about her long-term entanglements with the official welfare system, Christine revealed how the surveillance that bureaucrats exercise over poor urban residents—most directly, women with children—depends on what they know or imagine about kinship relations, a dynamic that lends itself to acts of co-optation such as that of her former mother-in-law. Christine spent a great deal of time waiting in crowded and dingy offices in the Rath Building downtown for appointments with various social workers to negotiate benefits due to herself and her children, as well as to contest their denials and claims brought against her through CPS. Caseworkers, many urban residents claim, "act like it's their money" (see Davis 2006; on intraracial enactments of class, Jackson 2001). Christine also devoted much time and emotional energy to preparing her home for visits from officials whom she needed to convince that she was a good parent (for instance, by having the correct number of beds and cleaning up the kitchen) lest they place her children in foster care. She also tried to enlist these caseworkers in her struggles with various landlords to fix the plumbing and heating. Many of the conditions under which Christine was able to claim benefits hinged on what officials claimed to know about her relations with Tony, her previous spouse, and her children. For instance, Christine's cash assistance grant was once inscrutably cut when she had a third child and was reduced on another occasion because she had not taken her ex-husband to court to claim child support. Officials were garnishing Tony's wages from his job at Walmart to support his own previous partner and their child, an arrangement that upset Christine because she and Tony were taking care of this child in their home every weekend. Christine discerned that "welfare is like pimping" because officials want to make you think that you depend on them. Her sister had been placed on a workfare program (see Dickinson 2016) in which she engaged in menial labor for low pay while working toward her high school equivalency diploma. Five years passed before she was deemed to have studied enough to take her exam, a period in which her workfare job had her picking up trash from the street for the low cash equivalent of welfare benefits.

Members of Heaven's Tabernacle and Victory Gospel often make reference to courts, welfare offices, homes, and "the street" in speaking of how God's designs supersede those of "the world." For instance, some women in Heaven's Tabernacle praise God for sending them checks via the welfare office to which the official rules do not entitle them. Pastor John related that he had once watched a judge pronouncing a lenient sentence she had not intended: he discerned that God was moving her lips. Pastor John and Pastor Hadley build on popular aspirations to make homes into refuges from external threats, encouraging the saints to "anoint" the walls of their homes with oil while "praying the blood of Jesus" during times of peril.

In particular, church practices of tithing elaborate in critical ways on "street" transactions. Tony and Christine told me that if someone in need turns to an OG (original gangster) for help, the OG will demand something in rapid return. Christine's father, she said, had been an OG who would recruit young boys who came from broken homes, advance them drugs on credit, and insist that they bring back most of what they earned. Church members speak of earnings from drug sales as a kind of "fast money," contrasting them with the blessings that God will provide in the time he knows is best in recognition of their tithes and additional monetary offerings. However, they worry that they may be "holding back" their own blessings because they are not offering enough or are demanding too much from the pastor. Christine expressed concerns that she might be exploiting Pastor John in asking him for help:

> I've been struggling, but I didn't want to ask him to do things for me. There's always something that holds me back because there are so many people who are asking him to pay their rent, pay their phones. Do you really need the money, or do you just want it? He helped me, and I'm feeling guilty: am I pimping pastor? … I don't want to feel like a burden to him. I cry out to the Lord, can you bless me so that I can bless him?

## Pastors' Insights

Important as insights into forms of exploitation and dependence are for urban residents in general, believers draw contrasts between "exercising wisdom" based on human knowledge and acting on the superior "discernment" that God provides to pastors and others who have spent many years developing insight into his ways. Having a mother who was a Jehovah's Witness, Pastor John recalls asking questions about the Bible from an early age but becoming dissatisfied with the answers he received from members of her congregation. As a nineteen-year-old living off drug sales, he came to a point of asking God for a sign of his existence. His girlfriend at the time invited him to a Pentecostal church service, where he saw people jumping about and behaving in other ways he found incomprehensible. "I had an eight-ball of cocaine in my pocket and I thought, I could sell to these people!" But he was struck by the discernment the preacher showed in his sermon of what had been in his own mind: "You've been asking God to show you He exists." The preacher concluded by asking the audience: If you were to die tonight, would you be going to heaven or hell? Pastor John knew that he would be damned, because he was living by "giving people poison." At the end of a subsequent service, he asked to be baptized, and the bishop called everyone back into the building for the event. Pastor John has repeatedly recounted to the congregation at Victory Gospel how his lived routines centered on the sanctuary from that time forward. As one of a number of novice male preachers serving under this late bishop, he endured a rigorous training over subsequent years, including being awoken at six o'clock for prayer each morning by elder women, including Mother Anderson, who became his "spiritual mother." These women told him that in order to hear God's voice he needed to "lay out" on the altar for hours. Nothing happened for two nights, but on the third night he was startled by a voice saying "My son." Since being saved, Pastor John has held a variety of jobs, including recreational director at a gym and a school basketball coach, and for some time was receiving rent from a property he had acquired.

Pastor John's wife, the First Lady of the church, has a nursing career and plays an important role in counseling new members of Victory Gospel, especially women.[13] Their marriage is a direct outgrowth of insights nurtured in the sanctuary. The two of them became acquainted soon after Mother Anderson told Pastor John the name of his future wife. He explained to the congregation that before seeking a wife, he had to consult not only God but the spiritual mother who had helped him hear the divine voice:

> I had in mind what I desired in a wife, someone to help me preach, but that's not what God wanted for me. He had to deal with me. My [spiritual] mother described her to me in her whole being, saying "she's no preacher." I had a ten-woman rolodex in my head of possibilities, but I had to talk to God first, because a king, if he chooses the wrong woman, is going to fall. My mother in the Lord did not know [my wife's] name. The Lord gave me a list of ten names, and her name was fifth on the list. My mother stopped me at that name. Then I went on a three-day fast and God gave me an instant love for her before I met her.

Like Pastor John, Pastor Hadley recalls having been a "hellion" as a teenager, rebelling against parents who were highly respected in the community. However, she had more exposure in her youth to Pentecostalism, and narrates her trajectory as one of returning to the faith of her family. "When I was young," she explained in an interview, "you just wanna go out, just do whatever can make you feel better. It was an ugliness about me on the inside. It was a miserable side of me that I could not, I just did not understand." As a young married woman, she came home to Buffalo on a visit while her husband was stationed on a military base overseas. Someone gave her amphetamine as a recreational drug.

> So I tried that but it scared me because I didn't like how I felt. And to make a long story short I ran into my aunt who I used to run from 'cause I didn't want to hear it. She was a pastor and I didn't wanna hear it. But this particular Saturday morning I sat at the kitchen table at my aunt's house. … She lived right across the street from my mother. I went over there and it was just routine and I was sick of doing the same thing, with the same people, and I was just miserable. I hated Buffalo. Buffalo was just ugh. It's nasty. It's dirty. I don't wanna be here because I was miserable on the inside. So this particular Saturday I didn't run. I actually remember saying to her, "Let's talk." She knew for me to say, "Let's talk," it was serious.

Pastor Hadley's conversation with her aunt led her to see Buffalo as a place transfigured through God's activity:

> She said, "Well, you miserable." I said, "I am just freakin' miserable." She said, "Well you've tried everything, why don't you try Jesus?" So I said, "Why the hell not" and put my hands up. And she led me in the sinner's prayer. From that moment the scales from my eyes fell off and all I did was cry because I didn't see Buffalo like I saw it. It was like I went onto a whole 'nother world and that was the night He delivered me from smoking. I had been smoking since I was twelve. That day He delivered me.

Pastor Hadley often speaks to her congregation of how God has brought about transformations in domestic space. For example, God proved his power to her soon after she rejoined her husband at his base overseas. She returned to find her home flooded; the devil, she said, had caused a faucet to turn on. The furniture was ruined, there was mold everywhere, and the woman responsible for housing at the base was very upset. Pastor Hadley heard God say, "Start cleaning." She began wiping down the walls with a sponge, although the mess was too great for one person to handle. She heard the person in charge of housing approaching and telling a coworker, "Wait till you see this mess." When they came in, they looked around in astonishment because the home was clean and dry.

In later years, Pastor Hadley moved to Atlanta, where she was employed as a nurse and owned a house she liked. At a certain point, God told her to move back to Buffalo to care for her aging mother. Disliking the prospect because of the winters and gray skies, she tried to negotiate with God, telling him that she would move out of her house, but only to the Atlanta suburbs. She had arranged the purchase, but a series of mishaps with the move convinced her that God would not be satisfied with her disobedience. Returning to Buffalo, she joined a large Baptist church attended by many in her family, where she imagined she could be relatively anonymous and not have to deal with other people's problems. When the pastor preached, though, she heard God speaking to her through him: "God's got your number. He's calling on you to do something." She took up an invitation to attend Bible study. At the study, she wondered why God had put her there, since all the lessons were familiar to her. When everyone was called on to introduce themselves, "God gave me a word about each person's life." The leader looked at her and said, "Sister Hadley, you look like you've got something to say." She proceeded to give each attendee the message God had given her about their lives, and everyone was in tears. Next thing she knew, a man was shaking her and saying, "Sister Hadley, you have to be teaching."

Soon afterward, Pastor Hadley had become the leader of a group of women who assembled to pray in the basement of her house. In many instances, these women had struggled with substance abuse, been subject to domestic violence, or had attempted suicide. She would sometimes invite a woman to live with her for a while as her situation stabilized. While God redesigned her living arrangements in this manner, his power to transfigure familial space transcended physical distance, extending even to places associated with drug use. Pastor Hadley's sister Kim was addicted to crack cocaine for many years. At one point while she was living in Atlanta, she heard God tell her to pray for Kim and immediately went into tongue speech to "send the angels of the Lord" after her. At that moment, Kim was in the midst of running from a scene of a robbery she had committed together with a friend named Brenda, and found herself immobilized. An angel, Kim realized, had stopped her in her tracks. She called up her sister and pleaded, "Stop praying!"

Kim eventually recovered from her addiction with the help of Narcotics Anonymous and Pastor Hadley's prayers, and she joined Heaven's Tabernacle. Brenda, who in her youth had known Kim and Pastor Hadley's parents, later joined as well. Brenda told me that she would thank God for delivering her from drugs, following Pastor Hadley's instructions, right before sitting down for a smoke at a crack house. After a few weeks of thanking God in this manner, Brenda was suddenly disgusted by the crack she tasted, and has not used since. Soon afterward, when she saw a packet containing a substantial quantity of cocaine on the sidewalk, she was able to deliver it to someone who "had a use for it" rather than keeping it for herself.

As these examples indicate, the powers and responsibilities of prayer extend far beyond the sanctuary. Pastor John estimated to me that the time he spends in worship service accounts for only about fifteen percent of the time he devotes to what Casselberry (2017) calls "the labor of faith." All the churches I am describing recruit members from both within and outside their immediate environs, as did pastors of those located in an African American neighborhood of Boston studied by Omar McRoberts (2003). However, unlike most of those leaders, Pastor John in particular devotes energy to programs aimed at benefiting the community at large as well as to assisting members of his own congregation, though not to formal political organizing. While Pastor John has many connections in Buffalo city government, he has had encounters with official influence peddling that have discouraged him from pursuing formal political work. Pastor John's labor includes couples counseling; praying for and otherwise assisting believers whom he knows are in need; acting upon prompts from the Holy Ghost about troubles they are in or might have caused; attending the ill or injured in hospitals; organizing community programs such as youth summer daycare and basketball tournaments; lobbying city officials and pastors of urban and suburban churches for resources to develop basketball courts, athletic fields, and other amenities; and consulting with his spiritual mentors who lead other churches. For her part, Pastor Hadley often remarks that she "does drive-bys"—in other words, she unexpectedly checks up on believers she is concerned about. To recognize and thank Pastor John and Pastor Hadley for their unremunerated work, members of their congregations try to "be a blessing" to them with money and goods, as well as by organizing birthday and anniversary celebrations in their honor.

Pastors sometimes coordinate collections of money and goods for saints in emergency situations. They do not actively discourage members from giving to one another informally, but since they are concerned about the formation of "cliques" within their congregations, they tend to encourage them to consult with leaders beforehand. On the other hand, once a service is over, believers will often linger in the sanctuary to share information about housing opportunities, health services, or job openings. At the suburban church of Eternal Hope, the pastor is paid a salary and there is less insistence on top-down coordination of material help. Members recall how other saints have supplied them with groceries during periods of unemployment. "Because of my association with God," Benny remarked, "I've always been provided for, never missed a mortgage payment." Eternal Hope operates a retail store that provides jobs for members, and believers give one another tips on openings there or elsewhere. The church also owns a private residence, which it was leasing to a family of one of the members during the period of my fieldwork.

## Geographies of Faith and Moral Peril

For members of Victory Gospel and Heaven's Tabernacle, God's designs for mutual assistance counteract the designs of racial oppression. While Pastor John, whose late mother was active in the Black Panthers organization, is quite articulate about the operations of "the world's system," Pastor Hadley does not usually feel a need to be as explicit. Yet she too makes clear to her congregation that the workings of "the world" make it all the more important to obey God: "The world don't want to have nothing to do with us," meaning Black folk. "You'd better raise your hands before God, unless you want to raise your right hand before a judge." While both Pastor John and Pastor Hadley acknowledge the importance of praying for political leaders, they point out that just as God allowed evil kings to rule over the Israelites when they sinned, he may do so in the United States as well. Pastor Hadley, who routinely referred to Donald Trump as "Goldilocks," attributed what she saw as his erratic, racist, and autocratic presidency to God's desire to punish the nation for legalizing same-sex marriage during Barack Obama's previous administration.[14] Since no one could tell what Goldilocks would do next, she often remarked to her congregation, there was all the more reason to rely on God's protection.

For their part, members of Eternal Hope aspire to make their sanctuary a place of colorblindness. Clary's comments about racial hostility as a matter of individual predilection have echoes in Eternal Hope members' reflections on ethnic diversity within their church. The national denomination to which Eternal Hope belongs has made efforts to promote people of color (mainly men) to leadership positions. "God is non-prejudicial," Benny told me accordingly. He and his wife Janet used to proselytize door-to-door on the East Side and drove a van to transport people from "the projects" to and from church until insurance costs became too great. Benny's work delivering mail continued to bring him to the neighborhood, which he described in disparaging terms: "On the East Side, there's a lot of chaos. Here [in the suburbs] when a child acts up, you can call a parent, but there you would have to call the police."

A middle-aged African American woman named Violet has been attending Eternal Hope since 1981, when church members knocked on her door in Buffalo as she was studying to become a speech therapist and invited her and her children to Sunday school. Raised Baptist in the college town of Ithaca, she told me,

> A lot of times I was the only Black person in my class, so being in a predominantly Caucasian church doesn't bother me. I've been here so long. God's spirit doesn't segregate. He created us all, we're like a beautiful flower garden. People want to be loved and accepted, that's a basic need in all people. If people come to our church and feel loved and accepted, more than likely they're going to stay.

Violet's husband, whom she met while they were in college, had previously been a member of Eternal Hope before "backsliding." He rejoined with her, and they were married in the church.

When Violet first came to Eternal Hope as a divorced young mother, she heard a sermon full of insight into her own circumstances, and experienced love and acceptance from the women who interceded for her at the altar. In her narration of this first encounter, she spoke of how God used people to show her that he knew her and her needs perfectly:

> God knew my innermost feelings, it was like [the preacher] knew me. The topic [of the sermon] was "An Answering To"—he went into how God has been with us all our lives, and there comes a time in our lives when He reaches out to us and calls us to make a decision to seek Him out. I was weeping and crying. The word of God is a discerner of the intents of the heart. The young lady next to me had some kind of discernment, she took me by the arm and led me to the front. The ladies there prayed for me. I was asking God to forgive me, but they told me that you don't have to beg Him, He's already forgiven you. They told me that "Hallelujah" was the highest form of praise, and I just started speaking in another language!

Like Pastor Hadley, Violet emphasized the ways God's activity transcended the space of the church, extending holiness into her domestic space. The devil tried to use her return to her apartment to make her doubt that the Holy Ghost was real, but God responded to her prayer there as well:

The experience of getting the Holy Ghost was so freeing! I had so much love in my heart for everyone. I forgave everyone for doing whatever they had done to me, because I knew God had forgiven me. I didn't know what getting the Holy Ghost was, because I'd never had a Bible study, but I felt free. At the time I lived with my mother in the projects, we didn't have a phone. I remember something else [i.e., the devil] telling me this wasn't real, you didn't get the Holy Ghost. I remember asking God, "If this was You, let me get the Holy Ghost right now," and He came on me right there in my bedroom! The enemy of your soul tries to snatch it away from you. If he can put an ounce of doubt in your mind that God did something for you, he zaps your joy.

Remarking "God's people are out there," Violet spoke of Christian believers in general as a kind of hidden community discerning other people's needs in ways that transcend personal acquaintance and boundaries between public and private spaces. I asked Violet whether she is able to discern what someone else might be going through in a public place. "Sometimes," she replied.

Yesterday I gave a woman an encouraging word. Another lady, she came up to me and I gave her five dollars and she just hugged and kissed me, and said, "God knows just what we need." Another young woman came by and encouraged me. God is so good that when you encourage someone, He sends someone else to bless you. That's quite an experience. Once when I was in the store, a woman came up and said, "You need someone to pray for you." She pinpointed a part of my body that I was having some difficulty with. She just knew. She said, "I'm going to pray for you."

I never heard racial inequality or any other economic issues preached about in Eternal Hope. In coded ways, however, Pastor Charles of Eternal Hope frames faith simultaneously as an affirmation of working-class identity and as a repudiation of the emotional toughness and xenophobia that often spring from the hidden injuries of class (Sennett and Cobb 1972). In so doing, he counteracts what sociologist Thomas Gorman (2017) describes as the cruel ways that white working-class boys commonly "reach for a little dignity" (147) by insulting each other and hurting one another's self-confidence. As Gorman points out, "This is what it is like growing up working class—you are never really certain if you are good enough, smart enough, or attractive enough" (160). Telling me that "church has changed Benny a lot for the better," Janet recalled that he had teased and bullied his siblings during his youth. Benny agreed: "That's what we did back then. The oldest would pick on the next one down, and so on." Pastor Charles often reassures the congregation on the issue of self-confidence by comparing them to the Corinthians addressed by Paul: "Brothers and sisters, think of what you were when you were called. Not many of you were wise by human standards; not many were influential; not many were of noble birth" (1 Cor. 1:26 NIV). In another common trope, he identifies the people of Israel in the Exodus story with God's people of today: while the Egyptians were in darkness during one of the plagues, the children of Israel had light, and it is mysterious why the Egyptians would not wonder what the Israelites possessed that they did not—namely discernment. Pastor Charles identifies the people "in darkness" by and large with the secular elite, whose self-assurance and sophisticated language reflect the fact of their entitlement. In a reenactment of the Azusa Street revival, a member of Eternal Hope played the part of a minister of an established religious denomination, speaking in multisyllabic words that sounded important but conveyed no literal meaning.

As do members of the African American churches, those in Eternal Hope speak of "being religious" in pejorative terms, as a kind of self-congratulatory conformity with external appearances of holiness. As Gorman (2017) argues, "those in the middle class are really the 'conformists' … but that conformity is what helps members of the middle class succeed" (7). Undoubtedly, much of this imagery of Pentecostalism as an embattled subculture (Smith 1998, 2000) reflects the well-financed efforts of the Religious Right to consolidate oligarchical power and white male supremacy in the United States by fomenting fears about moral impurity and violations of order (Du Mez 2020; Goldberg 2006; Mullings 2020; Posner 2021; Stewart 2020; Whitehead and Perry 2020; see Baker 2011; Curtis 2021; Griffith 2017; Lakoff 2002; MacLean 2017). Yet at the same time, Eternal Hope members' outreach to people of color underscores the work they devote on a general level to repudiating frustration and anger, emotions which often lead white working-class men and women to "lash out at middle- and upper-middle-class, white-collar workers … minorities, women, and … Muslims" (Gorman 2017: 6).

This complex dynamic lends itself to specific ways of thinking about locations of moral danger, as do the particularities of the landscapes of faith (Day 2014) on the East Side and the suburbs. The numerous churches on the East Side, including two large-scale African American Baptist ministries that hold ownership rights in low-income housing projects, make Christianity a ubiquitously visible presence in the city. There are several churches of various denominations within a few blocks of both Eternal Hope and Heaven's Tabernacle. While Pastor John and Pastor Hadley have close connections with leaders of some local ministries, their relations with others can be tense. In the case of Pastor John, these tensions often have to do with competition over scarce resources, while Pastor Hadley expresses concerns about malign spiritual influences that saints may encounter in other churches. Pastor Hadley does not discourage members of Heaven's Tabernacle from attending services elsewhere on occasions when she is out of town, but asks that they inform her beforehand of where they plan to go so that she will "keep them covered in prayer" if she happens to "know something" about the ministry.

In the suburbs, by contrast, houses of worship are more widely dispersed, and members of Eternal Hope are more disposed to locate moral peril in the activities of non-Christians. Several warned me about a town called Lily Dale, a community about sixty miles from Buffalo well known as a center for spirit mediums and other New Age practitioners. They say that the demonic influence over the surrounding area is so powerful that Pentecostal ministries struggle to gain a foothold there. They tend to be likewise suspicious of SUNY-Buffalo, the university where I currently teach, because (as someone said to me in an unguarded moment) "there are all those humanists running around." On the other hand, the fact that many members of Eternal Hope have known one another for decades has had the effect of multiplying and dispersing the places of their faith, and of countering the isolation and loneliness that some had experienced in their upbringing. A substantial cohort of believers has grown from youth to middle age spending time in one another's homes, and a number of their children have married each other. Alex, a man in his forties, mentioned that when he and his family moved within the area, their neighbors who also attend Eternal Hope bought the house next door so that they could remain close by.

Pastor Charles was raised in a Catholic home in the Buffalo suburbs in the 1970s but did not take faith seriously during his youth. In an interview, he recalled that his prayers as a teenager were "very self-centered: 'God, I want to be a millionaire'—they didn't have any spiritual depth to them at all." He was evangelized at age twenty by a Pentecostal minister from Texas during a period of unemployment. He recalled having felt at the time that the witnessing had "ruined my life" because "I knew I was lost" and needed to repent. Together with a friend, he had been experimenting with New Age practices such as self-hypnosis, aura reading, and astral projection. "I was open to spiritual things, and God saw that opportunity." As a result of the witnessing, he gained the insight that "you couldn't get good enough on your own to leave this world a good person," but that "God was gracious and good—the only catch is that He is the one who saves you, you can't save yourself."

In keeping with the admission that "you can't save yourself," believers at Eternal Hope often make a point of being open about their incapacities and of refusing to "put on a front" to impress other people, for instance in the workplace. In a sermon, Pastor Charles recalled that during a period of job scarcity in the early 1980s, when he was in his early twenties and had recently joined Eternal Hope, he needed to find work because he wanted to marry the bishop's daughter. "I had absolutely no marketable skills that a gazillion people didn't already have. I could have looked at the statistics and said, 'What's the point of even looking [for work]?'" Nonetheless, he repeated to himself "he that seeketh findeth," and regularly contributed tithes from his unemployment insurance and meager savings. He interviewed for a position as an electronics technician, a line of work he had studied in vocational school after having dropped out of college: "I didn't have parents who would kick me in the caboose and say, 'Get better grades.'" About halfway through the job interview, he said, "Stop—I'm not qualified for this job," and admitted that he did not know how to do the repairs he was being asked about. An hour later, the boss called him to hire him, offering to pay him twice the minimum wage while he enrolled in an apprenticeship program. "He was impressed by my honesty. Before you go out there and try to connive your way into a job, remember that so many people sit there and lie."

Pastor Charles's account signals some important differences between suburban and urban church members' insights into the distinctions between false knowledge fostered by "the world" and true discernment derived from God. According to Pastor Charles, God does not desire people to engage in posturing but rather to present their vulnerable selves to others with sincerity—a key theme in intercession, as I discuss below—so as, in this instance, to extend holiness to a workplace. Much more attentive to dynamics of exploitation, Pastor John argues that God does not necessarily value sincere self-expression, especially of a kind that insults are liable to elicit. For instance, he recounted that in expressing his true feelings to the police officers he had "failed a test" set by God. Clearly, the stakes involved in being honest with authority figures are generally lower for Pastor Charles than for Pastor John, who often remarks to his congregation that he must not question what his boss at a gym tells him to do regardless of whether he disagrees with him, since the boss is in a position of authority. Accordingly, Pastor John tells the saints at Victory Gospel, they must abide by God's order establishing a man as the head of the house (see Chapter 3).

Closely related to sincerity for members of Eternal Hope are qualities of wholesomeness, which counteract the angry and embittered dispositions that they associate with "the world." Alex, who works as a truck driver, remembered having been impressed by the "decent" appearance of the saints in formal dress when he first came to Eternal Hope in 1985 at age twenty. He too had been raised Catholic in a Buffalo suburb, but his home life was marred by domestic violence. Alex's father, also a trucker, had been "a big drunk" who smashed furniture during arguments; his mother disappeared from his life for a year during his childhood. As a teenager, Alex smoked marijuana and LSD but continued to search for God. He joined a Catholic Charismatic youth group whose participants "smoked grass" and said "Jesus was a hippie like us." He recalled, "I would go to bed stoned and out of my mind, praying to God: 'I know there's more.'" Foreshadowing the opioid epidemic that began to have a disproportionate impact on mortality rates in white working-class communities in the Buffalo area around 2015,[15] a number of other Eternal Hope members likewise spoke of how God had helped them in their struggles to overcome drug and alcohol abuse.

When Alex's sister, who had joined Eternal Hope, encouraged him to visit the church, he reflected, "You go for coffee with these people, they're really living it! I didn't find that in any of the other churches." Once when his car ran out of gas on a Sunday, the pastor impressed him by calling him to inquire about any problems. Now, "I find love in church. I cry so easily. I want to hug everybody, I want to get really close to people." Most of Alex's immediate family joined Eternal Hope as well; some were current members while others left after intervals of years. When Alex's father came, "he melted. You've never seen anybody flip so fast in your life. He got baptized, and he used to dance all around the sanctuary. My sisters and I can't believe it's the same person. He backslid"—that is, returned to Catholicism—"but he still lives very clean, no alcohol, no cigarettes, walks five miles a day." Alex asked his wife, whom he met at the church, to marry him on their second date, while he was driving her home in his beat-up car from a restaurant where he had had to ask her to leave the tip. Replying to my question of what she had seen in him at the time, he remarked: "I wasn't putting on a front, I wasn't trying to impress her by buying her a new couch like her other boyfriends. I had jeans with holes in them. She just saw a real guy."

## "Backsliding" and "Church Hurt"

To a greater extent than in the African American churches, where believers often pray to protect their unsaved kin from dangerous situations, saints in

Eternal Hope say "it's our goal to get everyone in our families saved." They joke that if you arrive in church as a single person, you likely won't stay single for very long. All four of Alex's sisters joined either Eternal Hope or another church of the same denomination. However, his youngest sister left following a divorce from her husband. Both had been very active at Eternal Hope, Alex recalled, but his sister had been so embarrassed by the divorce that she could not bear to come back to a place where she felt "everybody would be looking at me." In spite of Alex's assurances that everyone would welcome her enthusiastically, she felt a need to isolate herself from their gaze and touch. Her ex-husband, Alex recounted, "totally backslid—he parties and everything."

How do these churches handle withdrawals? In general, members calibrate their level of involvement so as not to take on more duties than they feel comfortable with, on the understanding that pastors and other leaders will assist them to the extent that they attend consistently and render tithes either in money or as labor. When they wish to leave church, they withdraw from these commitments. As the term "backsliding" indicates, these churches provide few means for speaking of departures in anything other than negative ways, though Pastor Hadley is comparatively accepting of occasions when members "have gone on to be with another body of believers." Unless negotiated with extreme delicacy, withdrawals frequently arise from and provoke a sense of injury. Pastor Hadley recounted at a Bible study that she was sitting on the front step of her house when a young woman whom she did not know passed by and struck up a conversation. Not realizing that she was a pastor, this woman shared her insight that church leaders are hypocrites: "They sleep with their members. I know, because I was one of the ones they slept with." In the African American community, the term "church hurt" describes the sense of deep betrayal that erstwhile members feel as a result of such abuses. For their part, pastors feel betrayed when saints who have been with them for many years depart because of apparently petty grievances. Pastor John was struck by a prophet's message at a revival that she had had a vision of fish in an aquarium swimming around with holes in their sides. This foreshadowed, he later told me, his own hurt at the departure of several members whom he had trusted and worked hard to support.

To withdraw from church means to refuse to see it any longer as a place of care, a possibility that pastors make concerted efforts to forestall. In a sermon following the departures, Pastor John recalled that when he was new to faith, he found that some of the other saints in the church to which he belonged at the time were gossiping about him. He had complained over the phone about this behavior to Mother Anderson. She listened carefully and then said: "I'm going to give you two words, so listen carefully: Shut up." Pastor John remembered nearly hanging up the phone at that point but continued listening as she told him, "Stop crying because you can't get your way." He needed, she said, to be responsible for making a decision to "humble himself before God" and to work as directed by senior leaders.

Addressing the congregation, Pastor John went on: "Why can you get blessed in this place? Because the atmosphere has been made conducive. Love, prayers, and healing have been released here. God expects you to be in a certain place at a certain time: He wants to bring you to an expected end [Jer. 29:11]. The problem is, we're trying to direct our own path." The combination of these chronotopic expressions "bringing you to an expected end" and "directing your own path" hints at the existence of enduring value conflicts, as does Pastor John's insistence that "if you don't go to church, this world is going to take you out. If you're sad or complaining about coming to church, the world has gotten to you." In attempting to resolve these conflicts in a direction that will counteract the world's designs, Pastor John feels it necessary to persuade others to reflect in the manner he does about space, time, value, and care. For instance, he spoke of the urgency that some members feel to make money, an impulse that precipitated one of the departures:

> It's getting hot and heavy for you, and you want to act the fool—what do you do, quit [believing]? No, hold on till the Lord does what He said He was going to do. Most businesses you work for are multimillion-dollar corporations and they're giving you peanuts. Is that where you put your faith? We don't live paycheck to paycheck, we believe God for the impossible. Why are you worried about that stuff? Focus on the kingdom!

In the following chapters, I discuss how believers understand their vitality as contingent on their willingness to abide by God's designs for care, value, and time. Turning first to care, I consider how believers distinguish themselves from "the world" by conveying what they know about proper kinds of communication among bodies and spirits.

3

# Openings and Enclosures:
# Designs for Communication and Care

Pastor Hadley was explaining to me how important it is for her to have a spiritual assistant known as an "armor bearer." An armor bearer has many duties, including arranging logistics for church events and helping to "set the atmosphere" at the outset of the service to make the congregation receptive to the work of the Holy Spirit. Having a faithful armor bearer is particularly important because she stands behind the pastor while praying in tongues, as the pastor lays hands on members of the congregation, delivering them from spirits of sickness or other demons. In so doing, the armor bearer "covers" the pastor, protecting her from any evil spirits that the pastor might "pick up" from the people who come before her for prayer. "To armor me means to cover me," Pastor Hadley explained. "Means that whatever gonna fight me gonna fight you." Speaking of her own armor bearer Evangelist Clarice, a woman who has been in her ministry from its outset, Pastor Hadley remarked, "She is so kind of connected to me spiritually that she already kind of know when I need something."

This chapter explores the themes of connectedness among spirits and bodies that informed Pastor Hadley's remarks. Having a "relationship with God" gives Pentecostal believers knowledge about how they are related or connected to spirits (especially the Holy Ghost), as well as to other people through those spirits. They have complex idioms for the insights into the character of human and nonhuman persons, themselves included, that they develop by virtue of these connections. As in the case of the spiritual protection provided by an armor bearer, they frequently conceive of such connections as matters of care. In this chapter, I discuss how believers' discernment of the character and doings of spirits and humans shapes the ways in which relations of care unfold over time, and conversely how trajectories of care shape believers' knowledge about those persons. What lived predicaments do these forms of care and insight reflect and potentially remake?

There are moral perils inherent in the connections among spirits and bodies. For instance, members of the African American congregations speak of "soul ties" and "generational curses" originating in great injuries that cause descendants of the perpetrators to suffer and/or repeat the offenses (Abrums 2010; Carter 2019: 58–9; Woodbine 2021: 203). However, the key source of insight into interpersonal connection for Pentecostals is "receiving the Holy Ghost," a supremely affirmative experience that convinces them of how God inhabits their bodies. Members of the suburban church of Eternal Hope can specify the exact day, often decades previously, when they received the Holy Ghost and/or were baptized by immersion. Pastor Hadley often remarks to her congregation that God may forgive you if you deny that you are a Christian, or even if you deny his own existence, but to deny the existence of the Holy Ghost after you have experienced his power in your body—she says with a shudder—is the only sin that cannot be forgiven.

To receive the Holy Ghost entails envisioning oneself as a porous being, a condition with wide-ranging implications. Writing of the moral perils of same-sex attraction for white evangelical Christians in the United States, Sophie Bjork-James (2018) points out that

> sexual desires and sexual acts are broadly understood in evangelical cosmology as communicative mediums for supernatural forces ... At least part of this emphasis stems from a view that sexual organs are openings to the body and thus are sites of literal porosity—and a corollary view that sexual intercourse involves penetration not only of the physical body but also of the soul. (650)

Many evangelical Christians involved in the "ex-gay movement" consider same-sex relationships to be "selfish" because those liaisons ostensibly close people off from God and promote the spread of evil forces across social and geographic scales. By ostracizing LGBTQ people, the believers whom Bjork-James describes attempt to close themselves off from the spiritual dangers that their connections to people in same-sex relationships would otherwise open.

Sexual desire apart, Bjork-James's argument may be extended to many different ways in which a "relationship with God" affords believers insight into how vitality and danger stem from closures and openings, as well as from the deployment of these metaphors in artful speech. Believers use such imagery to describe both what they know about the activities of human and nonhuman persons, and the effects that their own knowledge produces. For instance, members of the suburban church rely on idioms of opening to describe the bodily actions that foster worshippers' receptivity to the Holy Spirit. On the other hand, the phrase "to cover someone in prayer," used commonly in all the churches I am describing, signifies the power of a believer's words to shield another person from danger. Pastor Hadley routinely admonishes her congregation not to leave until everyone recites the final words of the service—"May the Lord watch—between me and thee—while we are absent—one from another;—Watch—as well as pray"—because this dismissal "seals" the word of God in the hearts of his hearers and prevents the devil from subsequently "stealing" the word. One Sunday, Pastor Hadley publicly apologized because she had forgotten during the previous week's revival to seal the word of the Lord in this fashion. As a result, the devil was able to try to prevent the great "deliverance" at hand by "attacking the body of believers," causing a spate of illnesses over the intervening period.

In her study of witnessing among fundamental Baptists in Virginia, Susan Harding argues that "speaking is believing": "in a coded way, they recognize language as a medium, even a subject, of religious experience, and they coach the unconverted in the linguistic dimension of conversion" (2000: 47). Harding advances this argument to explain how God becomes indubitably real for believers, a question that is key for Luhrmann (2004) as well in her treatment of the bodily techniques through which believers apprehend God as an intimate presence. In focusing rather on what kinds of difference it makes to gain insight into God's intents, I would add that believers understand God to have designed certain linguistic and other communicative expressions such as praise dancing (Elisha 2018) to be means of ensuring their own and others' vitality.[1] As a result, they understand speech and other bodily forms of communication to be mediums and subjects of care. In deploying imageries of openness and closure—together with related ones of connection, intake, emergence, expulsion, enclosure, and receptivity—they stipulate that God has designed vitality to possess specific kinds of content and not others.

My principal argument in this chapter is that as believers discern God's designs for communication and connectedness among bodies and spirits, they derive insight into various forms of divine and human care. In making this claim, I build on Bjork-James's suggestion that God shapes the ways believers comprehend kinship relations as sources of vitality and danger as he enables them to discern the body's porosity. Carrying forward my argument that discernment is both a source and a form of vitality, I show that insights into God's designs for connectedness constitute means of imagining and indeed creating kinship. In the suburban church of Eternal Hope, believers understand parenthood, siblinghood, and marriage as both models for and outcomes of "open" communication about the truth of the self, though communication with God involves forms of intimacy that may transcend the qualities of these relations. In the African American congregations, the emphasis lies on forms of covering and reception. In Heaven's Tabernacle and Victory Gospel, believers lay particular stress on receiving prophetic "coverings" that ensure protection, even as they express concerns about negative kinds of "covering" that they relate to misrepresentation and exploitation among kin. In scriptural terms, both sets of imageries draw heavily on Pauline concepts of the split between obediently willing and disobediently willful aspects of the self, which are common subjects of preaching in all these churches. I return to sexuality at the end of this chapter, exploring Pastor John's concerns about how "openings" and "connections" to demonic spirits contribute to improper forms of socialization within African American families.

## Opening the Truth of the Self

On two successive Sunday evening services in the suburban church of Eternal Hope, a twelve-year-old boy named Evan stood surrounded by a large crowd of adults as he tried to "get the Holy Ghost." The fact that Evan had not yet been able to receive the Holy Ghost was a matter of mild anxiety, since his older brother had done so at the age of eight. Evan's mother and father stood closest to him, laying hands upon him while others had their hands on them in turn, hoping that he would begin to speak in tongues or otherwise worship in the Spirit by shaking, jumping, or shouting.[2] While the other adults were all loudly praying in tongues, Evan's parents were speaking softly to him with expressions of concern on their faces. In a subsequent interview, Evan's father Bill, who worked in a factory making purchases, described to me how worshipping in the Spirit had been important to him in his own youth, and how encouraging his sons to receive the Holy Ghost was key to his parenting.

Bill's parents joined Eternal Hope when he was five years old, so that he has been going to the church for over thirty years. He described his own father, who worked in a tire factory, as having been emotionally distant. His parents' homelife was not the best: "There was no communication for several years, it was quiet, separate bedrooms, no love." This had given him a model, he remarked, for what not to do with his own children. His parents divorced when Bill was sixteen years old. Bill recalled how the large youth group at the church had helped him during that period, and remarked that they were still close as adults. Many in his group of peers have married one another, and they visit each other's homes regularly and watch their children.

Bill recalled that as a teenager he had been a "private person" who would "keep things to myself," but his experiences during altar calls at Eternal Hope provided him with lasting bonds at a time when his home life was difficult. Commenting on how worshippers pray at the altar, he remarked:

> That's the raw person. Where else in the world do you get to see that side to a person? You don't get to see the insides of a person anywhere. Maybe at a funeral sometimes. Very rarely do you get a glimpse inside to someone [other] than when you're at the altar trying to help them and you're encouraging them to reach their goal. It's very, very rewarding when you can participate in that. There's a kinship there.

"I never had that experience with anybody outside the church," Bill continued.

> Many, many times throughout our youth we had those times where we were emotionally open to each other, and that was okay and that was accepted. There's bonds that are created there that you don't find anywhere else in the world. You're not going to find those bonds with friends at school or at a job. Those are opportunities when you create not just friendships but a brotherhood and sisterhood.

Members of Eternal Hope call each other "Brother" or "Sister" so-and-so, as do members of the African American churches.[3]

The act of helping fellow worshippers to "reach their goal" of being "emotionally open" transforms erstwhile strangers into kin. For Bill, the communicative processes that operate in "the world" conceal a person's true sense of vulnerability behind expressive norms of the sort that he has encountered in school, work, and his own parental home. In my view, the formal dress styles at Eternal Hope, where women wear long dresses or skirts and men jackets and ties, help to highlight this contrast between interior susceptibility and external convention. In the enthusiasm of worship, the reserved demeanor ordinarily associated with such clothing is abandoned. It is as though the formal exterior exists in part so that it may be cast aside to signal the vulnerable self's exposure to God and other believers.

Bill related how he encouraged his son Evan to receive the Holy Ghost so that he would feel dependent on God and become receptive to the help of fellow worshippers—but also autonomous in his volition. He had waited for Evan to ask him about receiving the Holy Ghost rather than pressing him to do so. "It has to be the children's initiative," he said.

> You have to be careful that you don't get to the point where they're doing that [i.e., worshipping] just because you tell them to. They're going to get to an age where

they're physically and emotionally independent. I feel strongly in the church environment that they have to establish their own relationship [with God]. They're going to be men in a very short period of time, and if I push them, they're going to come to a time in their lives when they think, "I don't have to do this anymore." I want them to have this relationship with God because *they* started it.

At stake in Bill's efforts to promote his sons' "own" relationships with God is his desire to foster their independent volition without forfeiting their affection and respect for himself as their father. In this context, the paternal role of an intercessor is comparable to that of a coach encouraging a player to do his best. Bill indicated as much in drawing a connection between teaching his sons how to receive the Holy Ghost and his own work as a baseball coach. He has seen boys suffer "emotional breakdowns" on the field because they are on the team only because their parents want them to play.

In keeping with this emphasis on developing his sons' sense of autonomy, Bill told me that his advice to Evan about receiving the Holy Ghost was as follows: "Don't just say words and repeat words. Pour your heart out to God in worship and praise and repentance and ask Him for forgiveness for your sins. Concentrate on what you're doing, concentrate on praying to God and engaging emotionally with what you're saying. Don't be distracted by looking around to see what other people are doing." It might seem paradoxical that such expressions of autonomous sincerity (Keane 2002) must be elicited by means of the powerful involvement of others at the altar. However, the apparent paradox disappears in light of the kinship relations created and reinforced among worshippers and intercessors. Bill came to recognize the intercessors in his own peer group as "a brotherhood and sisterhood" by virtue of their potent bodily involvement in his well-being, which made it safe for him to be "emotionally open" with them about his struggles. It is the role of intercessors to encourage supplicants to be "open" in the same manner with Jesus. While Bill did not use the term discernment to describe how he had recognized these kinship bonds, the insights that his peers helped to give him into God's desires for openness—insights which had their source in God—made them into kin.

I asked Bill to suggest how I might explain to a secular audience why it is so important to receive the Holy Ghost. He replied that there had been many instances when God would "check" him when he risked becoming involved in situations that would tempt him to sin.

Many times through my life I've had a check, where I just know this isn't right. People have asked me to go with them on certain occasions ... This world is a scary place to raise children and a scary place to grow up. Drugs, alcohol, many things on the internet, temptations. I don't want my kids to get involved in premarital sex. I want them to be able to grow up and be mentally mature and raise families that way.

To summarize, Bill spoke of getting the Holy Ghost as an act enabling believers to overcome the moral perils of emotional isolation, self-indulgence, and pressures to conform. In this account, God cares for believers by performing a kind of calibration between autonomy and dependence. Bill wishes his son Evan to depend on the encouragement of other worshippers to become "open" to God—otherwise, he might become emotionally isolated and yield to temptations—yet not to the extent that Evan's own will to openness is diminished. Since his sons are "going to become men in a very short period of time," it is incumbent on Bill as a father to help them establish a sense of volition proper to themselves so that they may be "mentally mature" and raise their families properly.

The trajectory of care that Bill envisioned for his sons recalls aspects of George Lakoff's (2002) description of "Strict Father Morality," a worldview underlying conservative political thinking in the United States, in particular the principle that "at maturity, a child is assumed to be able to determine and act on his best interests for himself ... In the Strict Father model, the father must know when his authority ends, after which any illegitimate intrusion by him is resented mightily" (79). Bill's recollections of the "checks" that God has given him to warn him of danger, together with his remark that the world is "a scary place," dovetail likewise with Lakoff's account of Moral Strength, a central metaphor in Strict Father Morality, which posits a world of external threats and internal weaknesses that must be confronted. However, believers at Eternal Hope do not imagine that they can be strong in themselves; they depend on the connections among bodies and spirits that God causes them to apprehend. Bill imagines that Evan's sense of paternal authority will be transferred from himself to God, yet he insists that this transfer needs to be accomplished by an exercise of autonomous willingness and sincerity on Evan's part. Even so, God's paternal authority will be different from Bill's inasmuch as the Holy Ghost will create an intimate union with Evan of a kind that Bill could not and would not wish to achieve with his adult son.[4] In effect, then, Lakoff's account of Strict Father Morality holds true for this instance: the human father must know the point at which his authority over his son should end and let God take over, namely when the son exercises autonomous volition.

While Bill articulated a distinctively white masculine imperative to develop and calibrate one's volition, a middle-aged woman named Lynne who worked as a tour operator told me that in order to receive the Holy Ghost, a person needs to abandon her "pride" so far as to say, "I'm so sorry, God, for always trying to take control and do it my way." Lynne expressed remorse because prior to being saved, she had partied at clubs following a divorce and turned a blind eye to her teenaged sons' unruliness. Lynne narrated the experience of getting the Holy Ghost as beginning as a contracting sensation in her stomach that she likened to the impulse to vomit, culminating in a kind of full-body opening, arguably a transfigured and transfiguring childbirth:

> The Holy Ghost wants to come out … I think the contraction [means] I'm trying to suppress it. So, you can just feel it, and then when you let that go, you let it out, I'll never forget when I first started talking in tongues, oh my goodness … I just let it go. It's like a freedom! I let it go, and I started laughing uncontrollably. And I remember the girl [standing next to her at the time], she was amazing, she said, "Lynne, there was this ring of fire around you." 'Cause you know how they talk about how the fire still falls. I was jumping and I was laughing, I was drunk in the Holy Ghost. … It's an amazing thing when you finally let your head stop thinking about it. You have to pray through it … You can't think your way to the Holy Ghost. It's repenting and praying and praising and giving God the glory.

In contrast to the Catholic Charismatics described by Csordas (1994), who enter a calm and relaxed swoon as their injured selves become reconciled with the divine will, Lynne spoke of "letting it out" as a kind of ecstasy. I was often struck by the intercorporeal nature of such ecstasy, which in Lynne's account involved the woman who was helping her receive the Holy Ghost in a shared joy. The acts she narrated of repentance, prayer, praise, and giving God the glory for overcoming sinful inclinations all express a willing and sincere openness conveyed in a core scriptural injunction: "Repent and be baptized every one of you in the name of Jesus Christ for the remission of sins, and ye shall receive the gift of the Holy Ghost" (Acts 2:38). While such openings frequently depend on or stimulate the sympathetic involvement of others, they reflect moral ambitions to grasp the truth of the self as God knows it. A young man named Tom who like Lynne has struggled with alcohol in the past spoke of being drunk as "being in your own head," whereas getting the Holy Ghost is "freedom—you know that you are in God's hands." A person who has not received the Holy Ghost is not self-possessed according to a modernist ideal, but rather liable to the promptings of the devil. I often heard in Eternal Hope—though rarely in the African American churches—that every person is born with "a hole" open inside himself or herself that the devil will try to fill with destructive thoughts and behaviors. Arlene told me that after she first spoke in tongues, she realized that when she had previously thought about her body over the course of an unsatisfactory marriage, she had envisioned herself with a large black hole over her torso. Once she "got a relationship with God," she envisioned her body as complete. The devil, she told me, wants us to imagine that we are complete in ourselves, whereas the Holy Ghost gives us the insight that Jesus must fill the hole in us that had been open. This imagery of false versus true self-completion represents a particular stance on the Pauline predicament broadly shared in all the churches I am discussing: "For I know that good itself does not dwell in me, that is, in my sinful nature. For I have the desire to do what is good, but I cannot carry it out" (Rom. 7:18 NIV).

I experienced a comparable negation of self-sufficiency when I received the Holy Ghost at Eternal Hope. I tried to get caught up in the Spirit during worship sessions, and at one point began to speak unintelligible syllables. Standing next to me, Kathy thought (as she later told me), "Oh my gosh, Fred's praying!" and whispered some advice in my ear: "Don't think about what your mouth is doing. Just think about God." I drew a blank, and soon stopped. In a subsequent sermon, a minister spoke about the necessity to live for God rather than to live for ourselves. I was mentally busy comparing the content of the sermon to Max Weber's treatment (2003) of the Calvinist imperative to live a life of good deeds combined into a rationalized system so as to make oneself an instrument of God in the world. To adopt believers' idiom, I was "in my own head," though not (it is safe to say) in a way most of them experience. At a certain point, however, I said to myself—or the thought came to me, I cannot say which: "Just accept what the preacher is saying on its own terms. Think about living for God, not just for yourself." That did it. Without intending to do so, I began shouting glossolalia, my arms in the air, my body swaying, and my legs pumping. After one such episode, during which people held me up as I jumped and swayed in front of the altar, Arlene commented: "See? This is real." Significantly, a number of church members made a point of telling me that the sight of me worshipping had made the Spirit leap inside their bodies as well. They felt it important to tell me of the sympathetic connections between my own Holy Ghost worship and their own, in effect letting me know that we all shared one body in Christ. Arlene explained to me that as God is the head of the body of believers, he will use a person to take care of someone who is "going through" something, as one might use a hand to heal an injury to another body part.

Believers at Eternal Hope cultivate their capacity to intercede for others through bodily techniques that in various literal and figurative ways serve to open out what had been closed off. Lynne, who had joined Eternal Hope a few years before I met her, explained that "in the [Anglican] church that I grew up in ... they never taught us really how to pray the way Jesus taught us how to pray through the scripture. It was always just standing there with our mouths shut and thinking things." Rejecting this oral closure, Lynne made explicit that a relationship with God ought to be modeled on a marriage based on open communication: "We need to speak it—God wants us, it's a relationship y'know, like a husband and wife relationship. Like if you're going to speak to your wife, you communicate verbally." She had just been praying in a group with a woman who had gone to the altar weeping with her shoulders clenched. While Bill instructed his son not to "just repeat words," Lynne modeled intimacy with Jesus for the supplicant by encouraging her to use scaffolding expressions like "help me Lord" to express the truth of what she was "going through":

> Well, y'know, we were telling her, "Talk to Jesus, say it out loud, say Lord Jesus, help me Lord." And that's what we were saying to her, and then she started talking, and talking to the Lord. And we said, no matter what it is, He knows what you're going through, tell Him what you need. And she started—I don't know what she was saying, because I was y'know talking in her ear—so I was like, "Honey, y'know give it all to the Lord no matter what it is, let Him know Lord I need you, help me Jesus, I trust in You Jesus ... thank You for dying for my sins Lord Jesus, You died for me, I will live for You Lord." ... I was teaching her how to speak to Him and how to pray and just talk from her tongue, because we all start out almost the same way ... I don't know what her sins are, I just know that we're all sinners.

Taking Lynne up on an expression she had earlier used for the "tight" way the woman was holding her shoulders, I prompted: "You could tell that she was having trouble because she was all tight?" In her reply, Lynne figured bodily relaxation as an index of openness to Jesus:

> At first she was really tight, but we were telling her how much Jesus loves her, let Him wrap his arms around you and embrace Him and He will comfort you and He will give you that peace and that joy that you're looking for. She started—you could feel how she started—she lifted her hands just a little bit, that's good, that's a nice sign, but you could just tell that she was relaxing—and it was nice. And the same with her brother too, I've seen him a couple times come to the altar. He just stands there with hands at his sides and his fists clenched. Now today, when

[another woman member] went over and helped him just raise his hands, you can see, 'cause he used to be, almost like a stone, because he's got a lot of stuff going on with him right now … and all of a sudden, 'cause we were praying in Jesus' name, you could feel how his whole body was starting to relax, his whole body wasn't as stiff as it had been. And he was receiving it, he was moving his lips, like talking to the Lord, I couldn't hear what he was saying, and I don't need to hear what he was saying and that's what we were telling him: "This is between you and Jesus. Whatever it is, just talk to Him, ask Him to help you, and He will, He will give you that strength and that wisdom and He will teach you His ways." 'Cause I'm not in his face, I'm whispering in his ear, I'm not yelling at him, I'm letting him know in a soft voice that Jesus loves you and He already knows what you're going through, but He wants you to ask Him to help you.

In a manner recalling Kathy's characterization of intercessors as "oracles," Lynne made clear that her speech at the altar was designed by God to elicit openness. The devil works by trying to prevent openness, attempting to disrupt connections among the bodies of believers. In particular, the devil tries to disturb the timing whereby God induces a person to intercede for another at a specific moment. I asked Lynne what had prompted her to pray for a particular group at the altar.

I just felt led by the Lord to go over. There's a lot of people at the altar, but I just felt led. Sometimes I don't obey right away. I get a real strong feeling in the Holy Ghost, in my stomach, that it's like, you need to go pray for that family, and that young person. And I go like, maybe they're not ready. Because that's how the devil works: "Well maybe they're not ready to have somebody pray for them." Well, God knows best. So I went anyways, because the feeling got stronger in my gut. You need to go and softly pray with them, and they received it … Because they've been to the altar a few times, but I've never felt led [to pray with them] before. It's always in God's timing. You're kind of sensitive to the spirit of God. God knows what people need right when they need it. And today I just felt that, by the Lord, go and now gently lay hands and speak to them. And it had nothing to do with me. It was all God.

While being "sensitive to the spirit of God" consistently elicits "open" communication, believers adopt those communicative designs as models for care in some gender-specific ways. In contrast to Bill's expectation that the Holy Ghost will foster and calibrate his son's individual volition so as to render him autonomous, Lynne made use of her communicative relationship with God to foster intimacy with her own adult son in ways that countered his autonomy. Like other women in Eternal Hope who speak of "having a burden" to care for people, Lynne told me how she had metaphorically "carried" her adult son, who had been smoking marijuana and dealing illegal drugs, to God at the altar in his absence. Distraught, she asked God to "bring him to his knees," to do whatever it would take to get him off drugs. Her son, suffering from hallucinations and anxiety attacks, asked her to stop praying because although he did not attend church, he suspected that her appeals to God were worsening his anxiety. She told him that she would not cease praying—this, she knew, was "spiritual warfare." Finally, he called her at two in the morning, fearing that he was "going crazy" and needed to go to the hospital. Lynne recounted that as she drove to her son's apartment, she prayed for him over the phone: "Jesus, take this torment away from him. Honey, just think of the goodness of God, He loves you." As she prayed, she "heard a peacefulness come over him." When she arrived, she laid hands on him and rebuked the devil. "I prayed the name of Jesus over all the walls and every doorknob." Clearly, these activities were specifically maternal, in keeping with a gender ideology that identifies looking after dependents as women's care work and fostering autonomy as that of men.

Members of the African American congregations of Victory Gospel and Heaven's Tabernacle are similarly concerned with God's designs for verbal and intercorporeal forms of communication, and with the ways these styles of communication shape kinship relations. However, their idioms for those designs, centering on images of enclosure, protection, and reception, diverge significantly from those Eternal Hope members deploy as they foster openness. Before turning back to kinship, then, I need to discuss these idioms on their own terms.

## Receiving a Covering

At the beginning of Sunday services at Victory Gospel, ministers call out: "God woke you up this morning, you didn't wake yourself up, God called your name this morning," eliciting "hand-claps of praise" for God from the worshippers. One of the most important foundations of faith for these believers is the knowledge that they are alive only because God keeps them and protects them. At the outset of a service in March 2017, Pastor John related that he had heard of three nearly fatal incidents endured by members of the congregation over the previous week, including a traffic accident and a shooting. Everyone had escaped unscathed: "You better know that God has you under His covering." In 2014, Pastor Hadley told Heaven's Tabernacle that Apostle Cooper, her Overseer based in another US city, had been in a limousine that gang members mistook for a car belonging to rivals. The gang riddled the car with bullets, but not one hit Apostle Cooper or the other six church members who were with him. About a year later, Apostle Cooper was suffering from a severe lung infection, and the doctors were not optimistic. However, he made a full recovery. During a subsequent revival at the Apostle's home church in 2016, another prophet told him publicly of the significance of his illness: "God says, 'I'm sorry, but you had to go through that so the saints wouldn't be attacked by the enemy.'"

At the suburban church of Eternal Hope, Lynne likewise described to me the thankfulness she feels toward God for awakening her each morning. However, the insight that motivates her gratitude has less to do with protection than with her sense of her own limitations (an issue I take up in Chapter 4): "It's His blessings that have given us the gifts and talents that we have, it's not from me, it's from Him." By contrast, Pastor Hadley and Pastor John direct believers' attention to the ways they themselves elicit God's power to protect or "cover" the saints. In the remainder of this chapter, I describe various ways in which these pastors extend God's "covering" to believers by encouraging them to develop insight into forms of communication and connectedness among bodies and spirits (e.g., "*you better know* that God has you under His covering"). Covering is a form of protection or care that members of Heaven's Tabernacle and Victory Gospel speak of "receiving"—a communicative act involving specific kinds of listening and acceptance. They develop insights about connectedness centering on *what kinds of covering they have received and from whom*—ideally and ultimately, the blood of Jesus.[5] As a form of communication, receiving is both a medium and a subject of care: receiving must be fostered in specific ways if it is to convey protection. Hence, "receiving a covering" both provides and requires insight from God. I turn first to pastors' roles in extending covering, and then discuss the linkages between covering and reception.

In contrast to Eternal Hope, where the touch of the Holy Spirit is in a sense democratized—anybody can intercede for anyone else, albeit usually of the same gender, and stand over a person as he or she falls to the ground in the Spirit—there is much more concern in the African American churches with literally and figuratively "covering" those in vulnerable conditions. For instance, Pastor John commonly rushes around the congregation during the culmination of his sermons, laying hands on attendees and giving them a "word from the Lord" (usually, a promise of prosperity or healing) as the Spirit leads him. The people he touches are subsequently "slain in the Spirit," falling to the floor as he lays hands on them. At Heaven's Tabernacle, Pastor Hadley lays hands on saints or their relatives and friends who come forward after the sermon "for prayer." On these occasions, she frequently reminds the congregation of the miraculous healings that have taken place in the church, including those of a woman with a brain tumor and an infant whose doctors thought she needed a tracheotomy but could find no problem when she returned for a subsequent appointment. While speaking in tongues, Pastor Hadley touches the afflicted body parts of those who come forward or forcefully brushes demonic forces off them with either downward strokes of her hands or the flicking motions of a small towel. At this point, the person who has been healed usually falls to the ground. At both churches, assistants quickly cover those slain in the Spirit with a blanket (sometimes called a "deliverance cloth") for reasons of modesty, and saints avert their eyes from those on the floor. Members of Victory Gospel occasionally lay hands on one another in groups, but this is done only at the explicit direction of Pastor John as the Holy Ghost "leads" or instructs him, not when God moves an individual believer to intercede. In some African American Pentecostal denominations such as COOLJC, elders "tarry" for extended periods in intimate prayer with individual supplicants who wish to receive the Holy Ghost, but they too acknowledge that they must not pray for anyone to whom God has not led them (Casselberry 2017). At a Bible study, Pastor John publicly disparaged "people running around laying hands with no authority—all they're doing is transferring demons."

This emphasis on the authority of Pastor John and Pastor Hadley to protect and bless reflects aspects of the important roles African American churches have historically played in providing shelter and guidance in the face of injustice. C. Eric Lincoln and Lawrence Mamiya (1990) describe a "dialectic between priestly and prophetic functions" among leaders of Black churches, the former centered on "maintaining the spiritual life of members" and the latter on "political concerns and involvement in the wider community." While "some churches are closer to one end than to the other ... liberation churches also perform the priestly functions and priestly churches contain liberation potential" (12). Whether they are priests or prophets or both, the authority exercised by African American pastors stems from the historical fact that "black churches were one of the few stable and coherent institutions to emerge from slavery" (7). In 1903, W. E. B. Du Bois famously described the "Preacher" as

the most unique personality developed by the Negro on American soil. A leader, a politician, an orator, a "boss," an intriguer, an idealist,—all these he is, and ever, too, the centre of a group of men, now twenty, now a thousand in number.

The combination of a certain adroitness with deep-seated earnestness, of tact with consummate ability, gave him his preëminence, and helps him maintain it. (1990: 138)

This portrait of charisma concentrated in a single male figure needs to be qualified given that spiritual authority has historically extended to other officeholders within African American church hierarchies, many of whom have been women (Casselberry 2017; Gilkes 2001). Still, in Victory Gospel and Heaven's Tabernacle at least, "leaders" including subordinate ministers, evangelists, deacons, and elders derive their authority explicitly from their willingness to work under the direction of Pastor John and Pastor Hadley to lead prayer, teach Bible studies, and organize events including fundraisers and community giveaways. These hierarchies serve to concentrate rather than disperse charisma.

Members of Victory Gospel and Heaven's Tabernacle maintain that God sets up a "hedge of protection" around them and their kin in response to their pastors' prayers. Yet even as they pray, pastors become vulnerable to the attacks of the devil. The higher you rise in authority in God's kingdom, the harder the devil is said to struggle to bring you down, his logic being that if he can destroy the leader he will be better able to destroy the people. Those who are "advanced in the kingdom of God" by virtue of their prophetic gifts and long years in ministry protect others even as they themselves undergo perils of exposure. Following a service, an elder man in Apostle Cooper's congregation spoke to me of intercession as a matter of positioning oneself between the devil and the saints: "It's hard to be an Apostle because you're always interceding for people, so all the things that were supposed to be aimed at them are hurting you instead. Apostle woke up the other day feeling he'd just fought with Mike Tyson." In Heaven's Tabernacle and Victory Gospel, saints make concerted efforts to show that they in turn value the lives of their pastors, for instance by "lifting them up" in their own prayers—though usually not by covering them, since only other leaders have the spiritual authority to cover the pastors.

Some of the most striking instances of covering involve monetary gifts, which as I discuss in Chapter 4 commonly mediate spiritual realities within Pentecostal movements worldwide (Daswani 2015; Lindhardt 2009; van Wyk 2014). Prior to the revival at Apostle Cooper's church in 2016, Pastor Hadley together with a number of other pastors whose churches he oversees in other US states took up monetary collections from the saints so that they might "be a blessing to him."[6] This was enormously successful; it was later announced that over $2000 was raised for the Apostle, who works as a manager at a fast-food restaurant. During the revival weekend, Apostle Cooper told these pastors that he had written in a notebook the names of everyone who had donated to him, and that he was keeping the notebook in an inside pocket of his suit jacket so as to safeguard the donors against misfortunes. At a meeting of the pastors during the revival weekend, one of them pinned twenty-dollar bills from the collection all over Apostle's clothing as he stood before her, telling him that God would "bless his seed." Similarly, attendees at baby showers in the African American community clip cash to a pin on an expectant mother's shirt in order to "be a blessing" to her and her child, while guests at birthday parties do likewise for the honoree.

Like these monetary coverings, prayers for a "hedge of protection" convey blessings through safeguarding and enclosing. To grasp the significance of protection and enclosure, it is useful to compare the remarks that church members made about Apostle Cooper's vulnerability to demonic attack with passages from *Pigs in the Parlor* (2010), an enormously influential guide to "deliverance" (exorcism) composed in 1973 by Frank and Ida Mae Hammond, Euro-American Baptist ministers from Texas. Apostle Cooper, Pastor John, and Pastor Hadley use many of the same idioms as the Hammonds to characterize demonic forces, such as the "spirit of rejection" and the "spirit of fear," as well as to describe the ways demons enter the body through spiritual "openings" and depart through physical openings, via oral purgation or through the doorway of the building. I witnessed deliverance events perhaps once a month in Pastor Hadley's congregation and more occasionally at Pastor John's. These can be dramatic occasions when demons use the voice of the person they are possessing to speak or shout, or cause the person's body to run about or slide on the ground.

Frank Hammond argues that deliverance ministers have nothing to fear from evil spirits:

> Some of the reasons advanced for not laying hands in deliverance are based on fear. Some persons have been fearful lest the evil spirit make an attack upon them. I heard one person say that while laying hands on someone during deliverance he felt an evil spirit move from that person into his own hand and up his arm into his body. I personally have had no experience of such an occurrence. I have been laying hands on hundreds of persons over a period of several years and have never been attacked by a demon as the result of such physical contact.

> The principle is this: *no demon can attack us or enter us unless it has an opening to do so*. Fear can provide such an opening. If one is afraid that a demon can attack him, then he has given the demon the opening he needs. (2010: 94–5)

Apostle Cooper, Pastor John, and Pastor Hadley similarly disclaim any fear of evil spirits as they pray and lay hands, maintaining that "God has not given us the spirit of fear." However, their approaches to deliverance reflect their concern with protecting those who are less spiritually mature. They carefully instruct armor bearers as well as ordinary saints not to touch them while they are engaged in deliverance. People who are undergoing deliverance must be touched only by pastors, since only they possess the "power" and the "authority" to confront the demons;[7] Pastor John told his congregation that even he would not touch the head of a woman possessed by a demon, since the head is the "control center," containing "the natural brain" and "the spiritual mind." Likewise, when a person is lying on the floor having been "slain in the Spirit" after being touched by the Holy Ghost through the pastor's hands, nobody must step over him or her due to the danger of exposure to any evil spirit that might be afflicting that person, and nobody but trained assistants must catch these people as they fall backward or help them up from the floor. "It takes a lot of virtue out of me to pray for you at the altar," Pastor John told the congregation. "For a moment, I feel what you are going through."

Prophetic speech, often called "a word spoken over your life," is another kind of protective or covering activity. Prophets commonly convey blessings to their listeners by telling them of what God has planned for them. Pastor John often reminds his congregation that he knows he will prosper because a prophet once spoke a word over his life to the effect that enemies would set pitfalls for him but that he would avoid them all. He described to me the experience of being moved to prophesy as a corporeal "burning" signal that demands a response on his part:

> The best way I can describe it to you metaphorically, it's like a light switch. I can have the light on as much as I want. It'll click on whenever I get in tune. It won't click off unless I decide to try to turn it off. At times of emergency that He wants me to do something, I can't turn it off, He will just turn it on to alarm me that I need to do this or that. It's hard to describe because you will get a feeling in your body that is so unusual, the sensation is like a burning within you that says, "Get up and pray for this person now." It's a burning in my whole body. It's crazy, 'cause it's like a cool hot rush. And these are the times when I'm just sitting down and doing my natural man things and my home things, and just trying to tune out that part of me. And if it's something that I need to do, I won't be able to tune it out. I will have to say or do whatever He's telling me to do at that moment.

This kind of prophetic speech has implications for both covering and receiving that may be understood by returning briefly to deliverance. The Hammonds characterize the purpose of deliverance in terms that recall how members of Eternal Hope elicit sincere speech to Jesus during intercession. Spiritual warfare, the Hammonds (2010) write, is a means of "releasing ... a person's will in order that he can respond directly to the Lord and receive the help God has for him" (76). The aim is to allow a person to act on his or her autonomous will: "We must realize that we cannot control another person's will. Trying to control another person's will is opposite to the goal of deliverance and spiritual warfare, and is tantamount to *witchcraft*" (76)—an assessment that Pastor John and Pastor Hadley expressly share with their congregations, telling them that they must never pray in order to control what other people do. Yet when these pastors "cover" or "speak a word over" people's lives in order to help them understand "who they are in God"—that is, the truth of themselves as God sees them—they are concerned less with specifying their autonomy than with their receptivity to the speakers, namely God and his prophet.

An example will illustrate this point. Pastor John recounted to me how he had spoken a word over the life of a barber whom he happened to meet:

> I was in a barbershop last night, and I shared with a young man who cut my hair. My usual barber was busy, and this young man was in a hurry to get out of there, but he said, "Come on, I'll cut your hair." When he was cutting me up, I began to talk to him about some things that he had been praying about. Now I didn't know, I wasn't in the prophetic [frame of mind], I was just talking. And some of the things I was sharing, about credit, about restoration, about some of the things I've been working on through the church. [Pastor John had been prophesying in church that believers' debts would be forgiven and their credit restored.] And he was like, "Oh my God, just last night I was praying to God, saying how am I going to do this? I need someone to help me with my credit." And we end up talking for three hours after that. And he ended up stating: "This was God. This was God." He said, "I'm glad I told you I would take you [as a customer], because I normally wouldn't have. I had to go, but something was telling me to stay."

> Then at that point, the prophetic kicked in. I began to tell him what the Lord had told me about him having his own barbershop. He said, "Oh my God. I've been looking to do my own thing. I've really been looking to do this." It was like I couldn't break free from him. He was in awe of two confirmations he received in one night. The first was the credit restoration portion, when he was praying for the Lord to help him with his credit: "I need to find someone to help guide me through this." And here I am in the barber chair talking to him about credit, and the second confirmation was when the Lord showed me about his own

barbershop. He wasn't satisfied working where he was, but he didn't know which direction he should take until he heard those words coming out of me. He knew then, this is God now.

I revisit the important term "confirmation" in Chapter 5, which concerns the nature of events. For now, I wish to consider the imagery of "receiving" words from "the man of God"—that is, someone to whom God reveals things about other people's lives—and what reception has to do with covering. A striking element of Pastor John's account is the stress he places on the dialogic nature of his speech with the barber about God's word. Recall that Lynne related how the man for whom she was interceding at Eternal Hope was "receiving" the word of God, but she disclaimed any interest in the content of his responses: "He was receiving it, he was moving his lips, like talking to the Lord, I couldn't hear what he was saying, and I don't need to hear what he was saying and that's what we were telling him." By contrast, Pastor John found it important to hear and relate the barber's responses in order to make clear that his own words about what God had told him had been "received" by the barber, because the barber's reception confirms his discernment. "A prophet can be off," he tells the congregation, acknowledging the possibility that he might be misinterpreting divine communications. "If I'm telling you what God is showing me, I need you to let me know that I'm on it."

"Receiving" connotes not only hearing but acceptance and consequent action. The semantics of "receiving" reflect the prominence in African American language patterns of listener-oriented semiotic forms, in which the significance of an utterance depends on the responses it elicits (Kochman 1981; Smitherman 1977; cf. Robbins 2001). At times during ordinary conversation when I would have been likely to ask, "How did so-and-so respond to that advice?" my friends in the African American community would say, "How did they receive that?" At a certain revival, a preacher whom I did not know gave me a prophetic word. She asked me to stand in the midst of the congregation and publicly warned me, "The devil is after your mind." I approached her afterward to say, "Thank you for the word you gave me." She replied, "Thank you for receiving it," acknowledging my appreciation and in effect letting me know that it was my responsibility to act on the knowledge. Allowing the devil to shape one's thinking is likewise a matter of receiving or agreeing. When misfortunes or provocations occur, Evangelist Clarice said, it is important to "throw that demon into confusion by dancing or praising. The devil throws something at you and waits to see if you're in agreement." Evangelist Clarice alluded here to the exhortation "Let's touch and agree," whereby Pastor Hadley frequently calls other leaders to hold one another's hands in small groups near the conclusion of a service, amplifying the powers of each person's appeals to the Holy Ghost to bring about healing or other miracles in response to specific attendees' requests for prayer.

Within this semantic field, then, to "be covered" implies having *received a covering from someone* whether in the form of a prayer, a word spoken over one's life, a notebook enclosed in a pocket, or money attached to clothing. Ultimately, it is God who provides the covering, as believers point out in reference to the biblical passage "charity shall cover the multitude of sins" (1 Pet. 4:8), which they interpret to mean that God will excuse the sins committed by saints who remain faithful. Approaching the Bible as a spur to reflection on the order of things, Pastor John would take great pleasure in preaching and speaking with me about how "covering" helps to define the relation between humanity and divinity. Humans were designed by God, he remarks, to be spirit beings. In the Garden of Eden, Adam and Eve were "covered" in the glory of God, and their "natural bodies" were inside these glorified bodies. When they ate the apple, God's glory sank inside their physical bodies, becoming the interior "spirit man" (the male identifier is always used by members of Victory Gospel and Heaven's Tabernacle, even by women) that we have to "feed" by prayer, fasting, and speaking and reading the Word. Our goal as humans is to reclaim the full covering of God's glory that Adam and Eve inhabited while in the garden, which they were instructed to "dress" just as God had dressed their bodies. (In keeping with this understanding of covering as holiness, Pastor John wears a white button-down coat while preaching on Sundays though not when leading weekday evening Bible studies; Pastor Hadley wears formal but otherwise unmarked attire. Neither of them asks members to dress in a fashion that denotes holiness.) Unlike Adam, who was originally covered in the glory of God so that he would work according to divine instructions, Jesus had to "grow into his covering," preparing for his three-year ministry on earth by practicing obedience. The covering of God's glory will not endure dishonor, so that it departed from Jesus when he was flogged. This explains why he cried, "My God, my God, why hast thou forsaken me?" (Mt. 27:46) on the cross—he had become solely a "natural man" at that point.

For all these believers, the Crucifixion is an epochal event in which Jesus "looked down the corridors of time," saw what would happen to them if he were unwilling to undergo humiliation, torture, and death, and sacrificed himself out of love. Thus, the love for humanity that kept Jesus hanging on the cross when he might have released himself is a prominent theme in preaching at Eternal Hope, in keeping with that church's emphasis on opening the self to divine love. Struck by Pastor John's contention that the divine glory would not endure dishonor, I told him that the argument that God did not sacrifice himself on the cross is found in the Gnostic gospels (Pagels 1979), which he had heard of and immediately disavowed as non-Christian. Still, the distinction he draws between the suffering human and the divine glory underscores how for both himself and Pastor Hadley, the Crucifixion and Resurrection prompt a desire to tap into God's protection—that is, the "anointing" which can be released only once the olive is squeezed—but not to endure the squeezing for the sake of sharing in Jesus' humiliation, envisioning Jesus' solidarity with them in their own suffering (cf. Cone 2011), or admitting collective responsibility for the events of the Passion (cf. Werbner 1997). Rather, for them Jesus is the paradigmatic model of a pastor who undergoes the attacks of the devil so as to "cover" the less spiritually mature, and who endures betrayal only to overcome his enemies.

As God's vessels, pastors have an important role in providing or withholding a covering. Pastor Hadley recounted to her congregation that she has been asked by certain women to pray for their sons facing trial. During her prayers, God may reveal to her that they committed the crimes for which they had been charged. "God does not cover foolishness, He doesn't get in the midst of your madness," she commented. "I turn around and tell them: he did it and he has to come clean." In these African American believers' usage, in such an instance it is God's will to "expose" the person to punishment in the criminal justice system. A key point that Pastor John and Pastor Hadley make in their preaching is that people receive covering from God to the extent that they are "obedient" to his commandments. Drawing on the Pauline vision of the obediently willing and disobediently willful aspects of the self, they encourage their listeners to ask themselves whether they are in the "perfect will" or merely the "permissive will" of God—if the latter, God may be "getting ready to expose them" to violence, sickness, poverty, or humiliation. This, they know, may happen very suddenly and harshly: "Tomorrow is not promised to you." Yet pastors and elder women aim to provide covering for kinfolk who are "in the world" by praying for them. Believers commonly testify that they have come to realize in retrospect that God had been "keeping" them from harm in years past, and they attribute the protection to their praying mothers and grandmothers. As Mother Smith commented during Sunday school, "God puts pictures of persons in others' minds so that we may intercede for them. God is looking after people who are not looking after Him."

## "Put-On" Identities and the Meanings of "Strength"

For members of Victory Gospel and Heaven's Tabernacle, understanding "who you are in God" entails developing insight into how and from whom you have received a covering. In turn, it is important to discern the nature and source of one's covering due to the need to gain insight into the ambiguities of dependence and exploitation that often characterize kinship relations. This point became clear to me over the course of a series of weekly Bible studies at Heaven's Tabernacle on the subject of the "spirit of rejection" conducted by Apostle Cooper and Pastor Hadley, who elaborated on a list of "ten indicators a spirit of rejection is tormenting you" found on a Christian counseling website.[8] The overall thrust of the lessons was that the spirit of rejection "causes you to lose the identity that God desires for you," so that "you see yourself as a failure." Unlike the authors of the website, who do not address causality, Apostle Cooper and Pastor Hadley attributed this problem to a range of deleterious influences to which people had been subjected in childhood—for instance, being told by their mothers that they would never amount to anything—which have given them false understandings of their capabilities. "Most of us are not receiving God's promises because we are feeling rejected," said Pastor Hadley. As a spirit bestowed by more powerful others, rejection is in effect a harmful and distorting kind of covering. For example, Apostle remarked during the study that he was receiving a prophetic vision: "I'm seeing someone who's dealing with something in her body because of the spirit of rejection. You've been told all your life that you have to suffer under an infirmity."

As was the case with the "infirmity" identified by Apostle Cooper, important aspects of a person's identity are liable to be falsely "put on" him or her by others. This trope reflects these believers' concerns about exploitation and deceptive appearances. "If God gave you a vision" for your future, instructed Pastor John, "that vision won't fail as long as you are actively walking it out," in other words acting in accordance with what God is telling you. But "if you don't, whatever somebody put on you will become your reality." In other words, your vitality is liable to be negated by another person's hurtful speech-acts. Preaching about the scripture "his mother called his name Jabez, saying, Because I bare him with sorrow" (1 Chron. 4:9), Pastor John commented: "Look what mama tried to put on the son!" It is possible for pastors themselves to mistakenly bestow a false identity upon a person. Apostle Cooper admitted during the study that he had made people deacons in his church before they were ready to occupy the position, simply because he had needed someone to count the money taken during offerings. He commented, "Prophets can put identities on you before your season," that is, the appropriate time. In this connection, he pointed out that it is possible to misconstrue the word of God conveyed by a prophet: "You heard a prophet say something [i.e., speak a word over your life], but you have to go to God for yourself and ask: reveal to me Your love, and then I will know who I am." The devil, these believers say, is "the prince and power of the air" (Eph. 2:2), meaning that he is liable to interfere in the reception of words. Skepticism is inherent in the reception of prophecy, a fact that helps to account for Pastor John's interest in hearing his interlocutors affirm the truth of his words.

During the "spirit of rejection" study at Heaven's Tabernacle, a number of women shared stories about the "favoritism" that their mothers had shown toward their siblings, stemming in many cases from the complicated emotional dynamics of successive unions. Mothers, they said, sometimes tell their children that they dislike them because they resemble estranged partners who had hurt them. Trisha, a woman in her forties and a cousin of Pastor Hadley who was not currently working for a wage, recounted that "somebody dropped the ball somewhere" long ago in her family's history. Trisha's grandmother, to whom she has always been close, had recently surprised her by confiding that in her youth she had been angry and violent toward her husband. This fact, Trisha now realized, helped to explain why her own mother had been abusive toward herself. Pastor Hadley commented, "Rejected people reject people; hurt people hurt people."

The women in Heaven's Tabernacle identified learning "who they are in God" as demanding specific forms of emotional work that counter the effects of rejection. Trisha commented that "Faith takes work. It's all right to know that I'm feeling hurt as long as I get past that place." She recounted that she had had to deal with some insulting behavior the previous day. She had heard her children swearing on the porch, and when she told them to be quiet, her daughter responded defiantly: "We grown." Trisha had shouted at them and threatened to expel her daughter from her house. Then "I had to go into my room, lock my door, pray to God to help me. I went to Pastor's house to talk with her, and was there for hours in cousin and friend mode." The following morning, Trisha testified, her daughter asked her for her food stamp card to buy food for her own children. Trisha allowed her to spend the last six dollars on the card even though her daughter had $625 on her own card and had been so "nasty" to her. Susan, another woman in the congregation, asked whether Trisha would have been wrong had she refused her daughter's request, since Trisha is a good person. Pastor Hadley corrected Susan sharply: "The love in us will *compel* us to do right. Because you said 'Trisha is a good person,' something is going to come up on you. Now you're going to have to go through a test." A reflection of ostensibly inadequate emotional work, Susan's errant speech had set trouble in motion for herself. Trouble is often designed by God to be a "test" rather than a punishment. The latter is straightforward retribution, of which damnation is the ultimate type, whereas a person who "goes through" a test successfully will be strengthened in her faith. As Pastor Hadley says, "If you don't go through that test, you won't have that testimony."

The best covering is scripture, the word of God, which is said to "feed" a person's "spirit man" as it is read and especially heard. This metaphor of feeding conveys a refashioning of one's interior emotional language. During Bible studies, Pastor Hadley advises new converts to listen to an audio recording of the Bible, particularly Psalms, while going to sleep, so that "the moment the Word needs to come up, it will be in your spirit"—an excellent illustration of learning to know through "absorption" that it is God who speaks (Luhrmann 2007). If you haven't fed your spirit man, Pastor Hadley warns, when you want to speak God's word over a situation you won't be able to bring it up out of your body—"you'll get the dry heaves." Women at both Eternal Hope and Heaven's Tabernacle describe how receiving the word of God leads to changes in demeanor that are noticed by others. When she got the Holy Ghost, Lynne realized that she "didn't need the alcohol to laugh," while Pastor Hadley says that "your countenance will have a glow, it will match your speech." Like Bill at Eternal Hope, Pastor Hadley spoke of how getting the Holy Ghost enables a person to overcome isolation and in particular depression. "The devil," she preached, "has insight and knows how to give answers too—he knows your past, and uses you against yourself. He'll put you in a pity party so you won't want to bother with anyone. He wants to keep you isolated." There are proper and improper ways of being open with people, however. Elder Rebecca, who leads Bible studies at Heaven's Tabernacle, remarked, "It's hard to have faith in what you don't see [i.e., God and his promises]. But you have to learn to talk to your trouble about your God, not talk about trouble and talk to other people about your trouble. The Holy Ghost helps you not say what you think. Truth outside the obedience of God is a problem." It is morally dangerous, in other words, to be open with one's complaints, resentments, or anger.

Much of the emotional work that women at Heaven's Tabernacle say that God enjoins dovetails with popular imagery of the Strong Black Woman, a moral ideal that has come under critical scrutiny by feminist scholars (Collins 2000; hooks 1992; Jones and Shorter-Gooden 2003; cf. Mattingly 2014b). The image of Strong Black Woman, Tamara Beauboeuf-Lafontant (2009) argues, "advances a virtuous claim about any Black woman whose efforts and emotional responses defy common beliefs about what is humanly possible amidst adversity," yet it functions "to defend and maintain a stratified social order by obscuring Black women's experiences of suffering, acts of desperation, and anger" (2). Many of Beauboeuf-Lafontant's interlocutors, when prompted to reflect on how other people expect them to display "strength," described how they had had to conceal their sadness and frustration from both male and female kin in an emotional place "deep down inside" (4) for fear of losing their esteem and protection. They experienced "being strong as an imperative to exhibit an automatic endurance to a life perceived as filled with obstacles, unfairness, and tellingly, a lack of assistance from others" (Beauboeuf-Lafontant 2007: 37).

Without taking issue with the political implications of Beauboeuf-Lafontant's analysis—namely that images of Strong Black Women have legitimated unequal gender roles, and have buttressed the pernicious myth advanced in the 1965 Moynihan Report that dominating mothers rather than structural inequities are to blame for problems in African American families (see Mullings 1989, 2001; Thomas 2021)—I would modestly point out that women in Heaven's Tabernacle do receive assistance from one another. For instance, in line with Marla Frederick's (2003) account of how African American women generate empathy in Baptist churches, they encourage one another by sharing accounts of the miraculous ways in which obeying God's instructions can transform hostility into care. To illustrate, I provide another narrative about feeding. This exchange took place at a Bible study where the conversation, simultaneously moving and amusing, turned to the "strange things" that God can tell someone to do. Elder Rebecca recounted that many years previously, the Holy Ghost told her to invite a certain woman to dinner at her home. Elder Rebecca was pregnant at the time, and the other woman had slept with the child's father. The two of them told her that they wanted to marry when she was six months into her pregnancy. It was a "strange thing" for God to demand that she invite this woman to dinner, because "I couldn't stand her, and I knew she couldn't stand me." She protested to God, "But she—" and heard God reply, "I'm talking to *you*. Go bring her to the table and fix this." Elder Rebecca recalled thinking, "To the Jesus! I don't invite anybody to my house who I know don't like me and I don't like them. The friction is too strong! The kitchen is too hot, and I take authority over the ground. You want me to do *what*? And feed her *my* food? Satan, the Lord rebuke you!" Everyone laughed. "But in the obedience," she continued, "came the peace." After a few weeks of internal struggle, Elder Rebecca invited her over. The woman entered the house with trepidation, but Elder Rebecca assured her that no one else was there and asked her to sit down.

> I had set the table, I knew what she liked to eat. I said, "Listen. I'm saved now for real, I'm not playing with this. I understand what's going on here and it's painful to my heart, but I've given my life to God. It's more important to me to please God than to be at odds with you. Because me being at odds with you, or even you being at odds with me, is going to keep both of us from up there." We were in the same church, praying and reading the Bible, ain't speaking to each other—we got to fix this.

Another woman interjected: "And there was a child"—there needed to be some reconciliation. Both women started crying, Elder Rebecca recalled, and "what ended up happening, is he ended up going with somebody else anyway. Then her heart was hurt, because she believed he was better for her than for me, and now he done left her dry. And so now I'm strong enough to undergird her, to say, 'Listen, it's going to be all right, we're good.'" The idiom of "strength," in short, has many valences: by "going through" a test successfully, a woman may enable someone else to do so as well.[9] God may cause someone to "go through" so that she will later be able to witness to others in the same situation.

Women in Heaven's Tabernacle do not understand the performative requirements of "obedience" to God as a form of subjugation, but rather as a set of designs for care and kinship. Elder Rebecca's argument that "in the obedience comes the peace" reflects a view that vitality depends on covering and receptivity rather than on expressing injuries felt "deep down inside." Together with spiritual virtuosity acquired through docility (Mahmood 2005), "obedience" demands reflexive awareness of the connectedness among bodies and spirits. This awareness in turn fosters particular communicative styles, especially but not exclusively with the deity, that are ways of "speaking life," as God did to generate humanity.

## Submission and Sexual Connection

Pastor John, who is more concerned than Pastor Hadley with the difficulties faced by Black men, often says that his ministry is of a new style. He identifies himself as part of a younger generation of believers who deem it important to preach about sexuality and gender relations, and implies that earlier generations allowed problems to fester by refusing to speak publicly about how connections among bodies and spirits bear on these matters. He often remarks that "relationship problems" are some of the most pressing issues that the saints are facing, and encourages partners to engage in counseling sessions with him. Pastor John continually emphasizes how "submitting" to God provides a model for how a wife should "submit" to her husband: when she knows he is wrong about something, she should not strenuously argue but instead pray to God, who will set him right if her husband has a relationship with him. Likewise, Mother Smith remarks to women that "if you don't have respect for the man you marry, that's going to cause some serious problems in the relationship."

Johnnetta Cole and Beverly Guy-Sheftall (2003) point out that struggles for gender equality in African American communities are often complicated by the needs women commonly feel to compensate men for the oppression they endure, a dynamic that frequently leads women to avoid publicizing gender-based violence. Pastor John, however, attributes domestic difficulties within poor African American families to improper socialization and ultimately to lack of love for God. As he made clear during a Bible study, God regards submission as a model for love:

> I submit to God because I love God. If it weren't for God, John would have no being. So if you women love your husbands, you will submit to them just as I submit to God. A lot of you women are tolerating these men [whom you are dating outside church] because you just don't want to be by yourself. And some of you men need to learn that until you learn to love God, you can't love [your partners]. Because the sacrifice that the woman is making should be the same sacrifice that the man is making to her and to his family. We're in a world now where women's rights are being pushed, but do we not see the attack on Black men? ... The Black man is targeted from so many different angles. Then he has to come home and be targeted by his wife! If he can't be a king in his own castle, where's he going to be a king at?

Pastor John approved of a comment of a woman in the audience to the effect that because Black men are oppressed, women have to raise their daughters on their own, so that girls do not learn how to submit to men. When the daughters marry in turn, they argue with their husbands, causing the men to leave and perpetuating the cycle.

Pastor John often preaches to the saints that they have multiple fathers: God the Father, a natural father, and a spiritual father (himself), and that each relationship ought to be based on discipline (see Chipumuro 2014). "The Holy Spirit ain't enough. It will convict you [i.e., convince you of your sinfulness] and empower you, but it does not make you do anything. God puts a man in your life to help discipline you, so you can effectively receive God." African American children, he points out, all too often grow up without experiencing a father's discipline. This is detrimental both to boys, who will "wallow in their emotions" if they are raised only by a woman, and to girls, who would have "learned self-esteem" from a father who "would have told you not to settle for nothing" in a boyfriend. "I was disciplined to a pulp by my natural father and my spiritual father," Pastor John preached, recalling the beatings he received as a child and his late bishop's insistence that he rise early to pray, remain in church all day Sundays, render tithes and offerings faithfully, and fast according to direction. "God re-routes people to spiritual fathers who can bless them and speak over them," he went on. "Your natural fathers can't speak no blessings over you. Your mother can't give you those blessings" due to the patriarchal "order of God," who made Adam in his image, with a nurturing female spirit within him that God extracted to make Eve. Like God, Adam was a creator, bestowing names upon the animals. The devil destroys fathers knowing that "nothing can come to fruition without that father, because the seed is in the man, not the woman."

In Pastor John's view, state-initiated assaults on Black men have taken advantage of the body's porosity, resulting in a wide range of pathological sexual connections that provide "openings" for harmful spirits to afflict both women and men. During a sermon, he pointed out that some of these connections derive from secular hip-hop music: "Men are making songs, and have sold it to you women who are shaking your booty to it. This spirit is moving, plaguing young people to say 'Get rich or die trying' or 'Live fast and die young'—which was the last message my nephew wrote" before being shot and killed. "Folk want to keep being in the trap of music written by people you never know—you don't know what that life is like but you want to be connected to that life," which is glamorous but morally perilous. Pastor John identifies numerous "spirits of sexual perversion" that are "passed down" the generations, including homosexuality, fornication, incest, and child molestation. He continued:

> Noah's son sodomized him [an interpretation of Gen. 9:24]. That's why we got to deal with incest too in the church. Lots of us in the African American community have been molested. That spirit was passed down. We're fighting our demons and

the demons our parents didn't fight. Do not arise me before my time! A baby's joint can get high. Some girls who are molested get promiscuous, they can have their periods at age seven because they were aroused before their time. I had crushes on my teachers because I was aroused before my time: come on teacher, give me a hug! That spirit was passed down ... Some of you sophisticated people say we were experimenting—but some of the sexual perversions you have is because of the spirit that's been passed down.

"I can see you some of you cringing," said Mother Smith from the back of the sanctuary on an occasion similar to this one. "But people really don't understand the value of relationships these days. So they think, if it's not working out, we throw it away. We need to know this is a work, we can overcome this thing and still be together." In other words, it is necessary to know about and be delivered from harmful spirits in order to construct families based on love and proper submission. While Pastor John's approach is unapologetically patriarchal, his conviction that men as well as women need to be "transformed by the renewing of [their] minds" (Rom. 12:2) bears affinities to bell hooks's (2004) argument that "often black male children hear adult women repeatedly maligning adult black males, saying things like 'he's no good,' 'he ain't shit,' or 'there's not a black man on this earth you can count on.' All these messages reinforce the notion that he is flawed, that nothing he can do will make him be whole" (91). This dynamic, according to hooks, contributes to hopelessness, a sense of powerlessness, and continual anger.

To counter such destructive forces, believers enact ways of becoming "connected" to God.[10] Pastor John argued during the above sermon that God can transform the deadly connections forged through drug dealing and promiscuous sex into life-giving connections.

> You think I'm proud to have been selling drugs and act like I wasn't doing sorcery? I was having people bring me money every ten minutes. I was able to take one and make it look like two. But people's lives were being polluted. And when you were selling your body, you were allowing them to pour their spirits into you.

Pastor John went on to relate the story of the encounter between Jesus and the Samaritan woman at the well (Jn 4). His performance playfully dramatized sexual suggestion while overtly disparaging it—a dynamic that elicited laughter and other enthusiastic responses. The woman at the well, he said, "was a ho. She thought the only reason Jesus was talking with her was to procure her." She interpreted Jesus' statement "you ain't got the water I got" as a "game," an "offer to buy her," so she replied, "let me have some." Pastor John elaborated with a caress in his voice: "Women can take the pastor's hand in church to let him feel their tenderness" to try to seduce him. Given the multiple valences of "connection," such moral dangers are considered quite present in church.[11] "Jesus played the woman's game for a minute, but He flipped it on her when He started talking about husbands. The lady's eyes got big. She said, 'Oh!' Jesus hit her right there. He gave her her resumé of how many men she'd been with. The minute you sleep with someone who's not your wife, that's your wife too." He went on:

> Once I was taking life, but now I'm giving life. God can do that, but you got to be living holy. You got to start holding yourself accountable when you're not around me, and come to me saying, "Pastor, I've got a problem." … Women, stop being petty and going after your man if he just looks for a second at a woman with a big booty. He got eyes, he can see! If you keep looking through side mirrors, you got an issue. Sisters are looking through the side of their eyes to see who's looking at them—they got game. Brothers, don't be a fool: women are looking at other men too.

Clearly, some gendered power dynamics underpinned this performance. Pastor John is able to elicit respect from his congregation by playfully (and anxiously) giving voice to a heterosexual male gaze, but he does not encourage the women in Victory Gospel who often lead Sunday school to do anything comparable; if Pastor Hadley were to adopt such vocabulary, she would jeopardize her reputation as a respectable woman of God. Yet whatever might be said of Pastor John's approach, it illustrates the power of artful designs (in this case, those that lead to physical attraction) to shape the ways people imagine ethical and pragmatic possibilities. Pastor John presents "living water"—that is, the life-giving connections established by God—as analogous, even if overtly opposed, to the "spirits poured into you" via seduction, and he draws his audience's attention to the designs for care and communication inherent in both.

## How Knowledge Transforms the Body

In *Take Back What the Devil Stole* (2021), a biographical study of Donna Haskins, an African American prophet living in Boston, Onaje X. O. Woodbine describes how the knowledge Donna has received from spirits and other human beings affected her body over the course of her life. Subjected from an early age to parental and sexual abuse, Donna believed she was unloved by her mother, and she hated her own body for making her a target of male violence. Her poor performance in school associated with lead poisoning induced her to ask, "Am I ever going to be normal?" (72). She was hurt by male lovers who cheated on her, but she believed them when they told her she would be "worthless" without them (99). "And I couldn't take it anymore. The enemy put the idea in me, 'Well, kill yourself. If you're not here, [your lover] won't bother you'" (108). Donna rejected these false and dangerous kinds of knowledge at a moment when she was lying on her bed contemplating suicide but decided, "I can't leave. I can't leave my kids. I can't leave my grandkids. My daughters need me" (108). At that point,

> "I heard this song in my mind from Yolanda Adams playing: 'There is no pain, Jesus can't feel / No hurt He cannot heal / … For the battle is not yours, it's the Lord's.'"
>
> … Donna stood up from her bed and walked to her doorway. "I stepped out of my room, and I had to hear the rest of the song playing. I heard it, and I heard her saying, 'Hold your head up high. The battle's not yours, it's the Lord's.' Just that phrase, 'the battle's not yours.' It's like it's not my battle, I don't have to fight it. It's His battle. Just that little *wisdom I received* [my emphasis]. I opened the door, and I said to my sister, 'Maya, can I go to church with you?'" (109).

In later years, Donna received many other gifts of insight, for instance "treasures from heaven" bestowed by angels including "a beauteous bag … covered in splendid pinks, yellows, blues, and purples, with Hebrew letters scrolled across the sides" whose contents enable her "to bounce to different spaces and times in order to positively affect the present" (174–5). The insights Donna has received by virtue of her spiritual preparation give her an understanding of the true appearance of her body: in the spirit world, "her hair wasn't just silver, it was colored electric. Her face was more of a honey than ordinary caramel. Her eyes were two alluring moons. The garments draping her body reflected beams of fluorescent light" (11).

While Donna engages not only with the Christian Holy Spirit but with spirits derived from Afro-Caribbean and other traditions, her account highlights how the beneficial forms of knowledge she has received (that is, accepted) from God—which are directly opposed to the destructive varieties she had previously received from the devil—have transformed the ways she inhabits her body, enabling her body to generate new knowledge in the process. How to conceptualize these linkages between the ethical and the vital?

It is helpful here to turn to a non-Christian context. Discussing "knowledge of the body" among Kuranko in Sierra Leone, Michael Jackson (1983) focuses on connections between the ethical and the vital in order to draw attention to the parochialism of demarcating "religion" or "ritual" as distinctive domains of social life. Having relied on what he calls a "bourgeois conception of culture as something 'superorganic,' " Jackson admits that the approach he originally took to initiation was based on a "distinction which Kuranko themselves do not recognise: between 'pragmatic' work and 'ritual' activity" (332). In the context of initiation, Kuranko allusions to aspects of domestic and agricultural life, including processes of

> taming (unruly emotions and bodies), of moulding (clay), of making dry or cool (as in cooking, smoking and curing), of ripening (as of grain and fruit), of strengthening (the heart), hardening or straightening (the body) … are not mere figures of speech, for they disclose real connexions between personal maturity and the ability to provide food for and give support to others. Bodily and moral domains are fused. (338)

An important linkage between the ethical and the vital is thus to be found in caring activities, which fuse bodily and moral domains in ways Donna discovered when her thoughts of suicide were banished by her felt need to care for her children and grandchildren. In this chapter, I have shown that imperatives to sustain positive forms of care and overcome destructive ones constitute key reasons why Pentecostal believers make efforts to allow insights from God to transform their physicality. Their insights into the connections between bodies and spirits constitute "knowledge of the body" in Jackson's sense: discernment ideally becomes what the body knows and how it knows. Much as Kuranko initiates aim to inhabit their knowledge of having been properly tamed or strengthened, Pentecostal believers try to inhabit their discernment so as to become "who they are in God." In both cases, knowledge enhances vitality. The image of "feeding the spirit man," which has deep historical resonances with early Jewish and Christian concepts of food as God's blessing (Feeley-Harnik 1994), provides a clear case in point: learning to know that it is God who speaks (Luhrmann 2007) is a matter of allowing the Word to nourish the body. Importantly, this is a reciprocal process: the nourished body feeds others—whether through verbal instruction, laying on hands, or bestowing a covering—by virtue of the vital knowledge it generates.

Pentecostal believers understand that the designs for care and communication conveyed through God's word differ from their own. As a result, their "knowledge of the body," centering on susceptibility to beneficial and destructive connections with others, leads them to draw critical distinctions between God's designs and those that spring from human or demonic sources. God's designs for communication, which include prophecy, intercession, and worship in the Spirit, are consistently matters of wonder even for those well accustomed to them. Yet wonder and critical assessments take divergent forms in the majority white and African American churches I am describing, since these believers relate caring activities to bodily susceptibility in different ways. At Eternal Hope, wonder stems largely from experiences of comfort associated with opened bodies: God takes the role of a companionate spouse with whom one speaks openly, or he elicits expressions of emotional openness that become a basis for lifelong friendship/kinship of a sort not to be found "in the world." By contrast, the kinds of wonder that members of Victory Gospel and Heaven's Tabernacle express about care and kinship are more marked by concerns about exploitation and false representation, which lead them to develop insight into what kinds of protection, rejection, or improper connection they have "received" and from whom. Accordingly, idioms of enclosure, receiving, testing, and strength pervade these African American believers' accounts of God's designs for covering their bodies.

In either case, God both provides and enjoins insights that transform the body, and simultaneously causes the body to generate new insights. This point may be illustrated by the ways members of the majority white and African American churches respectively speak of how God cares for them either by carrying out moral calibrations between autonomy and dependence on the one hand or by organizing forms of receptivity and covering on the other. As Bill voiced his expectation that his son Evan would receive the Holy Ghost on his own volition at Eternal Hope, and as Apostle Cooper elicited God's power to remove the spirits of rejection that had been "put on" women at Heaven's Tabernacle, they each engaged with designs for bodily transformation that they knew they were not capable in themselves of bringing into existence. Yet how do believers understand the extent and limits of their own capabilities in relation to what they know of their dependence on God and other people? In Chapter 4, I explore this question by focusing on God's designs for personal value.

# 4

# Depending on God:
# Designs for Personal Value

"Just think about it," Pastor John encouraged me after describing his encounter with the barber.

> For people who are depressed, for people who are coming from an impoverished community, to have that peace, that assurance, to know that what I've heard or what I've received from the man of God—to know that some time in my week, it was confirmed what was said to me: that takes the mental stress off someone, to know that God is working on their behalf.

As I discussed in Chapter 3, Pastor John was reflecting on the power of language to extend care to other people, as well as on the ways God renders language itself a subject of divine care by showing the prophet what to communicate. What Pastor John left unsaid was the fact that some members of his church or their relatives have (while in "unsaved" conditions) expressed anger at God, even cursed him, because of deaths, homicides, or incarcerations in their families. Given the possibility that the poor and marginalized may feel that God is not to be depended on, Pastor John felt it important to assure the barber that God values his life and is able and willing to bless him.

Depending on God involves learning to express things about personal capabilities—one's own, other people's, and God's—on the basis of multiple kinds of authority, whether prophetic, intercessory, or lay. That such expressions may vary became apparent at the conclusion of an evening Bible study at Victory Gospel, when a Euro-American man named Albert raised his hand. Albert had recently become a member of Pastor John's church after relocating to Buffalo from another US state, where he had attended a majority white Pentecostal church. He addressed Pastor John, who had been teaching about how to "go through tests." It's important, Pastor John had said, to understand the difference between the "logical mind" and the "faith mind": the logical mind may tell you that there is no way to overcome a difficulty, while the faith mind "won't allow you to stay with what's logical." But, he went on, "you can't always be hocus-pocus either, saying 'I ain't paying this bill.' The spirit realm will help you see practical things too. When there's a flood, get in the boat." With some apparent diffidence—one does not publicly take issue with Pastor John—Albert said, "Pastor, when I pass a test, I give the glory to the Christ who dwells within me. That way, when I face the next test, I can lean on Christ who strengthens me." Pastor John immediately approved, calling out "Give God praise!" and everyone applauded. Nonetheless, it seemed to me that Albert was addressing what he perceived as a gap. Albert felt it necessary to verbally parse his own capacities and incapacities in relation to God's power in a manner that differed from Pastor John's emphasis on his own attunement to God's promptings and his willingness to obey them.

In this chapter, I explore how the meanings of depending on God hinge on what dependence signifies within believers' divergent lived situations. As they develop insight into their dependence on God, believers revise their understandings of their own capabilities in ways that shape and are shaped by the manner in which they depend on other people, especially kin and church colleagues. My argument is that these shifting configurations of dependence remake believers' understandings of their value as persons. Some basic Christian doctrines provide terms for connecting dependence on God to assessments of personal value, for instance Paul's exhortation "ye are bought with a price" (1 Cor. 6:20), namely Jesus' self-sacrifice which redeems believers by liberating them from slavery to sin. Yet the large anthropological literature on regimes of value within Pentecostal and Charismatic Christian communities provides ample evidence that a sense of dependence on God is apt to foster very different kinds of understandings about how and whether to depend upon other people. For instance, Simon Coleman shows that adherents of the prosperity Word of Life movement in Sweden are encouraged "to think of the most sacred part of themselves as becoming abstracted, removed from any confining social context and inserted into a realm of limitless possibility" (2004: 436) through monetary gifts and sacred speech. By Coleman's account, Word of Life members are not supposed to express any sense of vulnerability or incapacity—or at least, they do not value such expressions in religious terms. By way of contrast, Naomi Haynes (2013) describes how members of Pentecostal congregations on the Zambian Copperbelt express anxieties about dependence and loss of patronage. They worry that pastors will pursue relationships with wealthier believers—who are better able to "sow seeds" into the "good soil" that pastors' prayers provide—at the expense of poorer ones, a dynamic mitigated by the capacity of the poor to respond to improper forms of redistribution by starting their own congregations (Haynes 2015, 2017).

Pursuing this comparative line of inquiry, I explore how shared imperatives to depend on God may reflect different kinds of concerns about personal capacity. Specifically, Eternal Hope members speak of how important it is to admit their own lack of self-sufficiency and to become willing to ask God for assistance. Such admissions are key to assuring their vitality, as Albert indicated by speaking of the care he takes to thank the Christ who dwells within him. Some of the saints at Eternal Hope relate how experiences of divine love are contingent on distinguishing between affirmative and self-belittling ways of asking God for help, a distinction they link to retreat from Catholicism. For Pastor John and Pastor Hadley, by contrast, it is less important to admit that one is incapable of getting by through one's own energies than that one *should* not get by in a manner contrary to God's will. Practices of asking and giving in Victory Gospel and Heaven's Tabernacle do not reflect anxieties about self-sufficiency so much as concerns about the need to differentiate true from false sources of vitality and respect, an ability that must be cultivated by attunement and obedience to the prophetic word. Understood in this light, the engagements of these African American churches with the Word of Faith prosperity movement (Bowler 2013; Harrison 2005; Mitchem 2007; Rouse, Jackson, and Frederick 2016; Walton 2009) represent one among multiple sets of ways in which members of all these Pentecostal congregations ask and give in order to extend their selfhood to others while communicating their dependence on God (cf. Klaits, ed. 2017b). Importantly, they all express concerns about the moral and sometimes physical perils that spring from giving and asking in ways that do not conform to God's designs for those acts. In so doing, they articulate a range of critical outlooks on the nature and sources of personal worth.

## Asking and God's Love

Over the many years that Benny has attended Eternal Hope, he has gotten to know much about the life circumstances of other members. Many, he told me, had suffered from drug and alcohol addictions and had seen their finances and jobs ruined. "God brought them to a point in their life when they said, 'Everything I've tried doesn't work, help me God, help me!'" Benny spoke of recognizing one's own incapacity and consequent willingness to ask God for help as a key precondition for faith. Once people understand that they must depend on God rather than on their own abilities, and that God's love will assist them as they "go through" troubles, they will be able to extend God's love to others, whom they will help "bring through" difficulties by witnessing, praying, and interceding. "When you know God," Benny told me, "it's such a euphoric feeling that the creator of the universe will come into your life and work things out for you. You're just so grateful. If He hadn't been in my life, my marriage might not have worked out, I might have gone down a different path with alcohol."

Benny and his wife Janet contrasted this approach to asking and thanking God to the Catholic practices familiar to them from their youth. Both of them had been staunch Catholics until soon after their marriage, when they responded to the door-to-door proselytizing of a minister affiliated with Eternal Hope. Janet recalled being told during her childhood that "when you're sick, you pray to Saint Jude," but was never taught that she could "pray through" her troubles "to get back to the place where you should be in God" (about which more below). Benny and Janet remarked that they "had never been given rules to live by" or been encouraged to read the Bible during their Catholic upbringings—the Bible would lie on the table but was never opened. Janet's mother would simply tell her "Be good!" while her father was emotionally distant, favoring her brothers with whom he could talk about sports. For his part, Benny had been disturbed at the sight of elders in his Catholic church becoming inebriated at a celebration, and felt after surviving a car accident that God must have had a purpose in preserving his life. As a young couple, they both felt that they "knew of" God as one would a celebrity but wanted to know him personally, and therefore prayed together for deeper knowledge. When they first came to Eternal Hope, Janet seized Benny by the arm and took him to the altar, where a group was praying for the sick. They laid hands on the couple and "brought us through, had us talking in tongues." Benny found that he could "get to know God as a friend—when you pray to Him, He will use other people to speak to you."

Benny's and Janet's novel insights into "who God is" caused a shift in the texture of their dependencies on both God and their families. Their parents were all upset by their departure from Catholicism. Benny went so far as to call it a "disowning"; his parents felt it was "like a personal slap in the face." His Italian family "all came up in the faith, so to throw it away, how could you throw it away?" Benny recalled that his father would say, "That ain't no church, there's no statues, all they do is clap and sing songs." Many Eternal Hope members mentioned that they no longer attended Sunday dinners with their families because they needed to be in church during those evenings. While most of Benny's siblings live within a short distance from his house, he sees them far less frequently than his brothers and sisters of Eternal Hope.

Over time, Benny's and Janet's parents came to respect their commitment to God. Janet's mother attended her granddaughter's baptism, and at times of family crisis would rely on her and Benny. When a cousin, a woman in her thirties, contracted breast cancer, Janet's mother called them to pray for her. "They know that we're praying people," Janet said. "We'll really pray, not just say it. They rely on us for a lot of things in general, rides and everything else." Janet and Benny spoke of praying to God on behalf of their families as an important form of caring, comparable to such acts of giving as providing rides, cooking, and cleaning for aging parents.

Everyone involved understands the efficacy of such prayers as contingent upon believers' "personal relationships with God," connections predicated on specific linguistic forms associated with prayer. Arlene distinguished Pentecostal prayer from the styles of speaking to God that she adopted during her Catholic youth. As a girl, Arlene had wanted to become a nun, but when she decided against this course as a teenager she assumed that she was not going to be "living for God," since the only people she imagined doing so were priests or nuns. Like Benny and Janet, Arlene told me that when she was growing up, she was told to "follow the rules" of the Catholic church (i.e., abide by the sacraments), but "you still do everything the world does—you just confess your sins on Sundays." When she was a young married woman, she followed her husband to a military posting in another US state, where she encountered many more Protestant churches than she had seen in the predominantly Catholic suburb of Buffalo where she had been raised in the 1960s and 1970s. During the early years of her marriage, Arlene found herself wondering "who she was," puzzling over the fact that other people seemed confident about their directions in life. In retrospect, she realizes that she was searching for God, not for herself. She came to understand this point as a result of attending a Pentecostal church, where another woman convinced her of the scriptural necessity of getting the Holy Ghost. Nonetheless, she recalled in a conversation with me, at the time "I was still doing a lot of things Catholic in the way I prayed or in the way I talked to God. In the Catholic realm, you're always begging God." While Arlene struggled to articulate the precise differences between Pentecostal and Catholic forms of asking, she narrated a move away from what she perceived as pleading, a form of self-abnegation, toward an informal style of asking.

**Fred:** Rather than begging God, what kinds of language do you [now] find yourself using with God?

**Arlene:**   [At the time] I would be asking, Lord, please fill me with Your
             spirit. *Please* give it to me. I felt like I had to do something to receive
             it, rather than just receive it as a gift. Because I was already obedient
             by repenting and being baptized. When I was being prayed for at
             [the Pentecostal] church, they could feel the Holy Ghost on me,
             I could feel it on me, I could feel God [she felt goose bumps on
             her skin], but I didn't know how to just let it happen [i.e., speak in
             tongues, dance, or shout].

**Fred:**    Help me to understand the difference between begging God for
             things in what you say is the Catholic way, and speaking to God
             so as to—

**Arlene:**   Catholics have a way—Mind you, different Catholic churches are
             different. You're just never good enough. So even if you went and
             had your penance from the priest, you're just not forgiven. I never
             felt forgiven, because I knew what I was going to do again. Even
             though I was sorry that I sinned, you go to the priest—there was no
             change, there was nothing different.

**Fred:**    Rather than begging God for things, begging God for forgiveness,
             what you now do is—?

**Arlene:**   I had to unlearn that. What I do is, you ask. We can still feel ugly
             in our [self-] righteousness, 'cause we're not [righteous]. Character
             flaws and whatever. Now it's like a humbling, Jesus help me, change
             me, do this, intervene this in this situation or whatever, but not—
             You're asking more for help rather than begging Him for—because
             you feel—It's interesting, 'cause I never had to think about it before
             you asked me that. [Long pause.] I just guess there's a difference
             between begging for something and just being able to go and
             ask God.

For Arlene and other Eternal Hope members, "just being able to go and ask
God" on an informal basis is a principal avenue to the experience of divine love,
because this form of asking promotes a companionate relationship with God that
may be likened to marriage. Janet remarked in her husband's presence, "You think
when you're young that if you marry the right person you'll be happy forever.
But you get to a point in life when you realize that no other person can fill the
void in you. I realized I can only really depend on God early in my marriage—
He is the only one who will always be there." As I described earlier, believers
depict speech to God as a conduit of understanding and communication with
other people, a point that helps to explain why having "a relationship with God"

remakes the qualities of their dependence on others. Janet explained: "Prayer really helps get you through troubles in marriage. It gets you back to the place where you should be in God, ready to forgive."

What difference does God make by becoming a third party, as it were, to a conversation? Eternal Hope members consistently framed this issue in metacommunicative terms, pointing out that God gives them insight into how they ought to speak to people. Violet told me that God called her to be an intercessor, "a person who will pray for someone else who's going through some kind of difficulty." Benny remarked that he feels closer to God the nearer he is in church to Violet, "who's highly in the Spirit just being at her seat." Beyond interceding in ritual situations, Violet emphasized the importance of praying to God before speaking with someone else about a difficulty.

**Fred:** What difference does it make to speak to God in relating to other people, as opposed to just speaking to other people without speaking to God?

**Violet:** When you speak to God first, He can give you direction as to what to say that will help that person, more than you can. There's still that very human side of me that doesn't necessarily have to obey God. And rather than me tell the person what I think, I would rather tell the person through God's eyes, minister to them through the Holy Ghost.

**Fred:** So it's not you when you're ministering through the Holy Ghost?

**Violet:** It's a combination. The best way I can explain it is that sometimes I don't know what to do in a given situation, I really don't know how to approach a person about it. But once I pray, God will give me insight, if I'm seriously seeking to do the will of God. One way I always pray is: Lord, I want to please You. I don't want to say something or do something that God would not like ... Am I successful in that all the time? No. I have failed. But that's how I want to live and interact with people. If you do it God's way, you can't go wrong. If I do it with my own way of thinking, without consulting the Lord first, the end results might not be what I wanted them to be, even if my intentions are good. ... He knows people better than we do, but we're faulty in the way we think, we misinterpret actions. We think things that aren't really true because we speculate. But when I consult with the Lord first, really pray about it sincerely, and ask Him what to do, He gives me wisdom and insight and it turns out better every time. And when

I don't listen and I let the flesh get in the way, it doesn't always turn out so good.

As does Arlene, Violet performs a careful parsing of the significance and consequences of asking God. The insight necessary for intercession is contingent, Violet makes clear, on her prior acknowledgment of her own limitations—specifically, her intrinsic inability to know what to say—and her willingness to "ask God what to do." To the extent that she is so willing, God affirms Violet's personal worth, which transcends her occasional "failures," by showing her that she is acting in conformity with his designs for communication and care: "I know [intercession] is by His design. We're supposed to show love and compassion to one another, that's a reflection of who He is and He wants us to be like Him. So we join with that person in asking God to meet that need." Likewise for Arlene, the sense of companionship arising from her ability to ask things of God on an informal basis has enhanced her sense of personal worth, whereas the act of "begging" God as a Catholic made her feel that she was "never good enough."

## Sacrificing the Willful Self

In all these churches, the interplays between facets of the self that are willing to "ask God what to do" and those that are disobediently willful provide grounds for a "sacrificial economy" (Coleman 2011) involving fasting and tithing. Fasting may be considered a full-body form of asking that helps believers to distinguish and overcome the "flesh," identified as the aspect of the self that is incapable of apprehending God. Fasting is done "with a purpose," namely to reinforce dependencies on God and among believers. Benny and Janet explained that fasting is "an agreement you're making with God—if you break it, you're breaking your agreement to honor Him. When you fast, it's a victory because you've conquered your flesh. All you want to do when you're fasting is eat and cater to your flesh, so you're conquering that urge and that humanness." They have fasted to find jobs, to bring about healing within their family, and to help someone in church receive the Holy Ghost. Benny, Janet, and their daughters usually do not tell each other when they are fasting, on the principle that they should not be making the sacrifice in order to enhance their standing in another person's eyes. (Though it's hard, they said, to keep fasting a secret when someone calls you downstairs for dinner.) On the other hand, fasting can be a means of building relationships: when Benny and Janet's daughter Kathy was trying to solidify a relationship with a boyfriend, she asked him to go on a fast with her. On certain occasions when the founding bishop of Eternal Hope was actively presiding, he would ask sections of the congregation to commit to fasting and continual prayer on consecutive days of the week. These fasts were sometimes held to counter attacks of the devil, which at one point caused a number of serious illnesses among the saints. Fasting on such occasions, Benny and Janet recalled, was "a way of bringing us together spiritually, so the Spirit of God came down stronger."

Kathy identified tithing along with fasting as means of "cleaning out the pipes," of allowing the spirit of God to move through the self without hindrance. Setting aside ten percent of her income in weekly tithes—used in part for Pastor Charles's salary—is a way of "putting God first." While she was confident that the church would put the funds to good use, her principal motivation for tithing was "to honor God, to make a sacrifice." She recounted miraculous instances when God had unexpectedly provided funds for church members, but she was more inclined to speak of tithing as a "sacrifice" than as an "investment." During a period of formal unemployment, she paid tithes on money she received from a church colleague to help clear out her elderly mother's house, as well as from her father to do laundry for her aging grandmother. She told me that she never felt while putting money in an envelope in church that she could have used the money for something else she needed. As a result of "putting God first," she had never missed a payment on a car loan—"I've been really blessed"—but she was concerned about a decline in her family's overall financial situation that she attributed to her father's reluctance to tithe.

Benny and Janet compared fasting to another whole-body means of addressing God, namely "praying through." Believers both express and overcome anguish by "praying through" a problem until they begin to speak in tongues. Janet explained that "praying through" a severe difficulty is like "laboring when you pray: travailing, half crying, crying out to God. It's good when something is really bothering you—you feel better because you feel like you've connected with God again, you know that God's heard you. Sometimes I go into the basement and really let loose." Like fasting, "praying through" is a kind of "cleansing" that culminates in tongue speech, which she depicted as bypassing conscious intention and meaning. "When you're praying in tongues," Janet said, "you don't know what you're saying, so you don't have a lack of faith. But you're in communication with God then. Praying in tongues builds you up spiritually without your even knowing it." In effect, tongue speech marks ordinary speech as less capable of communication with God, because ordinary language is imbued with the believer's own partial and inadequate knowledge of what is to be said. As Csordas (1997) writes in relation to tongue speech among Charismatic Catholics, "because the speaking 'I' is not the self, one is already on the other side of the discourse—its charismatic side—safe from its fearsome, devilish, or uncanny features" (241). Again, the act of "praying through" locates those aspects of the self that are deemed less than fully capable, transcends those incapacities by reinforcing one's sense of dependence on God, and finally extends aspects of this dependent and transcendent self as a gift to others.

To elaborate, it is helpful to turn to Coleman's argument about the applicability of Marcel Mauss's (2015) treatment of the gift to the sacred words that circulate among Word of Life adherents in Sweden:

> Clearly, the recipient of language is not expected to reply with an equal or greater number of words, and is not "in debt" to the speaker in an obvious way. However, one who deploys sacred language expects a return on his or her linguistic investment. That return involves a belief that the words have taken effect, have made a difference to the world in a way that can be measured or imagined. Such a difference then becomes a constitutive part of the speaker's persona, a test of spiritual efficacy that they have passed. (Coleman 2006:174)

In particular, the kinds of words that extend the speaker's persona in Eternal Hope are those that convey dependence on God, so that asking becomes a means of giving God's love. Yet instances of fasting and tithing show that such gifted requests need not be solely verbal. In a remarkable narrative about "praying through," Arlene described a transcendence of language to me: her body was used by God to intercede on behalf of her unsaved former husband while he was undergoing a brutal hazing ritual in the military.

> When my ex-husband was in the Navy ... he was [being promoted] ... They put you through initiation ... It was at a time in my marriage when I was like, there's not a lot more that I'm going to be able to handle here. It was in the morning about 11:00, and I started feeling this burden to pray. You just start feeling this heaviness, you just don't feel comfortable, something's amiss, or something's drawing you. It was getting heavier and heavier, so I went to go in my bedroom and I prayed. I was praying next to my bed. And as I prayed, I went into deep prayer. For intercession, what we term it is travail. And when somebody travails, they're really crying, deep crying out, like you're in labor. [She imitated groaning.] That happens. This is not something you can make yourself do. ... I started feeling like I was going to throw up, something was very serious ...
>
> I began to feel that I was praying for my husband, not knowing what he's going through. So I'm praying for a long time, and I'm praying for our marriage and

for the man he was, he's a wreck. ... In my mind, I had a vision. And there was a little boy, he's about seven or eight, and he's in front of me and he's looking at me. He's looking at me and he's saying "Mommy." But I know I'm not mommy. He's looking through me to Mommy, whoever's behind me, and he's going, "Mommy, why?" And he starts to cry. And when I see that, I really go into deep prayer and cry. And the Lord let me know that the things my husband was struggling with had to do with his mother. And his mother died when he was twelve of cancer. And he was not able to say goodbye to her, and life was bad before, but it worse after mom died.

What happens later is he comes home in the evening ... And he looked terrible, and I wanted to know what happened. I wasn't even thinking about my prayer at that time. He goes, "Arlene, today I really thought I was gonna die." ... At the time I was praying for him ... they [were making] them crawl through slop, and then they made them eat it, and they had them on their backs. They were pouring whatever concoction they made of garbage and hot sauce. And they also had them open their mouths, and they were dropping from above raw eggs and made them swallow ... And while he's explaining this to me, I'm understanding that that's what I was feeling in my prayer: I felt that I had to take something in and vomit, and I felt like I couldn't do it and I felt like was going to die because it was so terrible. And he said, "We couldn't throw it up, we had to keep swallowing." ... He goes, "I really felt like I was dying, physically dying." And we know, sometimes in these situations people do die.

And I told him what happened. I didn't tell him about my thought about him as a child, but I let him know that God called me to pray for him today. He just looked at me. ... I [had only been] saved a few years, but ... God was letting me know: "I used you to intercede to help him that time this morning." I was literally feeling what he was feeling, because I was feeling that I was going to die ... That was a first-time experience for that type of thing, but there's been a couple times when I've felt the same sort of thing for somebody else ... It's terrible to really feel the emotions of what somebody's feeling, but God uses you to pray in that thing for them because they can't. They're in a situation of near death or sickness or a terrible situation in their home ... God is using you to pray because they can't.

Those who are in such extreme situations that they are unable to pray—that is, who cannot speak even their own incapacity—need an intercessor to express their dependence for them, sometimes in a full-bodied mimetic fashion. The intercessor is both a prosthesis of God, who "uses" her to ask on another's behalf, and a giver of her own empathetic expressions. Yet the suffering that Arlene underwent in this instance bore affinities to a martyrdom, an excruciating experience purposed by

God. In this respect, an intercessor may occupy a position analogous to that of a Catholic saint: a figure who has high standing with God by virtue of her suffering and therefore receives what she asks on behalf of another.

As her marriage deteriorated, Arlene came to depend on God more intensely. Her recollections centered on the ways that God had removed her from harmful dependencies on other people, changing her into someone upon whom others depended instead. The process transformed her from a victimized wife to a strong caregiver. She realized in retrospect, she told me, that her relationship with her husband had been "what the world calls co-dependent"—she was trying to preserve a marriage to a man who was deceiving her. "You have such a weakness, it's like an addiction, but it's to a person—you can't live without that person regardless of what's going on. I was so fearful of being alone. I was away from my family, I was a military wife, being taken advantage of." The Lord healed Arlene by letting her know that the "co-dependence" was in fact "idolatry," because she was giving her marriage higher priority than God. "Now I see it clear. I had to make a decision." She explained how God had smoothed her way over subsequent years through challenges of single parenting, relocations, and job losses in her nursing profession. Her ex-husband "was always trying to undermine everything I was doing" with their sons, and she had to hold them accountable for misdeeds without losing their respect or control over the household. "God was giving me this wisdom because I didn't know what to do in those situations." Her sons now honor her for her strength. At the time of her separation, Arlene was attending a Pentecostal church in another city, and she received advice and support from the pastor and another woman with whom she studied the Bible. When she first joined that church, she felt isolated as the only single mother in attendance. However, a number of other divorced women subsequently joined the church as well. "Since God did this for me, and taught me new ways of doing things, I have been able to minister to so many women who have been in my shoes. Unfortunately, we're a dime a dozen these days." Finally, God affirmed Arlene's role as a woman upon whom others depend by giving her a "prompting" (experienced by Arlene as a thought that was not hers) during a visit to Buffalo that she needed to move back to her hometown to care for her aging parents.

## The Labor Politics of Prayer

Eternal Hope members' practices of asking reflect some culturally specific predicaments concerning care and self-sufficiency. I often asked them what difference it makes to say "I will pray for you while you're going through this trouble" as opposed to "I really hope things will get better for you." I was commonly told that there was nothing wrong with expressing hope that a situation would improve, but that it was merely a polite comment: "It's just a gesture." Praying for someone, on the other hand, elicits the help of Jesus for the other person. As such, it is a form of labor in keeping with Arlene's term "travail."[1] Lynne referred me to the bestseller *The Power of a Praying Parent* by evangelical author Stormie Omartian (2005), who casts the work of prayer as an acknowledgment of her own personal weakness and as a request for strength and influence. Omartian frames the admission of personal incapacity as a condition of empowerment:

> The Bible says, "Whatever you bind on earth will be bound in heaven, and whatever you loose on earth will be loosed in heaven" (Matthew 18:18). God gives us authority on earth. When we take that authority, God releases power to us from heaven. Because it's *God's* power and *not* ours, we become the vessel through which His power flows. When we pray, we bring that power to bear upon everything we are praying about, and we allow the power of God to work through our powerlessness. When we pray, we are humbling ourselves before God and saying, "I need Your presence and Your power, Lord. I can't do this without You." When we don't pray, it's like saying we have no need of anything outside of ourselves. (18)
>
> …
>
> Whenever you pray for your child, do it as if you are interceding for his or her life—because that is *exactly* what you are doing. Remember that while God has a perfect plan for our children's lives, Satan has a plan for them too. Satan's plan is to destroy them, and he will *try* to use any means possible to do so: drugs, sex, alcohol, rebellion, accidents, disease. But he won't be able to successfully use any of those things if his power has been dissipated through prayer. (22)

Omartian begins from a premise of personal incapacity. She does not assert that she possesses prior abilities and character traits that she can bestow as gifts upon her children (or through a salaried career, a topic she does not discuss). Rather, Omartian casts herself as powerless in herself to refrain from repeating the mistakes made in her own upbringing.[2] It is her willingness to ask God for help, together with the labor she devotes to doing so, that she construes as empowering. To refuse to put in the work of asking God to protect her children would be to refuse to care; it would be tantamount, in Mauss's (2015) terms, to rejecting one's obligations to give.

Self-sufficiency, nonetheless, is the metaphorical ground upon which the figure of prayer is inscribed in Omartian's account. Crucially, she characterizes the unsaved condition of not praying as "saying we have no need of anything outside of ourselves" (2005: 18), in other words that we do not have to offer requests because we do not need to receive anything in return. In effect, people must be redeemed from a false sense that their security derives from their own efforts or intrinsic traits. By acknowledging their incapacity, they receive God's "authority," which provides true security. In a similar vein, Reverend Jerry Falwell Sr. remarked in a sermon to students at Liberty University:

> If I were to ask you to write down on a piece of paper your dream for your life
> that is ahead of you, I would get about ten thousand different answers. But then,
> I would ask you: Do you plan to do it out of your own energy and proficiency?
> Or do you plan to tap into the anointing of God's spirit? (Roose 2009: 45)

Like Omartian, Falwell frames prayer as a counterpart to the ideology of individual achievement: the admission of helplessness is a means of assuring security, and indeed a precondition for success. At the same time, Falwell and Omartian share a basic premise of white privilege, namely the ability to presume (rather than explicitly state) that security and success ought to be theirs in the nature of things.

This outlook on admitting helplessness differs from that of many in what Elizabeth Currid-Halkett (2017) labels the elite "aspirational class" in the United States, whose consumption habits index exclusive status and knowledge together with commitments to good causes. Those in the "aspirational class" are usually encouraged to feel (or at least behave in professional settings) as though they possessed intrinsic talents upon which to draw to achieve success, even as their financial investments in real estate and higher education help to solidify barriers to upward mobility faced by the majority of the population (Reeves 2017; Sandel 2020; Stewart 2018)—a dynamic that recalls the structuring power of bad-faith alibis. In Eternal Hope, believers often disclaim the efficacy of inborn talents, for instance by praying "I'm so sorry, God, for always trying to take control and do it my way." They combine these admissions with a readiness to labor in prayer on other people's behalf, through intercession and travail. As with other forms of labor, the extent to which the work of prayer is recognized and valued is a matter of politics. These labor politics of prayer provide powerful grounds for a right-wing critique of the exclusivity of the "aspirational class." I find it no coincidence that the 2016 Republican Party platform states, however cynically: "Every time we sing, 'God Bless America', we are asking for help. We ask for divine help that our country can fulfill its promise" (Republican National Committee 2016: ii). In a move lending itself to political revanchism, the notion that a person thrives by virtue of his or her innate talents is framed—not unreasonably—as arrogant. I regard this stance as a key basis for Eternal Hope preachers' condemnation of "humanism" as a conceited opinion that "man is the measure of all things," for their denunciations of the corollary view that individuals may create standards that they consider appropriate (about same-sex marriage, for instance) instead of adhering to the moral order established by God, and for their embrace of right-wing political figures. Yet arguments about the need to abide by God's moral order need not center on concerns about self-sufficiency. For members of the African American churches, the significance of requests made of God hinges instead on problems of respect.

## Negotiating Respect

"Living for God changes your priorities," Lynne remarked to me in a hallway outside the sanctuary of Eternal Hope. "You start to think more about salvation. I always tell my children that we are not just put on this earth to be born, make money, and die. Yes, you have to work, you have to pay your bills and all that, but really it's all about salvation." While I have no reason to think that Lynne was especially well-off, her comment conveyed a taken for grantedness about making money—together with a suspicion of its existential senselessness—whose like I never heard at all among members of the African American churches of Victory Gospel and Heaven's Tabernacle. Their outlooks have been shaped by the profound racial wealth gap in the United States (Baradaran 2017; Darity et al. 2018; McKernan et al. 2013; Traub et al. 2017) stemming from slavery and entrenched by systematic housing and school segregation. For them, much of the appeal of "living for God" is being "sick and tired of being sick and tired." However, they do not understand personal incapacity as a problem to be overcome in the same ways as do members of Eternal Hope. Pastor John and Pastor Hadley readily acknowledge that they themselves, like many in their congregations, have in the past found means to accumulation in the informal economies of "the street." They all know that they can get by, but can they do so in obedience to God?

"God will bless you emotionally, mentally, spiritually, physically, and financially," Pastor John often remarks. "The devil will only bless you financially, and he'll only do that for a short while." To be blessed by God is to be valued as a person in ways that transcend all other rubrics. As do members of Eternal Hope, when these believers acknowledge God's blessings, they express "thankfulness for a plenitude that could not have been planned or achieved on their own and through which the lack of control they experienced in other contexts might suddenly seem like evidence of transcendent care" (Seeman 2018: 342). Yet Pastor John's argument that the devil is a source of blessings, albeit false ones, suggests that for the urban poor, Christianity presents one set of approaches among others to questions of *whom* should be depended on, on what terms, and with what implications. To a much greater extent than in Eternal Hope, the problem of which sources of vitality to draw upon is thematized in religious terms in the African American churches. As these believers gain insight into God's blessings, they learn particular ways to respect and be respected while ideally unlearning others (cf. Bourgois 1995). Pastor John routinely says as much when instructing his congregation that they should "put nobody before God": he loves God first, then his wife, then his children, both those in his household and in his church. If his wife were to tell him to go against God's instructions, he would not listen to her.

For these believers, learning to depend on God is a process akin to what Brendan Thornton (2016) calls "negotiating respect." In the Dominican barrio Thornton describes, gang members and others in the community show Pentecostal believers respect "according to their perceived faithfulness and unwavering satisfaction of behavioral prohibitions" (191). While members of Victory Gospel and Heaven's Tabernacle do not obtain prestige in the eyes of unsaved neighbors in the same manner, they do perceive God's activity as countering the institutions that systematically exploit their labor and devalue their personhood. God's blessings bestow "favor in the eyes of men"—that is, extraordinary forms of prosperity and advancement, on the model of Joseph who was imprisoned in Egypt but subsequently elevated by Pharaoh to a position of power.

Yet the connections between respect and dependence upon God are not simple. Following a public dispute on the phone-in prayer line between two members of Victory Gospel, Mother Smith felt it necessary to deliver a speech at the conclusion of a Bible study session. "We have some strong personalities in this church," she said. "We have so little, and we want respect from other people so we're always on the lookout to see who's going to aggravate us." During a Sunday service a few weeks later, Pastor John told everyone to turn to the person sitting next to him or her and say, "Neighbor, I'd rather have truth than be real." Perceiving his audience's confusion, he elaborated: "We street people have got no problem being real. 'An eye for an eye' is real, but 'Turn the other cheek' and 'Vengeance is mine, saith the Lord, I will repay' are truth" (cf. Carter 2019: 140).

Mother Smith and Pastor John felt it necessary to carry out a careful parsing of respect. They argued that "we street people" ordinarily and wrongly demand respect in ways that contribute to "emotionalism" and tit-for-tat reprisals, yet if we "submit" to God and obey his word conveyed by the pastor, we will receive such "favor" that even our adversaries will be compelled to respect us, in accordance with the scripture "Thou preparest a table before me in the presence of mine enemies" (Ps. 23:5). The principle that one should avoid retaliation does not imply a refusal to recognize insults or betrayals. On one Resurrection Sunday (Easter), Pastor John preached about how Jesus had outmaneuvered Judas. He asked all in the congregation who had felt betrayed by someone close to them to stand, and everyone did so. He instructed each person to turn to his or her neighbor and say: "I've been betrayed, but I'm getting ready to rise!" He continued: "Every time you walk in Jesus, someone is going to turn their back. You've got to accept betrayal. Judas might be your wife, husband, mother, father, someone very close to you. It's inevitable if you're really saved." On the same day, Pastor Hadley preached: "Hell had a party when it thought Jesus had gone down." Addressing her audience, she continued, "How many of you know that they're gonna have a party when they think they've got you down? If you don't got a Judas, you got a problem. If you're walking with God, you got a betrayer." On another occasion, Pastor John preached: "The devil wants to take you out but can't get at you, so he tries to get in tune with the emotional side of you," tempting you to retaliate. "The enemy knows who to use at certain times to get on your nerves. There are already people out there talking, scheming about you. Tell them that they better do it quickly, because God's got a counter-move!" This speech elicited an enormous outburst of approval.

In what follows, I discuss a range of situations that have compelled members of Heaven's Tabernacle and Victory Gospel to consider how relations of respect have been or should be affected by their dependence on God. I turn first to requests for material assistance, focusing on how women living in poverty make claims to respect as they confront the difficulties of caring for their own and one another's children. I then discuss the concept of "sowing into people," a phrase associated with monetary offerings in churches whose significance derives from the ways requests and gifts circulate in wider contexts.

## Manipulative Requests and Conditional Love

Members of Victory Gospel and Heaven's Tabernacle encourage one another to evaluate forms of asking—including prayers to God and requests for scarce resources directed toward kin, friends, church colleagues, and social service agencies—along a moral continuum ranging from self-centered or deceitful "manipulation" to proper forms of "waiting" for help, which God often provides at the last minute. Elder Rebecca told me that she knows better than to ask God for what she needs in order to survive, because God knows what a believer needs and will make a way to provide it. A saved person who needs something, she explained, should thank God for what he has already done in heaven and is going to bring to pass on earth. Distinguishing "needs" from "desires," Elder Rebecca went on to say that it is legitimate for a saved person to ask God for the "desire of her heart," and then wait for God to grant the request at the time he knows is best. However, an unsaved person will think of God instrumentally, as she herself had done during her years of addiction to crack cocaine. Her requests will be pleas for help: "God, You got to help me get out of jail! I ain't no bad person!" Pastor Hadley recounted how a prayer partner named Emily related how she would ask God for help during emergencies by demanding, "God, You got to come through!" Emily heard God reply, "Oh, that's just Emily. She tells Me what to do." A better approach is to show respect. During her youth, Pastor Hadley recalls, she knew how to ask her father for things by getting into his good graces. Likewise, "To get what you want from God, massage His heart a bit. Tell Him how good He is. If it doesn't look like you're getting what you need, tell Him: 'Nevertheless, Your will be done.' Then you will delight in Him because He has your best interests at heart."

Women in Heaven's Tabernacle often speak in this fashion of how asking and responding to requests have been means of working out terms of familiarity and respect with kin, friends, and God. They comment that God is liable to afflict them by "moving people out of the way" if those people interfere with their sole dependence upon him. Pastor Hadley has repeatedly told her congregation that during her youth God caused the deaths of all the elder relatives whom she used to ask for material assistance, because while she wanted to rely on them, God wanted her to depend on him alone. Women recount during Bible study sessions how they have sometimes turned down requests for help with the excuse that they did not want God to "move them out of the way." This is a morally fraught move because they usually want to "be a blessing" to others who need resources, yet if God gives them a "feeling of peace" about the situation they will realize that a denial has been appropriate.

Elder Rebecca gave me a lengthy account of how God had moved her own child out of the way because she had made an improper request. At the age of eighteen, when she was newly saved, she made a vow to God that if he would give her a son, she would "give the child to Him" in imitation of Hannah, the mother of the prophet Samuel. Her elders warned her that this vow was a mistake, saying "that's a little too deep for you right now." When the child was small, Elder Rebecca recalled, she would not allow other women in the family to care for him. "He was handsome, he was gorgeous, he was a good baby. I didn't let no one feed him, touch him, change him. All you could do was say hi, and you had to say that at a distance. It was horrible." Elder Rebecca explained that God punished her for insisting on caring for her child in her own way. While at a church service with the baby on her lap, she heard a prophet say, "If you don't stop, God is going to take the closest thing to your heart." But, she recalled, "I didn't put it together"—in other words, she did not realize that the way she was keeping the baby to herself showed that she was "making an idol" of him over God. Within a couple years, the baby was diagnosed with an immune disorder, and Elder Rebecca felt that she needed to give him up for adoption to a family that could properly attend to his needs. "As soon as I signed the papers," she told me, "God brought back that prophetic word to my mind," letting her know that he had moved the baby out of the way. "I made a vow I couldn't keep," she concluded. "God made me keep that vow by taking him from me."

Comparable to Arlene's reflection that her dependence on her ex-husband was a form of "idolatry," the insight God gave Elder Rebecca was that her claim to be able to care for her child on her own was an overweening presumption. As Carol Stack (1974) shows, child sharing is an important means of creating kinship ties within poor African American communities. Especially in contexts of successive unions, a woman's willingness to share child-rearing with her own mother and her current and previous spouses' mothers helps to provide a child with an extensive network of kin. Since childcare requires resources, women commonly evaluate relations with particular kin by assessing one another's willingness to devote time, labor, and money to their children. As a result, the need to ask for assistance is liable to contribute to moral problems of "conditional love." Christine, whom I introduced in Chapter 2, recalled Pastor John's remarks on the subject of "conditional love" in a Sunday sermon, explaining ruefully in a conversation with me that most people think, "You do this for me, so I'll love you." But "if I asked you, 'Can you watch my kids while I'm going to the doctor's?' and you said to me you couldn't do it today, I'm upset with you now, I won't love you, you're not my brother in Christ, because you told me no. And it's not just in the church, it's outside on the streets too." Christine imitated someone saying, "'He looked out for me. He passed me a couple hundred dollars so I can get on my feet, so I love him.' Why can't you love him just because that's your man, that's your friend? That's a condition!"

To talk about someone's love as "conditional" is to criticize a person for being interested solely in her own well-being (or at least, that of someone other than the speaker's), and thus for being "manipulative."[3] Reflections of this kind are liable to fuel what is called "emotionalism." I asked Christine whether she could recall when she first became aware that other people's love for her could be conditional. In response, she described an episode that occurred when she was thirteen years old. Christine had run away from home because she disliked her stepfather, and was living with some cousins. She would accompany these cousins to steal clothes from department stores and then return them for gift cards that they could subsequently sell on the street for cash (on theft as labor, see Sullivan 1989). She told me that they knew they were "doing wrong," but that they were "just trying to make some fast money." One day, her cousin's mother asked her to steal for her. Feeling that her aunt was trying to exploit her, Christine refused, thereby apparently causing her aunt to feel disrespected in turn:

> You don't make your daughter steal for you, why do you want me to steal for you? You want me to make your money and my money too, but you don't make your daughters do that. I had to make my own money, I had run away from home. I told her, "I can't do it." Then we became like—she hated me, she didn't want me around, she didn't want to take me stealing to make my money. So I stopped stealing with them. I went back to school, tried to do right, and moved back in with my mother. But my aunt just completely cut me off all the way, told her kids I was a bad person. I was like, "I thought this lady loved me, but she only loves me under certain conditions."

Such surprises about "conditional love" and disrespectful attempts at "manipulation" are all too common in the context of the precarious circumstances of many members of Victory Gospel and Heaven's Tabernacle. Over the course of our four-year acquaintance, Christine related to me many such unpleasant surprises, but she has spoken of happier ones as well. Christine told me that she enjoyed my talks with her because they provided her an opportunity to "open out" about past events, whereas with most people she has had to be careful of malicious gossip. She also made a point of telling me that she appreciated the fact that I did not judge her.

Born in 1989 as the only child of her parents' marriage, Christine has six siblings from her parents' previous and subsequent unions. She was raised largely by her mother and grandmother, both factory workers, and by her father during weekends and summers. Christine's father sold illegal drugs—"he always told me he knew it was wrong," she commented, "but he said he had to support his family"—and was incarcerated for two separate two-year periods. Christine has a criminal record for petty thefts committed as a teenager, and she was once evicted, a circumstance that has made it difficult for her to find decent housing to rent for herself, her now ex-husband Tony, and her children (aged ten, five, three, and one in 2017). One of her greatest fears has been that she will lose custody of her children, as do many mothers whose precarious housing situations draw the attention of social workers (Desmond 2016; Lee 2016).

Over the course of four years, Christine lived in three different houses or sections of houses, all with various combinations of problems including faulty plumbing, lack of heat, smashed windows, dog feces in the basement, improperly installed water heaters, and bedbug and rat infestations. In addition, she has had to contend with arbitrary decisions on the part of caseworkers who periodically cut her Supplemental Nutrition Assistance Program (SNAP or food stamp) payments for various reasons: late paperwork, missed medical appointments, her ostensible failures to demand child support from her first husband (who was incarcerated and hence unable to pay), or because (she believes) caseworkers have been offended by her complaints. "It's too much," she often said. "They just don't care."

In April 2017, Christine's monthly expenses of at least $1,563 exceeded her household cash income of $1,476, equivalent to about $8.20 per day per person for a family of six. Her largest expenses were rent ($600, over 40 percent of household income, an unaffordable proportion by US federal definition), fuel for her car, which was in poor shape ($240), auto insurance ($200), utilities and phones (about $250), and a furniture bill ($1,350 principal at 20 percent interest, or $178 per month). Christine was receiving $756 each month as Supplemental Security Income (SSI) because her son had been hospitalized multiple times during his first year of life because of a congenital illness. However, she was worried because these SSI payments were contingent on the household income being lower than $9,000 per year. Christine had found a part-time job as a cleaner in a mental hospital, which brought in $520 per month, but the demands of childcare in her absence were taking a toll on her relationship with her husband Tony. Tony was working through a temporary employment agency, but most of his earnings were being garnished for child support for his previous spouse. As a result, he was bringing in about $200 a month in addition to $200 in SNAP food stamps. Christine calculated that she was owed $480 per month in food stamps, but caseworkers at the Department of Social Services were denying her claim because they had calculated her income based on the nonexistent child support she was supposed to be receiving from her incarcerated first spouse. She added that she ought to have been receiving $291 per month in benefits from the Temporary Assistance for Needy Families (TANF) program. These had been cut off on grounds that she was employed, even though the program is supposed to support minimum-wage employees who work fewer than thirty hours per week. Christine was able to supply her family with minimal amounts of bread, cheese, milk, eggs, and pasta from the Women, Infants, and Children (WIC) nutrition program. She was thinking about quitting her job in hopes of receiving TANF benefits, but in order to do so she would have had to enroll in a workfare program in which she would be paid in food stamps for her labor (Dickinson 2016). She was also considering making a request for a "fair hearing" at the Department of Social Services, but feared that all her benefits might be eliminated while her case was pending.

A couple of months later, Christine received a letter stating that her food stamp benefits were going to be reinstated (following a delay of several weeks) at $678 per month. She told me that one of her cousins once received six months' worth of back benefits on her electronic food stamp card in a lump sum. In their unpredictability and apparent arbitrariness, these bureaucratic decisions might as well be the work of God or the devil.

As Susan Crawford Sullivan (2011) notes, "Poor mothers' prayer narratives reflect a God who is both compassionate and judgmental" (38). At one desperate point when Christine was convinced that her children would be taken from her, a cousin told her on the phone to listen to a prophet delivering an online sermon from Florida. This prophet called out Christine's first and last name, exclaiming that God had a "great release" in store for her. Within two days, her caseworker called her to tell her that they were dropping the case against her. The knowledge that her struggles are part of God's plan for herself has encouraged Christine in her efforts to retain custody of her children and to maintain their health. More specifically, God has helped her understand who has been responsible and should be held accountable for various outcomes of these efforts. This awareness can take the form of self-reproach. While looking to move out of a house with multiple problems, Christine recalled the enthusiasm she had felt when she first arrived, because the rooms corresponded almost exactly with those that she had seen in a dream. However, the walls were painted a different color from those in the dream, a circumstance that should have made her aware that the dream was deceptive. She took the blame on herself for having decided to live there: "It's on me."

The knowledge that she is working to fulfill her maternal responsibilities has been an important source of self-respect for Christine, and her experiences in church have given her terms for understanding how she has or has not done so. She explained to me that while she was raised largely by her mother and grandmother, she had learned in church that God intends the husband to be the head of the household and the wife to be his support. As evidence, she referred to an incident when she allowed her ten-year-old son and a teenaged cousin to go to the movies by themselves at night, over her husband Tony's objections. They arrived home very late, having gotten lost on buses, and failed to keep their phones charged. This episode "convicted" Christine, making her feel that she was terribly at fault for having overridden her husband's instructions. Yet on the whole, God has affirmed Christine's sense that she has been a good mother, as have her own mother and grandmother. She attributed the survival of her first son, diagnosed with a life-threatening illness several weeks after his birth, in part to the prayers of her mother and grandmother, who knew better how to pray than she did at the time.

In 2014, Pastor John announced in church that God had awakened him at night to tell him to bless Christine with money and goods. She stood in tears at the front of the church as everyone embraced her, and church members spent a Sunday afternoon bringing furniture and a stove to her rooms on the second floor of a house. Due to a caseworker's enigmatic decision, Christine's monthly food stamp benefits had been reduced about six months previously from $526 to $225. Church members had been dropping by to ask her if she needed anything, and Mother Smith had put her in touch with a woman she knew at a food pantry who provided her with groceries, no questions asked.

However, after about a year such support from the church had waned due to perceptions that Christine had made some "manipulative" requests. In consequence, she relied more heavily on her kinship network in Buffalo, in particular her mother and grandmother, who made occasional gifts of food and money but who also asked to borrow her food stamp card when they were hard up. This circumstance is in keeping with Stack's (1974) finding that senior women often coordinate the distribution of resources within poor African American extended families, regardless of shared residence. Yet I was struck by the important impact that living arrangements within Christine's household have had on resource distribution and negotiations over care and respect. Over the course of several months, Tony's cousin, his brother, a brother of Christine, and this brother's girlfriend were sequentially staying with them against the advice of Pastor John, who had warned Christine of the dangers of having people in their house who were not "living for God." The men had recently been incarcerated and needed a place to stay. Tensions arose over food consumption and refusals to help with bills.

One day, Christine awoke to find that her brother had been preparing drug paraphernalia in the kitchen. She threw him out of the house, telling me that if her children had imbibed drugs, she would have had to take them to the hospital and would certainly have lost custody. Expelling her brother put Christine at odds with her grandmother, who did not want him either to go back to jail or to stay in her own house. Over the course of the next two weeks, the father of Christine's two oldest children physically threatened her in her house, and she was pulled over by the police for having lapsed auto insurance. She had her children in her car at the time, and was terrified that if she had been arrested then and there, she would have lost custody. In addition, Christine had a case filed anonymously against her with Child Protective Services (CPS), a situation that had occurred each year for the past several years. She suspected that women in her extended family had been calling in the state in order to pursue petty grievances, for instance that she had bought more clothes for her children than for theirs while shopping with them at the start of the school year. However, the social workers contacted by CPS had proved quite helpful to Christine in the past, advocating on her behalf with landlords, providing parenting classes that she found useful, and helping her in family court to retain custody of the children.

During this period of emergency, after Christine had left Victory Gospel, I asked her whether she felt any messages from God about what she was going through. "I don't know what the confirmation from God is," she replied. "I don't know what it is. Sometimes I just cry out, 'What do You want me to do? Where am I going wrong? Where am I failing at?' I really don't know, Brother Fred. I really don't know." A short while later, though, she told me that she had heard God's voice loud and clear: "Start packing." An aunt who had been staying with her while her own apartment was being cleared of bedbugs brought the insects into Christine's house, and then insulted her by talking about how well the apartment was being fixed up in her absence. When social workers discovered the infestation, Christine was forced to leave immediately and locate emergency housing for herself and her children.

While speaking about her struggles with kin, Christine commented that "God knows your heart," a statement I took to imply that God respects her even if nobody else does. Even if she is thinking or doing things she knows to be wrong, she understands that "your heart holds what you really want" and that God knows her true intentions. Christine implicitly acknowledges the conditionality of her own love, yet she understands herself as a responsible parent and generous kinswoman in part because she is able to imagine how her motives appear in God's eyes.

## Sowing into People

Sandra, a senior woman in Heaven's Tabernacle, was chatting over lunch with other church members about her hairdresser Linda, whom she liked very much: "Linda said to me, 'Miss Sandra, you don't have to pay me now. You can pay me next time.' 'I'm not that kind of person,' I said to her. 'I've got the money with me.' 'Oh, Miss Sandra,' Linda said, 'stop stopping my blessing.'"

As in many jokes, there was a lot going on. Sandra was remarking on Linda's caring attitude, which Linda expressed both by offering to cut her hair for free and by self-deprecatingly identifying her motive not as pity or condescension but as a desire for blessing. Sandra was not implying that Linda felt she would receive a blessing because of any special connection Sandra had to God as a believer. Rather, Sandra spoke of how she avoided presenting herself as a "manipulative" person who asks for help while giving nothing in return, while Linda playfully framed Sandra's insistence on paying as "stopping a blessing" that she herself would otherwise receive were she to make a gift of her labor. Even though Linda presumably wanted to be paid, pretending to elicit a request on Sandra's part for a free haircut was a means of framing their relationship in terms of gifting, whereby her own willingness to give would be recognized by God as well as by Sandra.

A counterpoint to this conversation occurred during a discussion at a Bible study in Heaven's Tabernacle. Pastor Hadley remarked, "We want God to move quickly on our behalf, but are we dedicated to Him? We're dedicated to our jobs, but are we dedicated to God's house? Did we move on time?"—a phrasing whose significance I discuss below. She told a story about a certain woman who was very poor but was expecting a large check for a disability claim. This acquaintance was always involved in church activities and promised to "bless" other women when her check came through. When she received the money, however, she moved to an upscale suburb. Instead of continuing to attend church and blessing the other women with gifts, she spent the money on vacations. When she subsequently lost her money, she had no friends. She had not recognized that she was dependent on God for her blessings; otherwise, she would have continued to give to the other women so as to "be a blessing" to them.

Both of these anecdotes suggest how respect is contingent on one's willingness to give in ways that enhance the vitality of others. In Victory Gospel and Heaven's Tabernacle, leaders build on such popular understandings of the sources of respect by vociferously encouraging their congregations to "sow into the life" of the pastor or visiting preachers by making monetary offerings in addition to the ten percent of believers' gross income that they "owe to the kingdom" in tithes. While the term "sowing into someone's life" is specific to churches, it resonates with a broader set of practices. I spoke with Clary about parallels between mentoring in church and on the streets, where participants in informal economies need to learn codes of honor (Anderson 1999; Duck 2015; Venkatesh 2006). Clary was careful to emphasize that the "direction" of mentoring on the street is wrong, unlike church mentoring. However, he distinguished his experiences with good street mentors, who were "actually trying to help me to know how to make it in this mean cruel world," from his involvement with bad street mentors, who were "just manipulating you to do their dirty work for them just for their gain." I asked him whether offerings made in church could be compared to deliveries of profits to one's superiors on the street:

**Fred:** In church, we often use the phrase "sowing into" the pastor. Is that expression used on the streets?

**Clary:** No, we use a lot of [words like] loyalty, being true to the game, keeping it real. A phrase I like to say is, I'm six o'clock, I'm straight up-and-down, there's nothing sideways about me. Some people that's been out here a little while might say "returns on my investment," but for the most part we don't say "sow into."

**Fred:** I'm wondering if it's sort of like the same thing, though, because when you're delivering the goods to someone who's looking after you, then you're enhancing his life.

**Clary:** Exactly. And in return, you get your return from a good mentor. As long as this person is making money, you're gonna make money. You can't worry about how much money this person is making. All you can do is focus on what you make. You do your part, and your team does their part. Another saying we like to say is, you're only good as your weakest link. As long as everybody is doing their part, everybody is going to eat. And it's the same thing with the church. As long as we come in there and we sow, and we being true about it, we'll get our blessings. As far as we make sure the church is good and functioning right, that helps us function right, so it's the same thing.

Clary had been privileged, he told me, to have been a mentor to many people on the street who had "come up under" him (a phrase also used in churches to describe long-term mentoring relations). He said that one of the greatest challenges he had faced as a mentor had been to build up subordinates' trust: "There's been so many people that has done them dirty that they don't even trust *me*. I can give them all the love in the world but they don't know how to accept it right because they're still waiting on me to flip [betray them]." Pastors express comparable concerns about trust. At a banquet held to commemorate the fifth anniversary of Victory Gospel's founding, the bishop of a prominent Buffalo church remarked that a pastor always has to wonder about a saint: "Can I trust you enough to sow my heart into you?" This question, reversing the usual direction of "sowing" from saints to pastors, reflects a concern that saints' love for their leaders might be "conditional" on material assistance or emotional support. Whether church members are trying to "manipulate" pastors is itself a focus of discernment. "When I give you love, I'm looking to see if your word is risky," Pastor John remarked during a service. "If I find that you're risky, I'm going to accept you and forgive you, but I'm going to back off." Unlike Arlene, who found an unequivocal source of affirmation in being recognized as a caregiver, Pastor John has been compelled to distinguish true from false expressions of respect. Yet discernment operates in multiple directions. Pastor John commonly tells his congregation that he must contend with members' suspicions that he possesses inappropriately intimate knowledge about their lives. Immature saints, he preaches, do not understand that when he speaks publicly in Bible study about what "some of you are doing outside church" (without specifying names), he is referring to what God has told him: "If God shows it to me, that means He wants me to see it." Rather than accepting "correction," they whisper that he has spied on them or is inappropriately airing their private business.

Beyond conveying concerns about trust, the expression "sowing my heart into you" implies that people obtain their capabilities and vitality from the blessings of others. To be blessed is to have been "sown into," as a visiting pastor argued at a Victory Gospel service while eliciting offerings. He pointed out that people derive all their characteristics from the "seeds" that other people have sown into them. "You're not beautiful or handsome in yourself," he preached. "You are beautiful only because someone sowed that beauty into you." While this pastor was making a case that the congregation owed a "sowing" into the kingdom of God in return for all these blessings, his argument hinted at a broader logic: senior or more powerful persons foster or impede the growth of juniors via the good or bad seeds they sow into them. Christine told me later that she found the preacher's words to be true: other people had in fact "sown into" her. She spoke of what Patricia Hill Collins (1994) calls "motherwork": Her mother had told her she had to go to school, and taught her how to be a woman, to cook, and raise children (see Abrums 2010; Carothers 1990). "Looking back on it now, I realize she was sowing into my life." I asked Christine whether she finds that the words people use make her feel certain ways about herself. She replied: "If people say, 'You ain't going to amount to nothing,' if you really think that—. Life does go by what other people say about you." She went on:

> If someone tells you that you're beautiful, you think that you are. I think that other people have sown that into me. My husband tells me, "You're beautiful," even though my kids tell me, "You're big today, Mom." The funniest thing they tell me is when I tell [one of her daughters] she's pretty, and she tells me, "Your hair is nappy today." But then when I comb it, she says it's pretty. Kids sure do tell it.

It is important to appreciate the urgency with which many of the members of these urban churches hope that God will "move on their behalf" in response to the seeds they have sown either as money or as labor for the ministry. Under the best of circumstances, they may find themselves lying awake at night wondering how they will pay their utility bills, and in emergencies they may worry that they will be evicted, lose custody of their children, or face incarceration. As women in Heaven's Tabernacle say, most of them are one paycheck away from being broke, so that they cannot afford *not* to tithe. Yet Pastor John and Pastor Hadley frown upon suggestions that the purpose of faith is to become prosperous. They instruct believers that they should "take God as your source and not your resource," and "seek His face, not just His hand." According to Pastor Hadley, the fact that the woman of her acquaintance left church as soon as she received her check demonstrated that she had been treating God as her "resource" rather than as her "source."

While believers routinely declare that God will "make you a lender and not a borrower," such assertions of prosperity are geared to fostering insight into the conditions under which they will be blessed. One such condition involves time: notwithstanding the urgency of their needs, they ought to inhabit the temporality of the gift rather than expect immediate returns. Christine's husband Tony explained that he did not contribute his tithes, drawn from his family's unemployment insurance and disability income, to receive "benefits" but rather blessings. A benefit, he said, is "something that you work for, you gain," but a blessing is "something that you already have coming to you. ... If a man on the street asks you for a dollar, and you give him a dollar, in return later on God blesses you with double what you gave that man. He doesn't benefit you with double." While a person intends to "benefit" from a business by earning a profit, Tony compared a person who tithes to a boat on the water that God gradually "releases from the chains" attaching it to other boats, which are "people in your life who are holding you down and using you." Eventually a saved person will be "floating" freely and be "able to think with a clearer mind even when you're in the darkness." Similarly, Pastor John and Pastor Hadley insist that you have to praise God when times are hard, putting your voice into "the atmosphere" so as to "confuse the enemy," who is expecting you to be depressed. A person should not worry about bills, but "rest" in the knowledge that "God's got this." Pastor John preaches, "You have to give up the belief that you have to keep doing those things that will bring you money: drug dealing, pimping, sleeping with a man who will do for you." You have to learn how to "trust God to stretch your finances." If you give tithes and offerings regularly, you find that your bills will get paid. Once you "believe God," you will no longer have to "chase money, because money will be chasing you."

Underlying this insistence on the need to trust God for finances is profound anxiety about the ambiguities of dependence and exploitation. One of the few times when Pastor John passed me the microphone during a Bible study (thereby authorizing my speech as instructive) occurred when I mentioned that the "spirit of capitalism" consists of believing that one has a duty to the increase of one's capital (Weber 2003). That "spirit," Pastor John elaborated, was of the devil: it both oppresses the poor and leads them to engage in destructive behavior. He draws a sharp distinction between "working for the man," who pays employees less than their labor is worth, and "working for the kingdom," which multiplies one's gifts "tenfold, a hundredfold, a thousandfold, a millionfold." In effect, he argues, you might think that your vitality depends on your job, but in actuality you are being exploited. In 2017, he publicly calculated that over the course of the nineteen years since he had been saved, he had made donations totaling about $200,000 in tithes, offerings, and gifts to prophets. He often reminds the congregation that he had been offered a job in Buffalo city government with a $60,000 annual salary, but that he turned it down in accordance with God's instruction to found a church.

As this suggests, the oppositions between wage labor and work for God's kingdom are constituted through the circulation of requests and gifts. Prophecies are themselves implicit requests for gifts, in that sowing into the life or the ministry of the prophet shows that the hearer has "received" his or her words and intends not to "miss the blessing." The same may be true of tithes and offerings, since as Peter Marina (2013) shows, church members who tithe regularly are more likely to be helped by leaders with resources to hand. Yet requests for tithes and offerings likewise generate anxieties among believers about whether pastors might be exploiting their sense of dependence on God (Klaits and McLean 2015). Believers speak of the work they undertake for the church as a matter of "serving" others in God's kingdom. Since the servitude of pastors is heaviest, they ought ideally to be blessed by members of their congregation with monetary gifts—but might they be "manipulating" people instead of serving? Pastor John routinely denounces pastors who "pimp the church" by demanding gifts in direct return for prophetic words.

To allay such concerns, church leaders insist on the efficacy of gifts that signify one's trust in God. When Mother Smith leads Sunday school, she often exhorts saints to follow her own example of rendering tithes and offerings: "People have come to my house and given me gift cards with money on them, so I know God has me on His mind." God will even "convict the hearts" of people whom she would least expect to change. On one occasion, she announced that her cousin, "the biggest flim-flam man in town," had recently paid back a $450 loan that she had made to him. "I never even thought to nag him for the money because I had faith God would enable me to receive it again." To be able to give out of abundance is a blessing that ensures more blessings. Mother Smith has connections at a local supermarket, which provides her with day-old groceries that she delivers to residents of Buffalo (not, for the most part, Victory Gospel members) whom she knows are in need. Yet she has related how she has had to "cut some people off" among her own kin even though it was hard for her to do so, because God had shown her that they would not learn to rely on him otherwise.

In ideal terms, the circulation of requests and gifts should render the body of believers a superorganism in which the health of each part is a concern of the other. Unfortunately, Mother Smith remarked, "some people's bodies tighten up when they hear the word 'obey.' The enemy wants us to resist someone who tells us the word, he wants us to be all jacked up and say, 'Get your own act together!'" Obedience to the word of God, together with willingness to submit to "correction" or rebuke, are key conditions of proper receiving. For example, those who have insight into the need to be "on time" not only attend church consistently and during proper hours, but follow pastors' directions to fast, pray, and provide labor both spontaneously and on specified occasions. To do otherwise is to be "out of order," a dangerous condition connoting alienation from God. A common saying is that "obedience is better than sacrifice" (1 Sam. 15:22), meaning that people who refuse to "put God first" will eventually be forced to sacrifice something important to them. "If you're not on time for God," Pastor Hadley remarked, "He might decide not to be on time for you when you need Him."

Mother Smith points out that the act of giving has physical as well as moral consequences. "People wonder why they're not being blessed," she remarked to open a Sunday school. It is because they are not giving tithes but complaining about their problems instead. "You'll feel a lightness in you if you are a blessing," whereas "our misery can make our bodies sick and others unhappy. We need to encourage people by telling them that God has blessed our lives, and that God will bless them too. Murmuring and complaining solidifies the problem. Don't pray the problem, pray the solution." More broadly, "praying the solution" means living in expectation of the gift, an attitude said to prevent bodily suffering.

Writing of cardiometabolic disorders in Samoa, Jessica Hardin (2019) shows how Pentecostal healing addresses collective problems through individual bodies. Faith practices, Hardin points out, constitute an "embodied critique" of the conditions necessary for a good life. For members of Victory Gospel and Heaven's Tabernacle, understandings of collective health problems take shape within an economy of blessings and the emotional work they entail. Evangelist Clarice, a senior member of Heaven's Tabernacle, remarked to me that unlike many middle-aged African American women and men, she has never suffered from high blood pressure. She did not feel the need to spell out that high rates of hypertension, diabetes, and obesity are outcomes of the stresses of everyday racism and the legacy of slavery, which "set in motion black people's diminished access to healthy foods, safe working conditions, medical treatment and a host of other social inequities that negatively impact health" (Strings 2020; see Abrums 2000; Mattingly 2010; Mullings and Wali 2001; Washington 2006). These believers are aware of the many structural issues created by "the world's system," but they emphasize the spiritual origins of cancer and other afflictions, which they say often arise from anger and resentment. For her part, Evangelist Clarice attributes her good health to the efforts she has made to allow Jesus to "transform her mind." Inspired by Baptist minister T. W. Hunt's devotional guide *The Mind of Christ* (1995), Evangelist Clarice has placed biblical passages on the walls and over the doors of her apartment so as to continually "check her mind" for spiritual awareness and responsiveness.[4]

As God's favor is contingent upon prior obedience, God may apply conditions to the blessing of health. Pastor Hadley made this point while relating an instance of divine back talk during a Bible study:

> We were talking about struggling or having a hard time with anything. We're to remember if we are Christians that we can do all things through Christ who strengthens us. If you go the Lord, He is able to deliver you from the thing that you can't do on your own. I'll give you something that was kind of funny. I remember telling the Lord, "You need to put me on a diet, show me how to lose this weight." He didn't say anything, and I kept on praying, "Show me how to lose this weight." The Lord says some funny things to me. He said to me, "Close your mouth." I'm like, okay—but I said, "Lord, You got to help me lose this weight." He said it again: "Close your mouth." The next day when I woke up, my tongue had swelled up in my mouth so thick that I couldn't talk and I couldn't eat. I said, "Lord, what's wrong with my tongue?" He said, "You told Me to show you how to lose weight, and I told you to close your mouth. Now you can't eat and you can't talk. Now go study your Word." He put me on an instant fast, praise the Lord, and it lasted for three days. And [the weight] went away just like that. So we got to be *careful* what we ask God for.

Playing with imagery of loudness and appetitiveness that Pastor Hadley and her audience found amusing—notwithstanding its troubling resonances with racial and gendered hierarchies (Collins 2004; Strings 2019)—God was making her understand that her health was a gift contingent on obedience.

In her study of Christian devotional dieting practices in the United States, R. Marie Griffith (2004) argues that ambitions for self-knowledge underlie believers' views that their true bodies, those which God sees and desires them to have, are healthy and fit. Griffith regards Christian dieting as a manifestation of the search "for fresh ways to become 'real,' to encounter the world in an authentic experience, to make the self—body, soul, or spirit, variously conceived—truly matter … [T]his authenticity is both the promise of Protestantism and its coercive power" (247). Yet Pastor Hadley's purpose in relating the biblical maxim "I can do all things through Christ who strengthens me" (Phil. 4:13) was not so much to claim a power to inhabit her true self than to illustrate how God is liable to reply to overly self-interested or demanding requests. Her conclusion—spoken seriously, not facetiously—that "we got to be *careful* what we ask God for" conveyed that if our prayers border on disrespectful "manipulation," God might respond by compelling a sacrifice of the willful self.

## Why God Talks Back

Kathy reacted negatively to my description of a revival attended by members of Heaven's Tabernacle at which a prophet asked for a monetary "seed" in order to "seal the blessing" spoken over an attendee. "That's not legit," Kathy commented. "God doesn't promise a blessing and then say, 'Give me money and then I'll give you the blessing.'" She went on to relate that when her parents Janet and Benny were searching for God early in their marriage, they responded to a televangelist's request to "send something of value" by sacrificing the shirts they had bought for their honeymoon—they cut them up and sent pieces of cloth to the station.

Who is to say what objects and activities are of "legit" value? In thinking about God's designs for bestowing value upon their lives, believers consider this question in remarkably explicit ways. To reiterate, their insights into the nature of value are critical in that believers aim to pass beyond what they consider to be ordinary, unsatisfactory ways of assessing personal worth. Such inadequate forms of assessment include but are not limited to individual earning power. They may involve improper styles of asking such as "manipulating" people or "begging" God, "co-dependency" on an abusive spouse, false imaginings of self-sufficiency, loving other people "on condition" of immediate returns, refusing to share or contribute to the care of children, or understanding time in ways that interfere with one's willingness to "sow." Of course, none of these ostensibly improper ways of assessing value would be concerns at all if they did not derive from lived conflicts over values.

An important reason God talks back, then, is to intervene in ongoing negotiations over what is to be valued and in what fashions. Pentecostal believers take as a premise that God's designs for personal value, as for all else, are not the same as human ones. God talks to believers because he has to "teach them His ways." Pastor Hadley compares God to a parent who feels compelled to "run" when a baby—that is, a new convert—cries to him for help: he will move quickly to see what he must do. However, God will not treat a grown child, a believer mature enough to understand his will, with the same solicitousness. Sometimes when Pastor Hadley asks for help, God replies simply, "My grace is sufficient unto you" and leaves it at that. The question of what counts as a respectful interaction is central for Pastor Hadley, in ways not shared by members of Eternal Hope who concentrate on how to signal their incapacities to God and respond to those of others.

The divergent critical bearings of these insights into value help to explain why God talks back to these believers in different ways, for instance by leading an intercessor at the suburban church to say, "This is between you and Jesus. Whatever it is, just talk to Him, ask Him to help you, and He will, He will give you that strength and that wisdom and He will teach you His ways," or by responding to the desperate pleas of a Black woman with "Oh that's just Emily. She tells Me what to do." In this chapter, I have used the phrase "the labor politics of prayer" to describe how Eternal Hope members' ambitions to be valued for the work they devote to prayer, and to admitting their own lack of self-sufficiency, often make them receptive to right-wing political appeals. The same descriptor might readily be applied to the ways in which members of Victory Gospel and Heaven's Tabernacle, laity as well as pastors, aim to elicit respect as they pray for protection and blessings. Yet the politics involved are quite different because their reflections on the content and sources of personal value are dissimilar. A telling point has to do with the reasons why God speaks. Pastor John remarked to me that he had surprised a group of urban and suburban church leaders by telling them that the Holy Ghost is not necessarily comforting. "He is a comforter, yes, but you have to discipline yourself to allow the Holy Spirit to lead you to all truth. God is a God of order. If you get out of order, He may expose you." Pastor John has spoken disparagingly to me about the kind of intercession practiced at Eternal Hope, remarking that worshippers are not necessarily encouraged to repent of their disobedience but rather made to feel sorry for themselves. As Pastor John sees it, respectful obedience is the only means of counteracting the operations of the "world's system," which extracts vitality from Black bodies in order to promote distorted forms of respect and value. By contrast, members of Eternal Hope take self-sufficiency as a ground of adult personhood: in principle, as it were, one ought to be self-sufficient but in fact cannot be, so that one's vitality depends on the help of the Holy Ghost. In becoming bodily extensions of God's love, these believers calibrate their sense of dependence on him against their autonomy or strength.

From this perspective, it becomes clear that the images of receiving and openness discussed in Chapter 3 have as much to do with personal value as with bodily susceptibility. In ways that reflect their different social positionings, the "knowledge of the body" that believers develop by inhabiting their discernment transforms how they physically apprehend their own value as persons (cf. Coleman 2006). For members of Eternal Hope, becoming open to Jesus is both an expression and a result of their insights into their incapacities. The devil wants them to imagine that they are complete in themselves, so that they will fail to recognize the hole in their bodies that must be filled by the Holy Ghost. For them, the moral peril of not receiving God's word consists principally of failing to understand that they need his help. As Baptist minister Reverend Campbell told Susan Harding (2000: 48), "You need the birth that's going to change you from the one you received from Adam, which is a sinful nature. You've already experienced that first birth and you're full of yourself." By contrast, the question "Who have you received from?" that interests members of the African American churches is closely linked to "Who do you respect?" To receive from the prophet of God is to respect both the prophet and God. Onaje Woodbine (2021) describes how the prophet Donna Haskins

> was sitting on the edge of her bed, thinking about all she had overcome, her multiple suicide attempts, segregated schools, illiteracy, unemployment, poor housing, the death of her nephews, breast cancer, asthma, being sexually assaulted, the men who cheated on her, and her promise of abstinence to the Lord. "No man should have dominion over me," she said. "I should never have given them dominion over me. I should not have handed it to them as if I was giving them my birth certificate. So now, I'm getting my birth certificate back. I'm getting everything back—my mind, my heart, my soul," she prayed. (147)

Donna attributes her suffering and her poor self-image not only to the actions of the devil who motivated the men who took advantage of her, but also to her own willingness to give Satan "dominion" over herself. In effect, she had respected and received false knowledge from the devil, whom I take to be an enslaver who tried to take away the name God gave her on her "birth certificate." Yet Donna takes responsibility for having received the devil's false knowledge, saying "I should never have given them dominion over me." In so doing, she hints at her own capacity to create or miscreate both her lived circumstances and her value as a person. I consider this topic further in Chapter 5, showing how believers locate vital elements within themselves as they pose questions about God's designs for time and events.

# 5

# Seeking Confirmation: Designs for Events

In *Black Gods of the Asphalt* (2016), a study of African American street basketball as lived religion, Onaje Woodbine relates a narrative by a player named Jason who explained how the sport has given him life. For Jason, basketball is a refuge from the demons that have tormented his family in Boston with drug addiction, anger, and depression. "Onaje, it's not my mother who is treating me so bad," Jason said. "I know something has a hold on her. I know it!" (92). He continued: "I love my mother to death, but [the devil] was working on my mom since the beginning. That was what honestly really got me started into just going to the court unconsciously. I would go to the court and eat." Eating, Woodbine explains, is "a slang word that means, in this case, to feed on life or the vital source of life." Jason went on: "I'm telling you dawg. I will go to the court and I eat, come back, my eyes are red. You think that I'm like—I'm just getting high off of basketball" (94).

Years later, while recovering from debilitating arthritis and a university coach's insults, Jason met the prophet Donna Haskins, "a lady of God" who received messages from Afro-Caribbean spirits.[1] Donna's exchange with Jason helped him return to the basketball court:

> That summer I met this lady who was a friend of my mother's and she's a lady of God, a voice of God you could say, and she thought she was coming to my house for my mother and it's like to bless the house. *We've come to the recollection that she was brought for me and around that time I met her.* She told me "you want to play basketball again?" She said "you going to play basketball again." She said "you also going to find a job." This woman when she told me that I was like, "for the league?" She was like, "nah, you want to play basketball again?" She said, "I don't see professional," and for some reason *all I needed to hear was her say* you're going to get back on the court even though she didn't say professional … I didn't know what was going on, but this woman she was sent into my life to tell me that message. (100, emphases added)

As a result of this encounter, Jason understands that the spirits with whom Donna communicated, together with the ancestral spirit of his great-grandmother, "mediate God's grace on the court" (104).

Jason's reflection that Donna had been brought to speak to him at a certain moment so that he would take a particular course of action constitutes a kind of memory work similar to what Pentecostal believers call "confirmation." To recall, believers distinguish between the *logos* word of God conveyed in the Bible and his *rhema* word with which he speaks to people about their specific concerns. They listen to divine words for "confirmation" of previous thoughts or awareness. Listening is a subject of ethical attention because, as I discussed in Chapter 3, willingness to "receive" is assumed to drive action. As Jason remarked that "all I needed to hear was her say … ," Pentecostal preachers insist that "faith comes by hearing" (Rom. 10:17). Most importantly, "seeking" and "receiving" confirmation are vital acts because they tap into sources of life that lie beyond oneself, namely God, ancestral spirits, or their human mediators. Thus, receiving confirmation helped Jason return to the basketball court, where he could "eat."

Confirmation is an instance of what Caroline Humphrey (2008) terms "decision-events," which "bring about the sudden focusing or crystallization of certain of the multiplicities inherent to human life and thus create subjects, if only for a time" (359). Humphrey's intent is to reassemble subjects, as distinct from the self or subjectivity, as "the concept most closely tied to action" (359). In consequence, she engages with Alain Badiou's (2003, 2006) writings on how the event divides time and makes subjects of those who acclaim its universal truth and its ruptures of previous knowledge, on the model of Paul on the road to Damascus. Humphrey highlights the issue of "what makes a person 'give way' to a happening" (2008: 374): in Inner Mongolia, "something in a person has to acclaim rather than reject the dream or divination" (371). In a similar vein, Joel Robbins (2010) points out that Pentecostal converts who have lived through the kinds of "evental transformations" envisioned by Badiou "inescapably have to negotiate with a past that rhetorically they often insist they have simply left behind" (649). Yet in acclaiming or rejecting the happenings geared to making a person "give way," Pentecostal believers are compelled to come to terms with multiple operations of time, including but not limited to breaks with "the past," in ways that render them questioners as much as decided "subjects."

Particular forms of vitality arise from different sorts of "giving way" to a happening. Here again Woodbine's analysis is instructive. As Pentecostal preachers insist that God has designed vitality with certain qualities and not others, so too does Woodbine make clear that the vitality associated with street basketball possesses specific rhythmic and expressive content to which good players should in effect "give way." For example, while playing as a student at Yale, Woodbine found that his mainly white, middle-class teammates "moved through the motions each day, performing set plays without joy or heartache. Trash talking, deception, and dancing were forbidden ... I felt isolated on the court, as if I was dancing to music that no one else could hear" (2016: 5–6). By contrast, street basketball games that are played to memorialize deceased loved ones are events in Humphrey's sense of inducing action based on a certain kind of decisive knowledge, namely awareness of the numinous presence of spirits on the court. While the sense of loss is palpable at these games, players draw upon and wonder at the vital powers of those who have gone before: "Striking the chest ... is *both* a strategy designed to obtain power and favor and a dance through which street-ball players play with the ineffable" (168). As players both create and "give way" to the aesthetics of this dance, the time they inhabit assumes qualities of both continuity and transcendence. A player named Chris recounted:

> There's no way you are going to stop me from getting to that goal. The whole game I was just thinking about my granddad, just thinking, you know, he's in heaven, he's watching this game, he's watching this game. Every time somebody hits me to the floor, he's up there jumping out his seat getting angry. And as the course of the game went on, I said "I can do this." (148)

In this chapter, I pursue the argument that particular forms of vitality and care lend themselves to specific ways of inhabiting time and constructing events, and vice versa. Because Pentecostal believers locate the source of vitality beyond the self, even as they insist that their vitality depends on their own responsiveness to that source, they express a need to be sure that they are apprehending God correctly in order to properly receive his care and extend it to others. Accordingly, what I find most applicable in Humphrey's treatment of events is her suggestion that action may be contingent on how certain elements in a person acclaim or reject various human or spiritual influences. I would stress that these are vital elements: Jason's decision to resume playing basketball, for instance, was predicated on the way Donna's words elicited his desire to "eat." Yet to a greater extent than in the instances Woodbine describes in *Black Gods of the Asphalt*, Pentecostal practices of "seeking confirmation" entail questioning the nature and sources of vitality and danger, together with the relations between God's will and believers' own imaginings of time and events.[2] In keeping with this point, I concentrate less on decisiveness or confirmation in itself than on the sorts of questioning that believers understand God as wishing them to undertake.

As they engage in such questioning, Pentecostal believers embark on trajectories of ethical discovery. In using the term discovery, I am drawing on Webb Keane's (2016) discussion of "ethical affordances," which bears similarities to Mattingly's (2014a: 15) treatment of ethical "vantage points." Keane argues on the basis of literature in child psychology that the "developmental relationship between the child and his or her surroundings"—whether those surroundings consist of "emotions, bodily movements, habitual practices, linguistic forms, laws, etiquette, or narratives"—"is not simply one of learning from others or just the expression of innate abilities: it is, at least in part, one of *discovering what they afford*" (2016: 30–1). For example, the phenomenon of "hearing voices" can afford "evidence of benevolent gods in Ghana, kindly relatives in India, or hostile strangers in the United States" (30). "Seeking confirmation" is an analogous process of ethical discovery in that the search affords various kinds of knowledge about how to specify and evaluate the sources of vitality and destruction. In a non-Pentecostal register, Woodbine indicates some comparable linkages between ethical discovery and designs for vitality. In "eating" on the basketball court, Jason was both feeding on "the vital source of life" and discovering and countering the destructive influence of the devil over his mother, and he discovered through his conversation with Donna that his participation in this source of vitality was sanctioned by the spirits. When Woodbine himself was at Yale, his teammates' play struck him not merely as unfamiliar but as ethically wrong, likely because it possessed none of the qualities that he has found to be life-giving in basketball. Here the discovery was that his white middle-class teammates did not much care about what gave him life—or, by extension, about his life.

Drawing on the themes of care, connectedness, and personal value I have discussed up to now, in this chapter I compare how believers' efforts to "seek confirmation" of God's designs for events shape their discoveries of connections between the ethical and the vital. The forms taken by these discoveries, centering respectively on how to receive God's word and how to become open to divine comfort, reflect believers' specific social locations. As we have seen, reception is key to respect in the African American congregations, while members of the majority white church concentrate on the ways God remedies their incapacities. I turn first to the musical qualities of services in the African American churches, focusing on a narrative of a keyboard player named Elder Matthew who explains how he seeks cues from the Holy Spirit and the pastor about how to improvise at particular moments. He makes clear that he would play into the destructive strategies of the devil if he were to fail to ask God how and when to "shift" the music so as to shape the course of events in a service. In Elder Matthew's account, vitality depends on and indeed consists of proper receptivity, which is causally prior to speech and sound.

Believers' trajectories of discovery do not usually extend so far as to call the rightness of God's designs into question, though when they do they can approach crises of faith. As a case in point, I discuss a self-described "faith crisis" undergone by Kathy at Eternal Hope. Kathy's analytical inclinations tended to set her apart from her church peers in ways that contributed to experiences of anxiety. Her impulse to "question God" about the layering of psychic events reinforced her sense that vitality consists of emotional security—a common trope in preaching at the suburban church—yet simultaneously sharpened her worries that God might not provide such security. Rather than focusing on emotional security, Pastor Hadley and Pastor John encourage members of their congregations to recollect how they have abided or failed to abide by "God's timing." In the process, they try to sharpen believers' awareness of their own capacities to create their lived circumstances and overcome forms of exploitation.

## Questioning God in Music: "If We Can't Hear Him, How Can He Speak?"

"Music ministry" is important in all the churches I am discussing. Believers speak of how God's presence in music blesses them and increases their faith. In each, Sunday services open with "praise and worship" sessions led by a chorus and solo singers. In Eternal Hope, singers are accompanied by a keyboard soloist at the rear of the altar and a brass and percussion ensemble at the side of the sanctuary, while in the more confined spaces of Victory Gospel and Heaven's Tabernacle a percussionist and a keyboard performer sit to the pastor's side. During praise and worship, gospel songs like Edwin Hawkins's "I Love You Lord Today" or Hillsong Worship's "Here I Am to Worship" elicit "sacrifices of praise," which include clapping, jumping or standing with upraised arms, flag waving, and other enthusiastic responses that pastors strongly encourage, sometimes upbraiding the saints if they lack fervor.[3] Benny and Janet explained that praise can sometimes feel like a "sacrifice" because it requires you to put aside the troubles that you might have been dwelling on and to think of God's goodness instead. At Eternal Hope, choir members rehearse in advance of services so that their singing may be properly "anointed." Musicians comment that when the "anointing" is strong, they can do things with their instruments that they had not thought themselves capable of. At the conclusion of services, as people come forward to ask for and provide intercession, the ensemble at Eternal Hope improvises melodies that move from soothing to triumphant, echoing worshippers' passage from supplication to reassurance or breakthrough.

At Victory Gospel and Heaven's Tabernacle, however, the interplay between the musicians and the preacher often continues over the course of the sermon and while he or she gives prophecies. African American Christian worship is renowned for call and response patterns, whereby leaders elicit the support of participants to create what Rev. Evans Crawford (1995) calls a "hum," a "homiletical musicality," so that the entire service may be considered an extended song (see Davis 1985; Sanders 1996). To a much greater extent than at Eternal Hope, musicians carry out an improvisatory set of dialogues with the preacher and the congregation. These dialogues entail a kind of ongoing questioning about the move of the Spirit.

Elder Matthew, who joined Heaven's Tabernacle in 2019, underscored the priority of hearing in relation to speech or music, explaining to me that as he plays and sings he has an obligation to listen to what God is trying to tell the congregation: "If we can't hear Him, how can He speak? If we can't hear what He's saying, how can we speak what He's saying? If I can't hear what He wants to say, I can't portray what He wants to say." Elder Matthew depicted God's voice as a combination of music and words: "He definitely will speak through music if we allow Him to." He played some bars of "I Love You Lord":

> If I'm in a familiar song like "I love You Lord" … He's maybe just telling someone that He loves them and explaining to them why He loves them—oh wow, that's just crazy, the revelation He just gave me—He's telling someone that He loves them and He breaks down for them why He loves them. "Because You cared for me / In such a special way." He's telling us that He wants us to love Him because He died so that we might have life and have it more abundantly. That might be simple to some people but it's so significant to the reason why we do things and the reason why we sing what we sing.

Raised in an African American Pentecostal church in Buffalo and currently working as a delivery driver for Amazon, Elder Matthew began playing the drums at age seven, started preaching at fifteen, and soon afterward took up other instruments including keyboard. Even as a committed Christian who never left church, he narrated a life trajectory of falling away, going through, and returning. While helping to train praise and worship singers as a teenager, he "started to want to experience what life was like outside of church. I'd never hung out with people my own age, I was just around the grandmothers. I didn't know at the time that I could be saved and have fun but live safe. I started to get into females and drinking and smoking." No one in the church knew that he was doing these things even as he was training other singers and could "see the power of God over people's lives." Elder Matthew recalled asking God,

"How can you still use me, knowing what I'm doing?" God said, "I wanted to show you: this is what I called you to, this is what I need you for … I needed to show you it's not greener on the other side. I used the drunk to send My word." The Bible says, him who He loves, He chastises. I was going through a lot of family issues, a lot of things in my life.

I asked Elder Matthew whether he thinks about these things as he plays. He replied,

All the time. I thank God all the time that I'm not what I used to be, that I'm not angry as I used to be. We don't know what young people are going through. We try to force them into the church, and all they have is music. This may be the only way that they speak, this may be the only way that gets them delivered.

He explained that while the words of a preacher might not "be for" a given person in attendance, that person might be moved by the music.

Even before I receive instruction to go physically talk to an individual, He might have given it to me in a song to minister to somebody … Sometimes we [in the congregation] might think, that message [from the preacher] wasn't really for me, I mean it was for me but it didn't really hit where I needed it to hit, but *that song* stopped me from wanting to commit suicide.

Inducing a worshipper to "give way" to the music in this fashion demands discernment on Elder Matthew's part. "The music may have a general meaning," he explained, "but to you it may mean something else." He took "Here I Am to Worship" as an example. "That may tell *you*, the King is here, let's acknowledge His presence, but to *me* it may mean I'm in a storm, but the Lord is saying I'm going to pick you up even when you make mistakes and see you through it." He demonstrated on the keyboard how knowing that he needed to convey a special message might cause him to shift his playing. Playing a series of chords unlinked to a melody, he remarked: "I can go to a place where I know I need to shift to a piano-strings layer bass." (This is a combination of synthetic piano and string sounds in the bass register. "Strings do a lot in the prophetic," he mentioned, pointing out that it is unusual for keyboard players to make use of strings.) "I know the presence of God is here, I know it's working, somebody just needs a touch, and the Holy Ghost may say, 'Okay it's time to shift.' The sound is there, but He might want to do something extraordinary. The sound and the tempo may change." As he played, the tempo slowed and the harmonies shifted. "There's something about that one note there. It puts me in a place of somewhat meditation, it calms. Everything going to be all right. It allows me to hear a little bit better what He wants to say to us." On some occasions, the "shift" is very marked. During a revival at Heaven's Tabernacle, things seemed to be winding down when suddenly the musicians began to play in a "prophetic" manner. "He changed it!" called out Evangelist Clarice, and Apostle Cooper began prophesying to people, laying hands on them as they swooned in the Spirit.

Elder Matthew made clear that "shifting" at the right moments requires close attention both to God and to his "leader" the pastor, a usage suggesting how the pastor may be understood as leading a musical performance. Elder Matthew demonstrated the various kinds of music among which he has to shift: "A lot of times God is trying to prepare us for victory, so we deal with a lot of victory music, He prepares us for battle, so we deal with battle music, and sometimes He wants us to be in a prostrated place, which is worship." Worship, he explained,

> causes the prophetic to come. If I was going to go into "Lord, You are good and Your mercy endureth forever,"[4] that's pretty much a celebratory worship song. … At that moment, so the prophetic movement of worship can come in, I like to switch through a combination of piano and strings. Or I could go straight strings.

By contrast, "if I'm in the midst of battle, it's to help break something in the atmosphere, where the adversary is trying to come against the people of God." He played a series of emphatic, separated chords. "The chords are letting Satan know, listen, you're in trouble. You can just hold it, it's like a rumble. … In the rushing mighty wind of Pentecost, there's like a rumble in the bass, something's coming, something's in the Spirit. We have to be sensitive to the atmosphere."

Sometimes the leader and the musicians are not properly in sync, as Pastor John indicates when he tells a keyboard player at Victory Gospel "Stay with me now" or "Don't go there yet." Emphasizing the moral dangers of improper responsiveness, Elder Matthew remarked that a lot of times God will show us what we need to see and we buck up against what we see. [Once] I wanted to go another way [while playing] and it didn't work out. It didn't sound right. It wasn't the message that He wanted, and I needed to make a drastic switch. Because music causes deliverance, it causes healing … the enemy tries to fight us in that area.

The devil "fights" him both by hurting him physically and by making him think that the saints are not responding well to the music:

My fingers begin to cramp up, [I get] pains in my chest, the enemy tries to attack you by giving you a heart attack or stroke, especially when you're in a deliverance ministry, where you're always on alert. He'll fight you with your voice. He tries to close your mouth, so you can't get anything out. There's so many ways the enemy will try to attack you. Even in people, where you think that people aren't in tune or discouraged, and that just isn't true. You can definitely get discouraged in music ministry. It can get twisted. You can take it like: They didn't like it, you were terrible. But it's working on your craft.

Elder Matthew engages in a process of ethical discovery as he tries to bring the rhythms of the music he plays into line with the rhythms God has designed. I hope to have conveyed something of the wonder and excitement with which he speaks of the insights he obtains into the "move of God" and into believers' responses to that move. In "giving way" to the different moods that "shifting" evokes, believers derive particular kinds of knowledge about their relationships with God. As a result, "shifting" opens an intersubjective arena, analogous to that created through intercession at Eternal Hope, in which Elder Matthew together with other leaders discover what the congregation needs from God. Significantly, members of Victory Gospel and Heaven's Tabernacle say that before he fell from heaven, Satan had been God's music director. As such, he remains "the prince and power of the air," adept at whispering inducements to sin and distorting other people's words into perceived insults. When Elder Matthew shifts into "battle" music, he acknowledges this power of the devil to create events based on false knowledge and opposes it with the music through which God designs events to unfold in time. Again, suffering is intrinsic to God's design, since Elder Matthew's experiences with having "gone through" enable him to minister to those for whom music is "the only way that they speak." By contrast, Eternal Hope members are liable to find deeper moral challenges in suggestions that God has designed them to go through suffering.

## Questioning God in the Psyche

Events that constitute ruptures with "past" ways of being are prominent in all the churches I am describing. In addition to narrating "God's plan for salvation" centering on the epochal event of Jesus' self-sacrifice, believers stress how the acts of receiving the Holy Ghost and being baptized move a person from an unsaved to a saved condition. In a more legalistic register, one of Pastor Hadley's favorite tropes in preaching is to tell her audience "now you're accountable" to God—from this particular moment, you cannot "plead ignorance" of his will. On the other hand, to listen to Pastor John as he told me of some expansion plans that he was developing on the basis of words given to him by a prophet several years previously to the effect that he would lead a multiethnic congregation, and then call First Lady so that she could confirm to me over the phone that she too had heard those prophetic words, was to be struck by God's designs for events that layer upon one another, indexing past and future events. In a similar vein, Harding (2000: 55) discusses how fundamental Baptists read the Bible in figural fashion, so that they may grasp the ways in which "earlier events prefigure later events, and later events complete, or fulfill, earlier, incomplete events" (see also Haynes 2020). Particularly in Victory Gospel and Heaven's Tabernacle, pastors set forth explicit ethical frameworks for interrogating such patterns of layering. Both Pastor John and Pastor Hadley insist that God will respond "yes, no, or wait—but never maybe" to prayers about a course of action. In so doing, they make clear that God encourages believers to question correspondences among events in certain ways but not in others.

While the saints of Eternal Hope do not use the term "confirmation" quite as often, they engage in comparable processes of listening in order to discern God's will and patterns in events. However, their approaches to questioning those patterns and listening for responses are shaped by their inclinations to frame vitality as a matter of emotional security, tendencies that are less broadly shared in the African American congregations. In his sermons, Pastor Charles tends to speak of the peace of mind brought about by God as a good in itself, indeed as an orientation that the saints should try to recapture in the midst of their difficulties by recalling the elation they experienced when they were baptized: "Do you remember how it felt? A closer walk with God will help you get back to that." During a Sunday evening service, he preached: "Jesus commanded the winds: 'Peace, be still!' The winds are the work of the devil in your life, and Jesus is the one who brings peace. This is what He meant by 'Blessed are the peacemakers': Christians are the ones who help you to Jesus' peace." A believer who has strayed from the fold, he preaches, has "no peace" wherever she goes in the world. Whereas God gives believers at Eternal Hope a calmness about their place in the scheme of things regardless of what they might be "going through," the devil works by creating conditions that trouble their peace of mind, such as depression or addiction.

Accordingly, when these believers discern evidence of God's orchestration of events, they often speak of what has contributed to or detracted from their emotional security, as did Kathy when she related a "faith crisis" to me. Kathy's faith is more inflected by psychotherapeutic discourses than that of most believers at Eternal Hope, an orientation that I think led her to tell me that I was giving undue analytical weight to intercession. When I told her of my impressions that God helped believers to feel for one another, she replied, "Yes, but that's not the point. Our relationship with God is primary, and our relationships with other people are secondary." Nonetheless, in a narrative below, Kathy relates how she questions God's words in order to develop awareness of the truth of her psyche, much as intercessors encourage worshippers to open the truth of themselves to God.

Around the age of fourteen, Kathy told me, she began to suffer from anxiety disorders and panic attacks, due in part to the ways her analytical personality made her a subject of gossip at school. During her junior year of high school, her mother brought her to a therapist who recommended that she read Lucinda Bassett's bestselling self-help book *From Panic to Power* (1995). In line with other therapeutic methods that prompt clients to give names to desirable and undesirable aspects of their selves (Lester 2017), Bassett's approach encouraged Kathy to understand her vitality as contingent on her ability to distinguish her true self from her anxiety. She recognized Bassett's list of anxious "What-if" thoughts as "something that happens with your anxiety." The book "helps you to recognize it and then counter it with compassionate self-talk," such as "If anybody did think anything [negative about me], it's okay … And even today, I have to remind myself, the things I always get worried about, it never happens."

Still, Kathy found most of her conversations with psychotherapists unsatisfactory because "it was just talk therapy": counselors wanted her to speak about her own self. Likening her therapy sessions to the ethnographic interviews I was conducting with her, she implicitly distinguished conversations aimed at eliciting speech about herself from the church services and online sermons that enabled her to hear and question God's words animated by other people. God, however, has not always acted for Kathy as an "empathetic therapist" (Luhrmann

2012: 297). She always prayed to God to heal her anxiety, but "He was choosing not to, for whatever reason," and she did not confide her illness to most church colleagues, fearing their gossip. This reticence likely played a part in making Kathy somewhat of a marginal figure among her peers in church. She recalled her unhappiness on occasions when other saints failed her trust by not interceding for her at the altar: "I know what it feels like when you want help and there's nobody there. I've had to walk with God on my own."

Kathy has indeed found help in God. She related an incident in which prayer had enabled her to overcome a sickness brought on by a psychotropic medication, and identified biblical passages that are "really positive, that will help you get through, and it's the same kind of principles that are found in [Bassett's] book." However, in contrast to "compassionate self-talk," Kathy described God's responses as contingent on "sacrifices" of various kinds. As Israelite priests had to sanctify themselves before making sacrifices in the Temple, she related, Pentecostal believers must fast, give up sinful behaviors, and dedicate themselves to reading the Bible in order to "draw closer to God." God will honor these sacrifices by showing them how he is working in their lives, so that they will love him all the more.

Yet in ways she links to her anxiety, Kathy has experienced God's expectations of sacrifice as deeply threatening. After graduating from college, she felt that God had called her to travel to a Middle Eastern city as a missionary. Kathy told me that she loved the city where she stayed but found the six months she spent there highly traumatic, largely because Christian missionaries in the country have been subjected to official harassment. She was afraid that the people she had befriended might turn on her once she revealed that she was a missionary and that she might be attacked or jailed as a result. She had to stay by herself in an apartment some distance from her missionary colleagues and feared being followed home. She would hear sounds of arguing at night and was terrified that someone would break into her apartment.

Kathy was convinced that God had called her to mission work but also that he had put her in danger, and she had no desire to be a martyr. For about six months after her return to Buffalo, Kathy felt no connection to God. She was unable to find consolation in church colleagues who had never been missionaries, and whose expressions of sympathy she found inadequate. She had difficulty reading the New Testament because of its passages on human sacrifice, and it was frightening for her to listen to songs in church about bearing the cross. Then, at a church retreat, Kathy's faith was restored. Kathy often enthused about the preaching at retreats, telling me that ministers' words are particularly "anointed" at such events because of their prior spiritual preparation, in particular intense prayer and fasting. In the following account, she narrated how she listened to anointed words for their bearing on events within her psyche.

When I actually got healed, it wasn't during a sermon, but it was at the altar call after the first speaker [of the retreat] ... I was just so upset and so not understanding what was going on. And sometimes, if you're so far away from God, and you are just going through the motions for such a long time, you can't feel God during the services, and I was kind of like that ... But I was there because I know in those larger services the presence of God is there so much stronger ... I was just like, "God, please just give me a clear mind, let me know what's going on." ... And so I just lifted up my hands and started praying in tongues, and what was going on in my head was me just questioning God. And all of a sudden, I just felt that foreboding sense of doom and gloom ... was lifted. I was just like, "What? This is the first time that I feel absolutely free of it, this is amazing!" But then the other part of me was really cautious: "Is this really true or is this not?" Because I've had a lot of instances with my anxiety and depression where it would be away temporarily but it wouldn't be healed ... But I was feeling ten times better, because that sense of foreboding was gone.

The sermon that really, really broke that stronghold that the devil had on me was the last sermon [of the retreat], when [the minister] preached about a chessboard. He said that not all moves on a chessboard are forwards, some are sideways. God has different ministries for us. And sometimes God sacrifices people, and they got taken off the chessboard, and then he started talking about John the Baptist, and how after his job was done he got beheaded. And I was starting to freak out again, I was like "Oh my gosh, I thought I [had gotten] healed, I thought I was going to be okay, what is going on?" And all those horrible feelings were coming back ... So then after that, he started talking about things that would impede you from moving [on the chessboard], and one of them is pride and the other one was fear. And he started telling a personal story about how he wanted to make a greater move and work for God in a city, but he just got this feeling one day that something bad would happen to his oldest daughter. So he was driving with his wife in the car, and she said to him, "Do you get the feeling that if we do this work, something bad would happen to our daughter?" And since they both got that feeling, they were freaking out, ... but then he spent a lot of time praying and fasting about it, and then God said "Nothing is going to happen, it's just the devil that's creating all this fear in your life, it's going to be okay." ...

And then the preacher said [to the audience], "If you're going through something similar ... God is saying that I'm going to protect you and you will go back, and this time you're not going to have any fear." And when I heard that, I was like,

"*What?* All I wanted to hear was that I was going to be protected and saved, I had no idea or thoughts about going back [to the Middle East], because I was so scared of it." But seriously, [the city where she had lived] is one of my favorite places in the world. All I want to do is live there and do work in the church there. When God works, He exceeds your expectations. I not only got healed and set free from that mindset of "I'm going to die," God told me that He was going to protect me. It's going to be hard to be in the Middle East in charge of a church, … but God said that He would protect me and I wouldn't have any fear. And that is one of the best gifts ever.

For many North American Protestants, desires for security of the kind underpinning this narrative give rise to moral problems when God does not appear to provide safety or reassurance in response to believers' fervent disavowals of self-sufficiency. Such moral problems are open to resolutions of various kinds. For instance, after Harding's interlocutor Reverend Campbell accidentally killed his own son, God gave him "peace in his soul" (2000: 53) by enabling him to draw on biblical narratives to frame the child's death as a sacrifice whose telling would reaffirm God's plan of history and allow Harding herself to be saved. However, unlike Reverend Campbell, who Harding comments "sacrificed his own son to his narrative tradition with a calm assurance, a peace of heart, that I still find difficult to accept" (60), Kathy envisioned the prospect of sacrificing her life to biblical narratives with real terror. Consequently, her account hinges on an oscillating set of connections between her sense of vitality or enervation, the kinds of time she was inhabiting, and the manner in which she "gave way" to narrations of events.

Kathy appears to have experienced her exhaustion upon returning from overseas as a kind of closed time, a "foreboding sense of doom and gloom" that she equated with "the stronghold that the devil had on me." She narrates her healing as transpiring in two stages on separate occasions, the first occurring as a result of her "questioning God" while speaking in tongues during an altar call, the second when she received assurance during a subsequent sermon that she would "go back" without fear. She does not frame her willingness to question God as a mandated act of faith or obedience in this instance, as Pastor John and Pastor Hadley often do in telling saints that they need to receive "confirmation." Yet in pleading with God to "let me know what's going on" she elicits "all I wanted to hear" to enhance her vitality, much as did Jason in Woodbine's account. The act of questioning prompts a "lifting" of the temporality of foreboding, along with subsequent questions as to the reality of the healing. During the second stage, Kathy is interrogating the correspondences between the preacher's narration of events and her own reactions. While the story of the beheading of John the Baptist threatens to derail her reconciliation with God by reinstating the temporality of sacrifice, the account of the preacher's conversation with his wife about dangers facing their daughter encourages Kathy to participate in God's reassurance of those who might be "going through something similar." In keeping with the emphasis on security, both Kathy and the preacher identify the time of "going through" as a discrete episode rather than as a trajectory of faith.

Kathy's narrative describes a process of ethical discovery: an attempt to recuperate a specific form of vitality by coming to inhabit a particular kind of time, namely one centered on willingness to receive God's gift of eternal life. Her conclusion that God's reassurance was "one of the best gifts ever" suggests how "something in [her] person," in Humphrey's phrase, wishes to bestow the love she has received as a gift from God on those who have not yet received it (cf. Elisha 2008). Yet while Reverend Campbell persuaded Harding to inhabit born-again language through his "willingness to ... narrate [his] experience and fashion stories out of it in dialogue with God's will and biblical truths" (2000: 59), Kathy's account is more tentative and marked by persuasive gaps. By its close, she remains much more hesitant than Reverend Campbell to embrace the prospect of self-sacrifice that he regards as a precondition for receiving the gift of life, even though as I related in Chapter 4 Kathy readily speaks of tithing and fasting as forms of sacrifice. Accordingly, her narrative represents an effort to reconcile an anxious subjectivity with one in need of Christian salvation, even as it highlights tensions between the two. Thus she concludes with thankfulness for God's gift of vitality, which she equates with emotional security, but stops short of situating this gift in a temporal framework together with past or future sacrifices of her own. To the extent she hesitates, Kathy remains dubious about the ethics of God's designs.

## Questioning Creativity

As I have shown, members of Victory Gospel and Heaven's Tabernacle make comparable efforts to live in line with temporalities of the gift, especially as they render tithes. However, in "seeking confirmation" they are more likely to speak in the related idiom of contract. During call-and-response praise sessions, they may call out that a blessing from God is "in their contract" and that God has to abide by his promises. They may also call out that they have "a constitutional right" as saved people to prevent the devil from making them enraged at other people's insults. Whereas Stormie Omartian and Jerry Falwell have the ability, as I remarked in Chapter 4, to presume rather than speak of rights to success and security, members of these African American churches feel a need to assert such rights on the basis of the contract that God has established with them. They conceive of God's contract as transcending social contracts, which are all too often fraudulent or violated. Following highly publicized police shootings of Black men and retaliatory killings of police officers in July 2016, a prominent visiting minister addressed the congregation of Victory Gospel:

> We have a crack in the foundation of this nation. If the foundation be destroyed, where can the righteous go?[5] ... The system keeps on operating to give privilege to those who created it, and most of the privileged see their benefits as their birthright. But what do I do as a child of God whose value is determined by the kingdom of God rather than by the uncashed check of the Declaration of Independence?[6]

In contrast to the makers of fraudulent contracts, God elicits believers' assent to a contract that will give them life. What these African American believers regard as problematic is the nature of their own assent. As I have discussed, they worry about how they might "get out of order" if they do not "move on time." For their part, when Eternal Hope members speak about "God's timing," they usually refer to how he unexpectedly arranges circumstances to bring about fortunate outcomes. As I described in Chapter 3, Lynne explains that "God's timing" leads her to intercede for people at the altar "right when they need it." In Victory Gospel and Heaven's Tabernacle, saints express much more disquiet about occasions when they might have "missed" God's timing by failing to "catch" (i.e., understand and act upon) his word.

More broadly, these believers' concerns about contract and timing reflect their efforts to foster a particular sort of vitality, namely creativity, which involves envisaging and bringing into being novel institutional forms, social commitments, and styles of relating to others.[7] During a powerful service, when "the wind is blowing as it will," causing people to dance in the spirit, speak in tongues, and prophesy blessings, low-wage employees are transformed into what they call "gods with a small g": beings with "authority" to speak words that will change their circumstances. Especially in Victory Gospel, Pastor John and visiting preachers compare the words people speak to seeds they plant: they bring forth either good or bad fruit over the course of time. When a believer publicly confirms that she has received a blessing that a pastor had earlier prophesied that God had in store for her, Pastor John often remarks that he himself has "spoken the blessing into existence." The explicit model here is Genesis 1, wherein God speaks the world into existence. This emphasis on a person's inherent creative capacity likely accounts for the fact that in Victory Gospel and Heaven's Tabernacle I seldom heard the kinds of speech common in Eternal Hope about how a person is incomplete without God.

Proper creativity depends on inhabiting time correctly. When I asked Pastor John in an interview "What comes to mind when you hear the phrase 'God's timing'?" his response was "Perfection." To the extent that they act in harmony with God's timing, prophets formulate courses of action that bring blessings to themselves and those who are obedient to the divine word. Pastor John drew on a biblical story about Elijah (1 Kgs 18:42-45) to explain how attentiveness to God's timing enables prophets to understand how and when to act:

> What people don't understand about God's timing, it's truly, truly about being discerning, having a discerning spirit, having a strong awareness of God ... A lot of people are just getting up living life, and they don't understand: You've got to [ask God], what are you saying to me today? It's an everyday thing. What's the plan for me? What am I supposed to walk into today? ... What made Elijah tell his servant, "Man, listen, go down to the river there and tell me what you see?" ... Something was coming to him in his spirit, to discern something. I know it's not humanity I'm feeling, this is divinity touching me, telling me that there's rain coming.

"It's like getting into a rhythm?" I asked.

> Yes. Because when you're in that flow, you don't miss God. He gives you all the promptings, all the warnings, everything you need to know, boom, this is what is gonna happen. So prepare yourself. ... And He wouldn't be who He is if He didn't prepare us for what was coming. Everything is about His timing, so in order for us to be ready for His timing, we have to have preparation. So God is so wise, He will give you all the tools: the signs, the wonders, the confirmation that you need to know: this is the time.[8]

Eagerness to be "in that flow" is broadly shared, to the extent that it provokes explicit instruction on where and how to listen. Midnight services on New Year's Eve rival those on Resurrection Sunday (Easter) for Pentecostal church attendance in the African American community, as large numbers of people come to hear "a word from the Lord" via the prophet about their situations for the coming year. Implicitly acknowledging the broad appeal of being in accord with God's timing, Pastor Hadley feels the need to warn saints against running to revivals held at any time of year to hear a prophet with an exciting reputation, telling them that they might "pick up" harmful spirits in some other churches and "come back and bleed" at Heaven's Tabernacle. In a similar vein, Mother Smith at Victory Gospel cautions the saints about overeagerness to act on prophetic words directed to them as individuals. "We are immediately looking for it when Pastor says something," but if he tells you that he sees that you will have a new line of work in the future, you should not suddenly alter your arrangements: "You need to just go ahead on." On the other hand, if you are specifically contemplating a move and the prophet tells you not to move, you had better rethink your plans.

To illustrate how one ought to act in response to a prophecy, Mother Smith explained to me that several years previously a prophet told her in church that she was going to be moving. "I received that," she recalled, but she had no such plans at the time. Rather, she had made an arrangement to purchase a house she had been renting. However, the owner subsequently died in a motorcycle accident, and his wife did not wish to maintain the purchase arrangement.

> Then I had to move. I didn't know where I was going, but God ended up giving me something better than I had. I got the house where I'm living now for $12,000. People told me I should take [the owner's widow] to court, but I didn't feel led to do that. If I hadn't received the prophecy, I might have been all shaken up, but I'd been attuned to the unctioning of the Spirit [i.e., she had learned to discern], so I just let it go.

In Mother Smith's narration, the creative aspect of "receiving" this prophecy consisted of her decision to accept God's will for her to move, which led her to "something better than I had." Mother Smith stressed that we need to be constantly attentive to God: "It's like walking through a minefield, but He gives us all kinds of guidelines to operate by. Trust God however much you're going through or however much it hurts right now."

The chronotope of "walking through a minefield" conveys the need to navigate carefully around ever-present, hidden dangers, but less perhaps the responsibility that many believers at Victory Gospel and Heaven's Tabernacle feel that they must take for creating their own misfortunes. Early in my fieldwork, I wondered why they felt it important to preach and listen to sermons about the terrible consequences of their proclivities to "get out of order," as though it were their own fault that they live under such precarious circumstances that any mistake can have devastating consequences. I came to realize that in making such discursive moves, they were asserting that they are not simply victims of fraudulent contracts, but rather take creative roles in shaping their circumstances even if they are injured in the process. For example, Mother Smith often related at Bible studies at Victory Gospel that before she became routinely attentive to divine promptings, she ignored God's warnings about cosigning on a car loan with her son.

> The whole while I was going over [to sign the papers], I wasn't comfortable with it, but I pressed [i.e., overcame my reluctance] and did it anyway … I could see that he was getting this car to make himself feel important, to be the man, … and I could see why—after the fact, you see, I didn't know about the unctioning of the Holy Spirit, I didn't know what that was then—God didn't want him to have that [car] at that particular time.

Soon afterward, her son was involved in an accident that totaled the car. The insurance paid the costs, and Mother Smith cosigned another loan, on which her son defaulted. Not having understood the implications of cosigning, she was surprised to find that her salary was garnished to pay the debt. "And like I said, I didn't understand at the time: God had cleared me, went and gave me an out. But then I went and did it again. … I went through all of that just by being disobedient. And I couldn't even get upset about it because I was forewarned."

While the judicial idioms in this account ("cleared me," "gave me an out") might suggest a reading focused on the power of carceral regimes to shape subjectivity (Mother Smith is a retired corrections officer), I view her narrative as stressing how these events resulted from the misuse of her own creative powers. Rather than blaming her financial hardship on her son or on lending institutions (which have a legal obligation to inform cosigners of their responsibilities in case of default),[9] she spoke of how she misused the vital element of creativity within herself by being "disobedient." Underscoring the importance of creativity in this instance is Mother Smith's recollection that when her son had the accident, God startled her by telling her, "Pray for your son." "It came from inside, but it was a thought that was not my own," she remarked to the congregation. "You have to learn to ask God: 'Is that You or is that me?' and then you need to yield to the promptings of the Spirit." In going into prayer at the moment God spoke to her, Mother Smith envisioned a creative role for herself in preserving her son's life.

## Discerning Wrong Events

God's words are not the only subjects of believers' concerns about "giving way"— they worry about giving way to the devil's suggestions as well. Pastor John commonly warns the saints against failing to "receive" prophetic guidance about whether their romantic or marital arrangements conform with God's contract, since the devil may prevent them from receiving the blessings God has designed if they do not seek confirmation in this area. In keeping with his concerns about patriarchal authority, he frames these issues largely in terms of ensuring that male "seeds" come to fruition in accordance with God's promises. For example, during a Sunday sermon Pastor John warned the congregation about "counterfeit blessings," attributing domestic difficulties to failures in detecting hidden sources of exploitation. He began by outlining the dangerous activities in which some in his audience might engage if they lose their expectations that God will provide.

> When God first called Abram, He had a conversation with him about his seed, promising him to make him the father of many nations. Abram left his home town, but walked right into famine. Whenever I feel faith, here comes the devil, trying to steal that word, trying to tell you that God didn't really speak to you. A famine is a place where everything is dried up, you can't pay your bills. In that season, there are some things I can make happen. Some of you know you make stuff happen when you get a little low on your finances. Abram went down to Egypt to make some quick money [i.e., by prostituting his wife], and some of you might gamble, do some white-collar crime,[10] run up your credit cards in times of your famine. But Abram went down to Egypt and almost lost his life. Abram was stupid, he went back to his old ways. And I know some of you would go back to pimping real quick—we revert.

There was a good deal of laughter at this. Pastor John went on to detail how "counterfeit blessings" in the shape of romantic partners take advantage of men and women:

> The counterfeit blessing appears like the blessing God has given you. Abram had a counterfeit blessing in Egypt, but then he got the boot. The enemy presents the counterfeit blessing because he understands that you have to receive the word of God in order to get the real blessing. You got to trust what the Lord is telling you, not what other people are telling you, or you will get the counterfeit blessing. You need to get confirmation after confirmation. This is the revelation to you all: if something went wrong when you were about to receive the counterfeit, your real blessing is right around the corner. Some of you [women] received the counterfeit, who is living in your house, eating your food stamps, not even paying one bill. You come home and you're cleaning up after him and the kids. Brothers: your counterfeit is a gold digger, asking for a ride to work, for help paying a bill even though she's working. You say, "That ain't nothing, babe." Then

she will call her girlfriends, saying "My rent is *paid!*" She invites you over to have food and complains to you, "My baby daddy, he ain't doing right." You start feeling bad for her. You take all the kids, they start calling you daddy, you feel like you're a man but you're being taken for a ride. The real thing is not going to be asking you for anything: she will be there to be found.

Sisters, how do you know if a man's the right one for you? He loves God more than he loves you. He won't take the opportunity to get into you. Don't try to present the nook-nook to see if he'll take it, because if he does, you're finished. You don't ask for nothing. Watch him to see what he does: you got more to lose. You're receivers by nature. It can take years to work its way out of you. Some of you women have been so hurt by someone that their spirit gets into you, and you run from one man to another until you're thirty years old and wondering where the time went.

Pastor John's allusion to what can happen to women if the wrong spirit "gets into" them has an analogue in the practice of "purging" (vomiting) that Pastor Hadley encourages when a worshipper is afflicted by an evil spirit. She told me that she first felt a calling to deliverance ministry while attending a church at a military base overseas. She recalled that when she sat on the left of the church, the right side of her face would be paralyzed, and when she sat on the right, she would feel the same on the left side of her face. Understanding that God was trying to communicate with her, she asked God to tell her what he wanted, and he told her to go home. She wondered what she was going to do with her young children, but another woman offered without prompting to take them home with her. "When I got home, I fell to my knees and purged over and over again. God was purging me of all the evil spirits I had been carrying in my body from other people."

As Pastor John encouraged his audience to understand events occurring within domestic partnerships in terms of the devil's power to undermine vitality, so may the vital act of purgation be a vehicle for comprehending and responding to such events. At the end of a Bible study in Heaven's Tabernacle, a woman named Diane whom Pastor Hadley had never previously met asked her for a "word of wisdom." Diane was uncertain about whether she should seek a reconciliation with her husband of seventeen years after living apart from him for one year. They are both saved, she said, but he doesn't go to church. Instead, he goes around to the churches where Diane preaches and tells stories about her. He is, Diane continued, also doing things that are ungodly. While Pastor Hadley like Pastor John sometimes holds women responsible for their mistreatment at the hands of men (as in her own case), her approach to domestic difficulties is not to apply patriarchal norms in order to augment the respect due to men. She exclaimed to Diane, "Run! You're all tied up in red tape, you don't have to wait for him to sign the papers, you can get a divorce in two weeks by getting an injunction from the court." Diane replied that they have two children, one a teenager and the other in her early twenties, and that she was wondering whether she ought to stay married for their sakes. No, Pastor Hadley replied, they are grown now. Diane should follow Pastor Hadley's own example: she and her own ex-husband are now the best of friends.

In this instance, confirmation took both verbal and somatic forms. Pastor Hadley asked Diane to remove her jacket and brushed the "spirit of rejection" off her body with vigorous downward strokes of the hand while speaking in tongues. Diane began speaking in tongues herself, and then purged while Pastor Hadley and Evangelist Clarice stroked her, encouraging her to rid her body of the evil influences. Afterward, Pastor Hadley had Diane lean on her own back as she walked around the perimeter of the church while speaking in tongues, carrying the burden of her body's suffering on her own. Suddenly, the Spirit struck me too while I was sitting on a pew, and for several minutes I was speaking in tongues and shaking uncontrollably while the women in the congregation laid hands on me. I felt an impulse to purge but restrained it, wrongly perhaps. Once everyone had returned to ordinary habitus, Diane confirmed the pastor's words about her need for deliverance, reporting that God had instructed her while she was in the Spirit to tell Pastor Hadley that she would deliver many women from far and wide, as in childbirth, and that her armor bearer Evangelist Clarice would be her midwife.

## Moral Ambitions for Vitality

A purgation may seem distant in practice and consequence from receiving an inspired word or improvising a harmony. Yet all these activities reflect how certain vital elements in a person acclaim or reject the care given by spirits or other humans. I have suggested that acts of "giving way" to such influences help to construct events because those acts provide grounds both for decisive action and for ongoing discoveries of the sources of vitality and danger. By the same token, acts of "giving way" shape linkages among particular forms of vitality and ways of inhabiting time. Examples of such linkages include the need Elder Matthew recognizes to "shift" his playing as he listens to what God wants to tell the congregation at a given moment, Pastor John's warnings about "counterfeit blessings" people may receive if they fail to listen for confirmation, and Kathy's reflections on the ways a preacher's words interrupted the closed time of her anxiety. The vital and generative power of listening—indeed its priority to speech, sound, and movement in all these accounts—underscores the principle that "faith comes by hearing."

All the same, the need Kathy felt for God to restore her peace of mind represents a markedly different moral ambition from those expressed by members of the African American churches to fulfill the terms of God's contract and make proper use of their creative capacities. It is instructive, for example, to consider the overlaps and differences between Mother Smith's and Kathy's respective accounts of seeking confirmation. They each narrate how events unfold in ways contingent on their willingness to listen to God's communications. However, they are posing different kinds of questions about the vital elements in themselves that are to "give way" to those communications: Mother Smith worries about misapplying her creative powers to the contract God has made, while Kathy wonders whether she will be able to overcome her anxieties so as to become capable of extending God's gifts. These respective concerns about vitality structure the different kinds of time that they hope to inhabit. Kathy narrates how God's words interrupted the closed time of her anxiety, reaffirming her place within biblical narratives about which she nevertheless continues to express ambivalence, while Mother Smith speaks of how events unfold in accordance with the degree of her readiness to "receive" divine guidance.

These alternative framings of vitality as a matter of creativity or peace of mind reflect divergent understandings about the place of affliction in God's designs, an issue that prompts me to offer some concluding thoughts in what follows about the ethical intelligibility of suffering for Pentecostal believers in this highly unequal society. In emphasizing that "Christians are the ones who help you to Jesus' peace," Pastor Charles of Eternal Hope makes a restorative move, presenting suffering as an episode, however acute or long-lasting, within trajectories of faith. By contrast, Pastor Hadley and Pastor John stress the creative roles believers must take in shaping the rhythms in which affliction and miracles unfold. These different approaches to temporalities of suffering have some profound political implications.

# Conclusion:
# Ethics and Politics of Pious Vitality

Discernment has its limits. There are numerous experiences into which many believers claim to want no insight, for instance ostensibly "unnatural" same-sex desire and nonbinary gender identities, about which it is commonly said in the African American community "nobody is supposed to know" (Snorton 2014). While some "radically inclusive" Black Pentecostal churches help to celebrate these forms of vitality (Lewin 2018), they are prohibited in the churches with which I have become acquainted. In addition to rendering certain forms of vitality immoral, Pentecostal insight may make them unintelligible in ways that recall what James Fernandez (1982) labels "the inchoate"—"that which is *un*formed, undeveloped, the material on which the culturally *in*formed imagination is going to work" or has not worked (Coleman and Dulin 2020: 8). For example, in a conversation with a Euro-American minister affiliated with another church of Eternal Hope's denomination in the vicinity of Buffalo whom I met at a revival, the subject somehow turned to democracy. This minister was enrolled in seminary coursework to obtain formal licensing and was inclined to systematic thinking in ways I find useful for my purposes here. Pointing out that democracy is a non-biblical concept, I asked his opinion about its merits. He reflected that the Bible depicts undemocratic arrangements such as slavery in the epistle to Philemon, but that "God cares only about saving the lost." As he put it, "What does it matter to someone that they had been a slave on earth, if they are dancing before the Throne for all eternity?" He went on to speak about debates over gun ownership rights in the United States, which were then current in the aftermath of the December 2012 massacre of schoolchildren in Newtown, Connecticut: "God doesn't care if you or I own a gun. What will it matter ten thousand years from now, when we'll all be in either heaven or hell?"

This minister's statements, whose like I heard voiced by several members of Eternal Hope on separate occasions, illustrate to the point of caricature Elizabeth

Povinelli's (2011) argument that injustice is legitimated in the future perfect tense under conditions of late liberalism, as well as Jane Guyer's (2007) point that millenarian outlooks render the near future unintelligible for planning. These ways of thinking about the good (Robbins 2013) have real structuring power. Why should future bliss necessarily compensate for excruciating suffering in the present? From Povinelli's perspective, clearly, the question is an aporia, an unresolvable puzzle demonstrating that this millenarian worldview leads to an ethical dead end because it can justify anything, including the "economies of abandonment" that consign the majority of humanity to bodily exhaustion. The minister went on to speak anxiously of his unsaved neighbor in her sixties who was suffering from cancer, worrying that she needed to get to know Jesus. To him, one form of vitality (the potential death of an unsaved aging woman from cancer) was ethically intelligible in a way that another (the potential deaths of unsaved gunshot victims) was not.

That Pentecostal insights in all their diversity should generate multiple kinds of aporias and areas of unintelligibility comes as no surprise. Their purpose, after all, is not to provide access to all truth regimes or to grapple with their various ethical entailments. Nor, I would argue, are Pentecostal insights fundamentally devoted to managing what Matthew Engelke (2007) calls "the problem of presence," that is, "how a religious subject defines and claims to construct a relationship with the divine through the investment of authority and meaning in certain words, actions, and objects" (9). However instrumental a role disclosures and concealments play in making the activities of spiritual beings intelligible and authoritative (Coleman and Dulin 2020), to dwell on *how* those beings become present is to risk neglecting questions of *why* their presence matters in the first place. For the believers I have described, Pentecostal insights are critical practices, geared to overcoming the conditions that inhibit their knowledge of and willingness to abide by God's artful designs for vitality. In order to explain, then, why for some (but clearly not all) believers dying from gunshot wounds might be less ethically intelligible than dying from illness at an advanced age, or why a person's enslavement could be seen as a matter of indifference to God, we need to grapple with how they do or do not understand these forms of vitality as conforming with God's designs.

This is where a comparative perspective can prove helpful. I have been arguing over the course of this study that a key source of political sensibilities is to be found in connections between the ethical and the vital.[1] One such nexus consists of how believers confront the prospect of the afterlife. Pastor John and Pastor Hadley often remind saints to strengthen their relationships with

God given the imminence of the rapture and the frequency of unexpected and premature deaths due to disease and violence among their kin and friends in Buffalo and elsewhere. As Pastor Hadley says, "It looks like every day I get a call telling me that someone has passed on. I don't want to miss heaven on a technicality." However, I never heard anyone in Victory Gospel or Heaven's Tabernacle suggest that what they are going through now will not matter in ten thousand years. On the contrary, their eternal fate depends directly on how they go through now. In other words, their "knowledge of the body" (Jackson 1983) does not lead them to abstract the temporality of eternity from places and social relationships, as the rhetoric of the minister I met at the revival so thoroughly did. What kinds of knowledge of the body motivated his remarks? The issue, it seems to me, hinges on the position of suffering in God's designs.

Strikingly, the minister implied that the sufferings endured by enslaved people have had no bearing on their salvation—according to him, their afflictions are literally meaningless in God's scheme. It seems to me that this argument, which amounts to yet another devaluation of their labor, is grounded in ways the body generates knowledge of salvation—ways which I found generalized among members of Eternal Hope, and which underlay statements like those of the minister that some of them made as well. The forms of suffering to which Eternal Hope members assign ethical content consist of discrete moments such as "travailing" in prayer or intercession, or distinct episodes like a period of trauma. However, they do not usually speak of these periods of suffering as constituting faith trajectories in themselves. Neither Arlene, in conjuring stasis-in-duration with her image of an endless road, nor Kathy in depicting the closed time of her "faith crisis" spoke of suffering as intrinsic to God's designs. While excruciating travail is sometimes necessary for overcoming trouble or bringing another person to Jesus, God has designed travail as a means to an end, namely opening a self to divine love. For these members of Eternal Hope, moments of intimacy and openness, not episodes of affliction themselves, are key to salvation—that is, they do not frame their prospects of salvation as contingent on how they have undergone affliction.

Consequently for them, in ideal terms salvation does not justify previous suffering so much as supersede it. While Arlene's salvation, for example, transformed her from a victimized wife to a strong caregiver, she did not describe the Holy Ghost as justifying or designing the pain of her divorce but rather as bringing her through the pain.[2] Such felt needs to displace affliction, which Pastor Charles likewise articulates in preaching that Jesus restores one's peace of mind, disincline Eternal Hope members from conceptualizing salvation as a just reward for having endured suffering. It is not that salvation has nothing to do with justice—after all, God saved Arlene from an unjust marriage, and has done likewise for women in other Pentecostal churches she has attended—but God has not designed "going through" as a precondition for salvation. Accordingly, I never heard Eternal Hope members express concerns that they might not be saved if they have not suffered.

On the other hand, the minister's suggestion that past enslavement has no significance in God's eyes ironically finds an echo, if not a direct parallel, in Povinelli's claim that bodily exhaustion in the present exposes the ethical emptiness of promises made in the future perfect. The minister considers the future so transcendentally important that present sufferings are meaningless, whereas Povinelli regards the future as illusory—yet in either view, the future does not or cannot justify the suffering that has preceded it.[3] In both moves, perceptions of time are severed from bodies and places in ways that ultimately distract our attention from how discernment transforms the physicality of all these believers, and from the range of political possibilities latent in the reciprocal processes whereby insights reshape the body and bodies generate new insights.

Pastor John and Pastor Hadley, for instance, insist on some causal connections between present suffering and future well-being. They argue that ultimate salvation together with prosperity in this world depend on one's willingness to go through trouble properly, for instance by refraining from inappropriate openness about it. From their standpoints, it would make no sense for God not to recognize the intrinsic value of faithful struggle in the midst of suffering. Thus Pastor Hadley often remarks that the devil attacks us "because Satan don't break into empty houses," so that "if you're not going through anything, you'd better check yourself, because there might be something wrong with your faith." As she often reminds her congregation, "God will cause you to go through some things so that you can witness to other people who are in the same situation. You have to be tried and proven." Pastor John draws his favorite scripture about slavery not from Philemon but Exodus (1:12): "The more they afflicted them, the more they multiplied and grew," a passage implying that vitality may be grounded in suffering.

For all these believers, discernment ideally constitutes what the body knows and how the body knows—and how the body extends to others what it comes to know of communications among spirits and bodies. Pastor Hadley takes a further step, insisting that suffering provides means of apprehending how God inhabits the body, so that suffering is in effect a form of discernment. Upon returning from a visit to her son and grandchildren in another US state after the children's mother suddenly passed away, Pastor Hadley preached on the subject of "valuable pain," words she saw on a television screen while sitting alone in their home. Her Bible had happened to fall open at that moment to Ps. 119:71, "It is good for me that I have been afflicted; that I might learn thy statutes." As she reminded the congregation, "when you are really going through something, that is when you talk to God." By way of comparison, Baptist minister Reverend Campbell's knowledge of salvation enables him to justify the accidental killing of his son as an element of God's plan (Harding 2000). Yet he does not attribute his moment of redemption, namely receiving "peace in his heart," to the experience of going through the pain of the accident, which is conspicuously elided in his narrative. As a result, what salvation justifies for Reverend Campbell is not his own suffering but God's plan for redemption.

Within the broad trajectory of African American religious traditions, sensibilities based on shared insight into the sources and content of suffering have long given shape to artful practices such as hip-hop that counteract social erasures (Jackson 2015; see CERCL Writing Collective 2014, 2017; Pinn 1995; Price 2012; Zanfagna 2017). Such sensibilities have motivated formal theological debates about God's activity in the world as well. A key point of departure for womanist theologians (e.g., Cannon 2006; Cannon, Townes, and Sims 2011; Townes 1995) is that for many Black women experiences of "making a way out of no way" are foundational to faith and to witnessing against social injustice. Notably, Delores Williams (1993) reads Black mothers' endurance in the face of oppression through the biblical story of Hagar, arguing that "if the incarnation in and the revelation of God in the oppressed mother is ignored, it is of very little significance to black women that black male theologians … connect the revelation of God in Jesus, the Oppressed Son, with liberation and reconciliation" (176). On this reading, the Crucifixion appears less instructive given that Black women have suffered enough for other people's sins. As Rebecca Carter (2019) writes, "The opportunity, therefore, is to gather and articulate the ideals by which the Black Church has formed while asserting its position as a productive site through which new awakenings and movements might be directed" (220).

While neither Pastor Hadley nor Pastor John espouses a liberatory theology, their stances resonate with Martin Luther King Jr.'s argument that "unearned suffering is redemptive" in that the "oppressed are the only ones who will bear the burden of the struggle against their oppression because they are the only ones with an interest in doing so" (Chappell 2004: 50). Thus, even as these two pastors expect God to bless them and their congregations, they also express moral ambitions to retain some aspects of precarity, in particular an awareness that God has designed them to go through. This point returns us to how the insights that all these Pentecostal believers receive from God reveal to them specific kinds of connections between the ethical and the vital. As Povinelli indicates, connections of these sorts have implications extending far beyond religion. The linkages are explicit, though, within Pentecostal and Charismatic forms of Christianity and perhaps piety movements generally. Believers perceive God as having designed true knowledge of his will—as distinct from ordinary, partial, or false knowledge stemming from human or demonic sources—as essential not merely for life in a generic sense but for specific forms of vitality with particular and varying content.

Within a broadly shared Pentecostal framework in which having a "personal relationship with God" is always key to "life more abundantly," these urban and suburban church members frame their insights into possibilities for future vitality in chronotopic terms that differ from one another. For example, Eternal Hope members responded enthusiastically to a preacher who depicted Jesus on the verge of coming back for the rapture experiencing an excitement like that of lovers about to be reunited after a long separation. Pastor Hadley evokes a different sensibility in relation to time and endurance, frequently telling her congregation that "we are living in the dash" between the dates of our birth and death: "All we have to do is walk it out, and we know how the story ends—in our victory. Isn't that comforting?" The respective moral perils that these expressions of movement through space and time aim to guard against—namely, failing to anticipate moments of communion with the deity in the one instance, and failing to abide by the rhythms of God's designs for events in the other—resonate as well with what these believers regard as faulty approaches to care, communication, and value. These perceptions, as I have shown, reflect distinct predicaments stemming from believers' different social locations and life chances. Eternal Hope members voice imperatives not to close off the vulnerable self from contact with God, and not to imagine that they can be self-sufficient. In the African American churches, believers focus rather on the dangers of exposure and improper reception, together with possibilities that they will misapply their own creative powers, for instance by bestowing respect on the wrong beings or becoming self-interestedly "manipulative."

All these forms of knowledge entail various actual or imagined movements through space-time, so that discernment embeds believers' bodies with other beings in particular places (see Hovland 2016).[4] Images of going through, bringing through, walking it out, being reunited after a lengthy separation, and inviting the Holy Spirit to cleanse one's body as though it were a dirty house express such processes in metaphorical terms. However, the insights believers derive from moving in and between places are far more than metaphorical. In all three churches, the altar is at the center of communicative relationships among human and spiritual beings, the key site where believers powerfully apprehend God's designs for vitality in and with their bodies. The insights they draw from these encounters both affect and are shaped by what they know of events and relationships in their homes and other places in and around Buffalo. Likewise, the complex semiotic processes through which believers discern how God has designed specific kinds of communication to be means of carrying out care work and remaking kinship relations take shape in church spaces where worshippers receive a covering from or become open to powerful others.

This perspective on the socially embedded and embedding qualities of discernment sheds new light on what Csordas (1994, 1997) calls the "self processes" whereby believers come to know "who they are in God." Csordas works with and beyond Weber in conceptualizing charisma, exploring how among Charismatic Catholics the gifts of the Spirit are dispersed among believers rather than being concentrated in a single authoritative figure. Pnina and Richard Werbner (forthcoming) bring Foucault's (1990) later writings on ethical formations in classical antiquity to bear on dispersed charisma, pointing out that the "aesthetic self-fashioning" Foucault describes "enables the individual to achieve critical distance from a taken-for-granted order" and allows for possibilities of dissent. At the same time, the Werbners argue,

> Foucault ... has in common with Weber a shared stress on personal mastery ...
> For Weber, it is a mastery that leads to authoritative leadership of the follower;
> for Foucault, it is the mastery of the self leading to an emancipatory loving of
> the beloved by the true lover and, ultimately, to mastery over the self, the family,
> and the city.

But must we conclude that Christian discernment necessarily amounts to a wish for mastery after all?

The argument that believers' charisms bestow a sense of mastery over unsatisfactory or uncanny aspects of their selfhood dovetails with James Laidlaw's (2014) point that piety movements foster desires for positive freedom. Laidlaw maintains that a common tendency in the "ethicizing 'world religions'" is to diminish what he calls, following Bernard Williams (1993), "moral incapacity." Moral incapacity is the ability to decide not to commit bad actions; in Laidlaw's view, religious training instills habits that erode a person's freedom to make such decisions. "Moral incapacity ... makes me incapable ... of pulling wings off butterflies, of betraying my friend, etc.—but not ... because I know that if I try I shall fail ... A moral incapacity ... is the *outcome* of a deliberation" about the consequences of an action. "I recoil from the course of action as being shabby, disloyal, cruel, or whatever, and therefore I conclude, 'I couldn't do that'" (153). On the basis of a reading of Charles Hirschkind's (2006) and Saba Mahmood's (2005) studies of Islamic piety movements in Egypt, Laidlaw argues that religious training replaces deliberation with sets of embodied dispositions that ideally make performing a bad action so impossible for the adept that contemplating it would cause the moral equivalent of vertigo: if one were to try, one would fail.

Laidlaw is critical of this aspect of religious learning, arguing that "individuals are invited to exercise individual ethical choice to embark on a path of self-formation, the end result of which is the extinction of exactly the capacity for wilful decision that enabled them to take the path in the first place" (154). He argues that piety movements place limits on "what one might be able to choose to do" in order to advance the "quite different value of positive freedom, ... the realization of one's true self in absolute and involuntary fearful obedience to God" (154). Laidlaw draws here on Isaiah Berlin's (2002) classic distinction between "negative liberty" from coercion and principles of "positive liberty," which entail mastery in the sense of becoming one's true or best self in relation to an objective good.[5]

On this reading, the sources of one of the aporias I discussed above—the minister's claim that "God doesn't care if you or I own a gun. What will it matter ten thousand years from now, when we'll all be in either heaven or hell?"—lie not only in soteriology but in the invitations that believers extend to God to diminish their moral incapacity. These invitations might lead them to avoid tracing linkages between current collective decisions and future outcomes (such as what might happen if everyone were to have a gun)—or, more to the point, might render such an avoidance rhetorically plausible and politically persuasive. As long as we remain our best selves through our dependence on God, our decision to own guns is as inconsequential in God's eyes as any of our other sovereign consumer preferences (though no less inviolable: we have both negative and positive liberty!). Considered in light of the white-supremacist implications of the rhetoric of the National Rifle Association (Gilpin 2020), this obfuscation of the vitality of potential gunshot victims really does reflect identification with the power of the master.

Laidlaw's argument that religious training diminishes moral incapacity is broadly applicable to many of the Pentecostal believers with whom I have worked. Ideally, as they see it, God would so remake them that even if they tried to perform a bad action they would fail. For instance, they commonly speak of how God has taken away their desires for cigarettes, alcohol, and illegal drugs, explicitly denying that their own deliberate decisions could have brought about the change. Members of the African American churches in particular see good reason to call on the Holy Ghost to eliminate their "emotionalism," since they are well aware of how systemic and interpersonal forms of exploitation frequently eventuate in gun violence. From their standpoint, the power of the Holy Ghost to "take away the spirit of rage" constitutes strong evidence of God's care for them. Both Arlene and Pastor Hadley attribute the fact that they did not murder their ex-husbands to divine activity of this kind.

Yet understood in comparative perspective, such forms of divine care reveal how religious practitioners' desires for mastery and freedom (of whatever sort) may be productively reframed as specific aspects of many possible linkages between the ethical dimensions of religious subject formation and what I have been calling designs for vitality. Less suspicious than Laidlaw, for instance, of God's ability to care for believers by overriding their freedom to make decisions are Amira Mittermaier (2011, 2012), in her work on the humbling power of dreams among Sufi devotees in Egypt, and China Scherz (2018), in her discussion of God's power to eliminate feelings of disgust among Catholic nuns who care for disabled adults in Uganda. Scherz points out that to focus on God's grace is to attend to the "unpredictable element in [believers'] ethical lives" rather than identifying ethics solely with "the intentional, the conscious, and the reflective" (108). For the Ugandan nuns, physical contact with the disabled is a form of vitality designed by God as a vehicle for his grace. As these encounters afford the nuns knowledge of the mysterious ways God has suddenly transformed them into caregivers, so too do many artful forms of speech, listening, and movement afford Pentecostal believers insight into the spatiotemporal trajectories over which God cares for them.

For example, a women's group at Eternal Hope enacts periodic disclosures of both human and divine care by circulating notebooks of "prayer needs." At the beginning of the year, each woman writes the names of her own family in a notebook, along with their birthdays and particular prayer needs—for instance, for healing after an accident or finding God after backsliding. The books are then distributed anonymously within the group, so that no woman knows who has received her book and is praying for her family's needs. She may receive anonymous notes and gifts from her "prayer partner" throughout the year, handed to third parties for delivery. At the end of the year, the identities of the prayer partners are revealed. "You find out who it was," Janet enthusiastically told me, "and then you think, 'Oh, it was you who did this for me!'" This process of concealing and subsequently disclosing the identities of benefactors is likewise a means of revealing the (erstwhile known but concealed) presence of God, together with his loving and sustaining activity over the course of one year.

The socially embedded and embedding insights derived from this circulation of requests and gifted responses show how God may care for believers by sustaining tensions between the reflective and the uncontrolled, rather than by resolving them into a teleology as Laidlaw would have it. The element of ethical unpredictability, apparent in the women's ignorance of their partners' identities and of how those partners' prayers might be operating, is inextricable from their reflections about how to provide appropriate and effective gifts themselves. More directly relevant to Laidlaw's concerns about ethical decision-making, though, are the questions that members of Victory Gospel and Heaven's Tabernacle pose about why they go through trouble and how to endure it properly. I once presented Laidlaw's argument to Mother Smith, asking her whether she thought that a person could become so advanced in God's kingdom that she would be unable to perform a bad action. She answered, "Once you are perfected to *that* point, God will say, 'I need you up here' and call you home." As long as we are in this world, Mother Smith continued, we need to deliberately listen for confirmation before we act.

Still, Mother Smith effectively acknowledged that spiritual "perfection" would entail the erosion of a person's moral incapacity. The availability of this ideal, in conjunction with the principle that God tests believers with affliction in order to gradually diminish their capacities to do wrong, opens room for them to speculate about the degree to which spiritual maturity might obviate the need to go through suffering. I draw this inference from a very unusual sermon I attended at a revival conference held in another US city together with Pastor Hadley and leaders of some other churches. The preacher at this conference, who was not personally acquainted with most of the attendees, remarked that she was addressing an audience composed of people who were advanced in God's kingdom, and that she could therefore give them advanced teaching. She took as her text a mysterious passage in Genesis 5: "And Enoch lived sixty and five years, and begat Methuselah ... And Enoch walked with God: and he was not; for God took him." The preacher distinguished "walking" with God from merely "living." To be "walking" with God as Enoch did is to understand so thoroughly "how God will move" that you don't need to have expectations of what he will do. "Enoch moved so far in God," the preacher asserted, "that he didn't need faith anymore to operate." God wants us to walk with him so closely that, like Enoch, "we are not." The preacher went on to remark that "spiritual warfare is fine, but at a certain point you get tired of warring," and that God had given her a powerful word about what to do during times of trouble: "Acquiesce." Later, as she laid hands on people in attendance, she called out: "Be consumed!" (on the model of Enoch, who "was not"). While she did not make the point explicitly, it was clear that Enoch had gotten to a stage where he no longer had to go through.

The audience received these words with marked hesitancy. There was none of the excited byplay in which believers signal to one another that the preacher's words are confirmation from God of what they had already been thinking—and which had been going on during an earlier portion of her sermon, when she spoke about how God was going to thrust believers to "an unexpected new level." When the preacher stated that Enoch did not need to have faith, some people did call out "Wow!" but with noticeable tentativeness. She appeared to recognize her audience's discomfort, mentioning that when God instructed her to deliver this message, she had asked him whether this was really what he wanted her to tell the people. At the conclusion of the service, once offerings had been collected, Apostle Cooper publicly remarked, "That was different." Over a cafeteria lunch the following day with some of the other church leaders, I mentioned that I had been struck by the statement that we can get to a place where we don't need faith, whereupon one elder very politely replied with a smile, "I haven't yet received that revelation."

And yet Pastor Hadley continued to reflect on this sermon when she returned to Buffalo to lead Bible study. As everyone in her church already knew, she had heard God say to her one morning about two years previously, "This is the dawn of freedom." Later that day, she was laid off from her job as a nurse and has been unemployed since. Pastor Hadley concluded that God had taken away her job so that she could devote herself entirely to him, but as she told the congregation after returning from the conference: "The bills don't stop just because I'm not working. If I take a moment and give over to the enemy these days, anxiety and fear will get into me. Satan will put a magnifying glass on your bills and you'll say, 'How will I get out of this?!' But you're trying to figure out what God has already figured out." (She has hinted to me that she receives help from her wide network of spiritual daughters.) Recalling the preacher's remarks about walking with God, she continued:

> It's one thing to trust Him, another thing to walk this thing out. I got to remind myself every day, "God, You called me to this." I got to just back up into Him. The safest place in a storm is the eye of the hurricane. It's like silence hits, you're at peace. I don't say, "If You don't come through, God, I don't know what I'll do." I go to sleep. There's no worry in God.

On the one hand, Pastor Hadley's proleptic narrative about how God has already solved her problems corresponds closely with the conference preacher's advocacy of "acquiescence." On the other hand, she went on to make an implicit criticism of the preacher's remark that advanced believers do not need to expect things to happen: "I've learned that faith is an action word. If you need to travel somewhere, you don't say, 'God, You need to help me,' but you pack and go online to find a ticket." This sort of action-in-expectation aims to bring human desires into correspondence with God's timing, based on a recognition that the two are not identical and that one's requests are in need of discipline. Pastor Hadley's chronotopic metaphor of being in the eye of a hurricane—so powerfully evocative of precarity and its unpredictable, hurtling placetimes, as well as of the insights that might be acquired in the "eye"—encapsulates the tension between the reflective and the uncontrolled aspects of this ethical formation: there's no hurricane without an eye, but equally there's no eye without a hurricane. In her view, God cares for believers both by inducing them to reflect on how and why they have gone through and by eliminating their anxieties and sinful inclinations in ways that they cannot control or predict—ways that Povinelli does not anticipate in her concern with present exhaustion, and that Laidlaw too readily dismisses in his preoccupation with freedom. I think that the discomfort that greeted the preacher's sermon at the conference arose from her attempt to resolve this tension in one direction only.

The forms of vitality that Pentecostal believers regard as compatible with their best or truest selves, or as conforming with the timing of God, are not simply given in advance as Laidlaw's reading of piety might suggest. As a socially embedded and embedding phenomenon, discernment gives rise to forms of ethical discovery that are simultaneously vital and political in nature. To be sure, some of these discoveries are limited and profoundly limiting in their exclusionary effects. Yet other discoveries open possibilities for spatiotemporal movement and placement that counter or at least complicate some believers' inclinations to use the future perfect tense to reinforce willful ignorance about the unequal distribution of suffering in the world. A case in point is the circulation of notebooks of "prayer needs" in Eternal Hope, whereby women discern who needs what from God and one another, and who has given what to whom, over one-year timeframes. Some discoveries may be more painful. For Arlene, communicating with God provided insight into the complexities of gendered expectations over the course of a bitter divorce. Her relationship with God became stronger as her understandings of those complexities developed, since the pain caused by her insights enhanced her need for the Holy Ghost to help her "see it clear."

In concluding, I would like to emphasize the vital qualities (such as Arlene's pain) that forms of discernment and ethical discovery can evoke. In a recent conversation with me, Pastor John was nearly in tears. He had been hospitalized for ten days with Covid-19, was facing a range of budgetary difficulties associated with church expansion plans, and was deeply upset by the unresponsiveness of some white suburban megachurch leaders to his requests for financial assistance. All of this, he pointed out, had taken a heavy toll on his health. After telling me this, though, Pastor John began to relate how he had discerned prophetically that "God is about to bring about a great wealth transfer" because "history repeats itself." When the Hebrews left Egypt, Pharaoh was so distraught that he said, "Take whatever you need and get out!" They took silver and gold with them, the reward God had laid up for them because they had been enslaved. "God is a just God. He wants quality of life for those that have been poor in spirit. They have a right to live in a place where there's not lead poisoning. He's about abundant living, He's about people being healed, He's about people being resurrected from wherever they were at." As he spoke these words, Pastor John's demeanor changed dramatically. He became animated, cheerful, full of expectation. How could it have been otherwise? How could ethical discoveries forged through relationships with powerful spiritual and human others not be vital discoveries as well? To address the "So what?" question about God's existence with which I opened this book, discernment consists of discovering how to become embedded in these relationships, and for this reason is both a source and a form of vitality.

# Appendix: Commentaries and Conversations

This appendix contains commentaries on the ethnography by a former and a current graduate student, Michael Richbart and LaShekia Chatman respectively, together with transcripts of my conversations with each of them edited for length and clarity.

## Commentary by Michael Richbart

*Michael Richbart holds Master's degrees in Anthropology and Biostatistics, as well as a Bachelor's degree in Biblical Studies and Intercultural Studies. His fieldwork has examined practices of "treasure hunting" carried out by members of majority white Pentecostal congregations in the Buffalo area. In "treasure hunting," believers learn to discern clues that they receive from God through prayer, and use these clues to identify people in public places who are in need of divine love and healing. Prior to studying anthropology, Richbart worked for four years as a youth pastor at a Wesleyan and Southern Baptist church.*

### The Magi

When Fred Klaits asked Pastor John what he saw as the value of the endeavor of anthropology, he replied quite cleverly by comparing anthropologists to the Magi. Unlike the shepherds, the Magi did not find Jesus through a specific divine call but rather through their own intellect and observation. This analogy raises an important question: what value does Klaits's ethnography have for Christians?

First, Klaits's observation that discernment itself is a form of vitality correctly identifies believers' own underlying motivation for following God, namely that God is the designer and source of life. This point, I find, is often overlooked by anthropologists but is crucial for understanding a believer's relationship with the divine. Second, Klaits's work provides a starting point for believers to reflect on how their own insights into God's designs may be shaped by an unequal distribution of life chances. The different life possibilities believers envision do not stem only from their contrasting scriptural interpretations but reflect different forms of vitality that God has designed. Careful attention to how and why these forms become ethically or politically sensible opens a renewed critical perspective on how God cares for believers. For example, proclamations of prosperity are seen by many evangelical Christians as a misuse of authority. Kathy expresses such a concern when she claims that a monetary seed is "not legit." Klaits poignantly shows that in taking responsibility for their misfortunes, the African American Pentecostal believers he describes claim a creative role in shaping their own circumstances. These believers do not have the luxury of presuming rights to success and security, so that they assert them on the basis of their contract with God.

## The Blues

In thinking about the connections Klaits suggests between the blues and imagery of "going through" in African American churches, I take as a starting point what evangelical author Donald Miller (2012) said about jazz: "I never liked jazz music because jazz music doesn't resolve … I used to not like God because God didn't resolve" (ix). In music theory, resolution is about movement or progress, coming to a period of rest after a time of tension. Miller's desire for resolution recalls Arlene's description of an endless road, an image that conveyed her troubled sense of lack of progress toward a destination. While blues and jazz are different genres, I would suggest that the "reaping what you sow" imagery commonly used by blues players in the early twentieth century (Spencer 1989) might induce a similar unease for some Christians. Instead of easily resolving, "reaping what you sow" represents a kind of wrestling with the temporal trajectories over which events occur. For believers at Eternal Hope, resolution is found in specific occasions of "bringing through," while believers at Victory Gospel and Heaven's Tabernacle seem to desire not so much resolution as to move by God's rhythms. This comparison helps to highlight how as certain forms of vitality are made ethically and politically sensible to believers and nonbelievers alike, those forms might obscure other vital possibilities. Onaje Woodbine (2016) illustrates such a dynamic in his account of playing basketball with his mainly white middle-class teammates at Yale: "I felt … as if I was dancing to music that no one else could hear" (6).

## Contract and Covering

It comes as no surprise that as a white male raised as an evangelical Christian, I found some of the insights into vitality provided by the African American churches rather distant from the forms of resolution in God to which I have been accustomed and which I encountered in my fieldwork with Pentecostal "treasure hunters" in Buffalo (Richbart 2019). In "treasure hunting," believers from various majority white, middle-class Pentecostal congregations learn to discern clues that they receive from God through prayer and worship. Treasure hunters ask God to reveal locations, names, appearances, and prayer needs of people ("treasures") who are in specific need of the gift of God's love. These clues are written down by each treasure hunter and then combined to form a "treasure map." When evangelists find "God's Treasures," they demonstrate his love through prophetic words, deliverances, and healings. "Treasures" are people whom "God has on his mind" because they have been buried in loneliness, hopelessness, or pain and need God's love.

In my fieldwork with treasure hunters, I heard many analogues to Pastor Hadley's discussion of the "spirit of rejection," Pastor John's conversation in the barber shop, and the speech of both these pastors about prophetic timing. However, I did not hear them talk about the risks these pastors associate with failures to abide by God's designs. For Pastor John and Pastor Hadley, not properly acknowledging the connections between bodies, spirits, and words is akin, in Mother Smith's words, to "walking through a minefield." Believers must not "get out of order," and they must be careful not to mistake a counterfeit blessing for the true blessing. These dangers were not acknowledged in my fieldwork or, I gather, stressed at Eternal Hope.

Concerns with "getting out of order" or failing to live in harmony with God's will are prominent themes in the Old Testament (Mann 2013). To better understand how Pentecostal aesthetics are shaped by the distribution of life chances, it may be fruitful to ask how life possibilities are shaped by how believers relate to the Bible. Many of God's designs for vitality at the African American churches appeared unfamiliar to me until I considered them in light of God's relationship with Israel described in the Old Testament. Whereas many white evangelical Christians focus mainly on New Testament theology and emphasize individual sin, the African American believers whom Klaits describes draw heavily from themes of obedience and contract found in the Old Testament. To account for this disparity, I suggest that as believers envision how their conduct or characteristics appear in God's eyes, they are also envisioning who God is and the kinds of human beings he has created. For example, Klaits shows in his discussion of creativity that members of Victory Gospel and Heaven's Tabernacle envision themselves as "beings with authority" to speak blessings into existence. At Eternal Hope, by contrast, believers explain that getting to know God personally has transformed how they ask for and accept the gifts that God gives.

The book of Leviticus outlines a set of ritual practices by which the Israelites could experience life as God designed it. The sacrificial system was one way to keep their relationship with God "in good order" (Fretheim 1996: 128). The most well-known type of sacrifice is called the "sin offering." The blood required for the "sin offering" was considered expiatory not necessarily because it involved the death of an animal but because it represented the gift of life that God had already given the Israelites. Sacrifices atoned for sin by interposing something between one's sin and God (Erickson 1998). In Hebrew, atone (*kaphar*) means "to cover." The idea of covering can most clearly be seen during the ritual Day of Atonement (Yom Kippur). Here atonement is pictured not just in individual terms but as a corporate practice. Through the sin offering the priest made atonement for himself, the sanctuary, and the whole community of Israel. The Israelites were covered.

This type of covering seems closely analogous to the ways the African American pastors whom Klaits discusses "go through" various sorts of affliction so as to "cover" other believers. Whereas in the Old Testament a sacrifice was interposed between sin and God, Klaits describes how an elder spoke of intercession as a matter of positioning oneself between the devil and the saints. These forms of covering do not atone for sins, but rather protect believers from the devil or other harmful spirits. Pastor Hadley points out that people receive a covering only when they remain obedient to God's commands and pass tests successfully. This is analogous to God's covenant with Israel whereby obedience to divine commands brought about protection, while disobedience led to Israel being exposed to its enemies (Deut. 29). In many Old Testament passages, God's people call on him to abide by his promises. Likewise, believers at the African American churches call out the blessings "in their contract." According to Ps. 119:49–50, these promises were a source of vitality: "Remember your word to your servant, in which you have made me hope. This is my comfort in my distress, that your promise gives me life" (NRSV). These parallels shed light on the frameworks that inform designs for vitality within the African American churches.

Believers at these churches also interpret Jesus' life using the language of covering. According to Pastor John, Jesus was not born with a covering but had to "grow into" it through obedience. Pastor John's narration of Jesus' life downplays phrases like "lived a perfect life" that are very common in white evangelical discourse. This move makes sense given that he understands "going through" as intrinsic to faith, yet it also signals an important set of differences concerning how believers understand the effects of sin. Members of the African American churches stress the consequences of sin for being in line with God's rhythm, whereas for Eternal Hope members, awareness of individual sinfulness is closely linked to acknowledging their own incapacities.

At Eternal Hope believers focus on God's gift of love, which requires an acknowledgment of individual sin. The New Testament is full of passages describing God's love for humanity, the universality of sin, and Jesus' victory over death. It follows that believers at Eternal Hope emphasize that Jesus' love kept him on the cross and express a desire to open the self to divine love. Yet when I first read Klaits's description of the African American churches, I felt that Jesus was rarely mentioned. Upon reflection, I realized that this reaction stemmed from my own religious background. Many of the evangelical churches I've attended are part of renewal movements emphasizing the salvific work of Jesus. A compelling example of this discourse is found in a sermon[1] entitled "God is for God" preached by Southern Baptist minister Matt Chandler in 2012 and incorporated in a recent documentary (*American Gospel* 2019). Chandler argues that believers should not improperly identify themselves with the heroes of biblical stories, but regard Jesus as the hero instead. The story of David and Goliath (1 Sam. 17) should not be interpreted as one's own triumph over the enemy, but rather as Jesus' victory over sin. Chandler likens Christians to the frightened Israelites rather than to David. This message that believers should rely on Jesus rather than their own abilities dovetails with the needs Eternal Hope members feel to admit their own incapacities.

In the African American churches Klaits describes, sin and Jesus are not connected to personal incapacity in this fashion. For Pastor Hadley and Pastor John, Jesus modeled what it looks like to "go through" trouble successfully so as to receive divine protection. Just as these believers understand sin in different ways, they also envision the effects of Jesus' life, death, and resurrection differently. Taken as a whole, these distinctions speak to a larger theological tension between faith and works made prominent by the Protestant Reformation. The doctrine of justification by faith alone (*sola fide*) has led some Protestant denominations to downplay the importance of works in comparison to God or faith: "Our righteous deeds are like a filthy cloth" compared to God's holiness (Isa. 64:6). For some evangelicals, faith hinges on recognizing their incapacity to perform righteous deeds, while they cast obedience as works.

## Openness and Incapacities

For evangelical Christians, passing from sinner to saint requires a careful parsing of one's own condition in relation to that of God, who is "set apart" in his holiness (Mann 2013). Thus for many believers, recognizing who they are in God also entails a proper recognition of their own (human) condition. Klaits describes how Eternal Hope members' practices of recognition involve acknowledgments of their own incapacities, which lead to moments when the self is opened to divine love. To enrich this discussion, I briefly comment on John Calvin's and Blaise Pascal's understandings of incapacity.

Calvin (2008) argues that knowledge of God and knowledge of ourselves are mutually connected; believers feel displeasure with the "depravity and corruption" of the self and are made more aware of this by a reflection on the "divine purity" of God (4–5). For Calvin, an awareness of one's own weakness and incapacity is intrinsically tied to God's redemptive work. He argues, "And it is of no slight importance for you to be cleansed of your blind love of self that you may be made more nearly aware of your *incapacity*; to feel your own *incapacity* that you may learn to distrust yourself; to distrust yourself that you may transfer your trust to God" (Calvin 1960: 704; emphases added). Pascal likewise acknowledges the importance of incapacity but is more concerned with futility, "the condition of being condemned to pursue happiness by means *incapable* of attaining it" (Moriarty 2020: 115; emphasis added). For Pascal (1995) an acknowledgment of one's own limitations allows the believer the possibility to trascend them through fulfillment in God:

> What else does this craving, and this helplessness, proclaim but that there was once in man a true happiness, of which all that now remains is the empty print and trace? This he tries in vain to fill with everything around him, seeking in things that are not there the help he cannot find in those that are, though none can help, since this infinite abyss can be filled only with an infinite and immutable object; in other words by God himself. (45)

Though a devoted Catholic, Pascal was heavily influenced by Calvin's thought. Notwithstanding the subtle differences in their accounts, both emphasize that a believer's knowledge of the self, whether in futility or depravity, leads to a relationship with God. For both theologians, the root cause of this incapacity is sin. In the New Testament the word for "sin," *hamartia*, is an archery term, which means "missing the mark." Although sin often refers to moral decision-making or the tension between the willful/willing self, in a broader sense it locates humanity in a fallen condition. While Calvin and Pascal wrestle extensively with what that condition entails, each concludes that people must recognize their own incapacities in relation to God's holiness, goodness, or love.

Klaits shows how for believers at Eternal Hope moments of openness and intimacy with God and one another contribute to the formation of novel kinship relations. One key aspect of this process is an acknowledgment of a common condition of sin. Lynne describes this awareness when she remarks, "I don't know what her sins are, I just know that we're all sinners." Similarly, Bill urges his son to ask forgiveness for his sins among other things. Eternal Hope members' imagery of a "hole" in every person directly recalls Pascal's emphasis on futility. As a result, believers are in a common position: in need of God's help and more importantly of his love. Although believers intercede and help one another, they position themselves in intentional ways so as not to come between God and the supplicant. Thus, Lynne explains that she was "not in his face," but "whispering in his ear." She further remarks that she was "not yelling at him," but rather speaking "in a soft voice." Similarly, Bill tells his son not to be distracted by "looking around to see what other people are doing." Klaits glosses such acts as carrying out a moral calibration between autonomy and dependence. In this language ideology, words that convey one's own incapacities and need for help are valorized, while omitting such expressions could be a source of sin or idolatry. Members acknowledge that during intercession language itself may even come between God and the believer given their own "partial and inadequate knowledge of what is to be said" (105–6), an important rationale for tongue speech.

Albert's discomfort with Pastor John's emphasis on his own attunement to God's promptings, described at the beginning of Chapter 4, aligns with what Calvin (1996) writes in relation to the apostle Paul's "thorn in the flesh" (2 Cor. 12): "For men have no taste for [God's power] till they are convinced of their need of it and they immediately forget its value unless they are *continually reminded by awareness of their own weakness*" (161; emphasis added). Reflecting on one's own incapacities reminds the believer of the value and need for God's power. From Albert's perspective omitting this point was akin to not giving credit where credit is due. By continually admitting their own incapacities while asking, believers at Eternal Hope also enhance their self-worth, as they recognize that God's love and acceptance are not based on their own performances. Klaits's observation that this perspective underpins a right-wing political stance is insightful. I would add that an emphasis on admitting incapacities may also obscure the connection between personal responsibility and social injustice. As believers concentrate on admitting their incapacities, they find it easy to take for granted the conditions that have led to their comparative security and prosperity.

## Limits of Discernment and Treasure Hunting

While Eternal Hope members view travailing in prayer as a means to an end and members of the African American Churches understand "going through" as intrinsic to God's designs, the Pentecostal treasure hunters with whom I worked think that suffering should simply not be present in a believer's life. In heaven there is no pain or suffering, so on earth there should be none either. The idea that God gave or allowed someone to have a disease or infirmity to teach them a lesson is considered a "demonic" thought.

I return here to treasure hunting because it combines reflective and unpredictable aspects of ethical decision-making of a kind that Klaits discusses in his conclusion. Believers spend a great deal of time reflecting on what their "clues" could mean and where they should go to find "treasures" (malls, grocery stores, airports, retail stores, parks—that is, places of alienation and/or anonymity associated with the nature of the public that are transformed through believers' activities into spaces of care). Treasure hunters and the people they approach often marvel not at having "gone through," but rather on the intricate timing and connections God has used in order to bring about his kingdom. The "treasure map" gives tangible evidence of God's intricate timing and connections showing God's treasures just how valuable they are in God's eyes.

Although there are many unpredictable aspects of the activity of treasure hunting, I found over the course of my two-year fieldwork that many clues on the treasure map remained the same. In other words, God's timing and care had stereotypical patterns: the names received were mostly common English names, locations were always in a wealthier part of town, and prayer needs were usually about healing a body part or meeting an emotional need. When I asked why these patterns exist, I was sometimes told, "God uses what we know." Notwithstanding the novelty of insights into God's designs, discernment is limited by "what we know." Thus, certain potential ethical discoveries remain closed off—an important example of how Pentecostal aesthetics are shaped by the ways life chances are distributed.

While a relationship with God might diminish believers' capacities to decide not to engage in sinful behaviors, as James Laidlaw (2014) maintains, it also provides them freedom to discover God's designs for vitality and, importantly, experience God in ways they find unpredictable. This freedom is possible because discernment is a source of life itself designed by God, and outside of God there is no life. Laidlaw's disapproval of the obediently willing self frames the outcome of religious obedience as a negation of freedom. Believers vehemently reject this idea, since their insights motivate them to choose life-giving activities while avoiding life-taking situations or relationships.

I end with thinking about the imagery of "going through": for these Pentecostal believers, does God provide resolutions? For believers at Eternal Hope, God is believed to offer resolution through peace of mind and moments of openness to God's divine love. For believers at Victory Gospel and Heaven's Tabernacle, believers find resolution in God's protection and blessings as they navigate the moral perils of being out of rhythm with God's designs. Yet the unequal distribution of life chances raises the question, does God truly resolve?

## Conversation between Mike Richbart and Fred Klaits

**Mike Richbart:** Susan Harding (2000) describes a near-death experience that caused her to ask herself, "What is God trying to tell me?" You mention in Chapter 1 that you have not allowed God to reorganize your own sense of time or its patterning. But I wonder, to draw on Baptist minister T. W. Hunt's (1995) terminology, did you develop a critical awareness of the conditions that God has designed for your own vitality? For example, did a relationship with God reframe your sense of responsibility to God or to other people?

**Fred Klaits:** I would say that part of me is responsive to God—you could call that the willingly obedient aspect of myself. This is the part of me that feels the Holy Spirit in my body. There have been many occasions when I have received a word of knowledge from a prophet about my life that was surprisingly appropriate (and sometimes morally uncomfortable). Also, there have been times during my fieldwork when I've been involved in some tricky situations and felt the need to pray to God for guidance, following the model of believers who say, "In all your ways acknowledge Him and He will direct your path." In these ways, God has become one of my own "personal symbols" (Obeyesekere 1981). But on the whole, I think the answer to your question is that I find it impossible to dissociate the vitality that I derive from God from the vitality

I derive from the work of ethnography. Outside the contexts of fieldwork and writing, I think about God only sporadically. As a scholar and an educator, I feel that important aspects of my vitality do hinge on my ability to make critical assessments of my own, but I don't go about with the thought that God has a call on my life to do this scholarly work. In other words, my own moral ambitions really are very different from those of the believers I'm describing. Here I'm following Tanya Luhrmann (1989) and Adam Klin-Oron (2014), who point out that whether ethnographers' "interpretive drift" becomes complete or permanent has to do less with the persuasiveness of the epistemologies they encounter in their fieldwork than with the social and intellectual networks in which they themselves are immersed. But I'm wondering about the impulse behind your question.

**Richbart:** I mentioned Harding's account of how language is a medium and a subject of conversion because I was thinking of how members of the African American churches in particular speak of how they have to "go through" in life. Did you find yourself thinking in those terms about struggles you've had or difficulties you've faced yourself? In Eternal Hope, believers speak about bringing one another through difficulties. So I was wondering how you navigated "going through" or "bringing through."

**Klaits:** I want to be clear that I do not go through anything comparable to what the people in these African American churches go through. My circumstances are much more privileged, and I don't apply the same kinds of the language about "going through" or for that matter "bringing through" to my own concerns. Not only am I privileged, my own moral ambitions as I've said are very different from those of any of the believers whom I've written about. I argue in the book that an important reason why believers feel that they need to receive insights from God is that those insights help them to adopt critical perspectives on what they see as ordinary understandings of personal value, care, placement, and how events unfold over time. But the lived predicaments in which those concerns become important to them are not predicaments that I share. I'm concerned with this set of issues because I'm broadly preoccupied with questions of how and why people come to feel that they need to care for one another's well-being, or alternatively refuse any such involvements. Those questions can be framed in terms that we might label religious, but they don't have to be. They bear on what we call medicine, economics, politics, and kinship. I do feel that much of my vitality depends on my ability to raise critical questions about these issues. But the people I've been working with don't share my preoccupations. Why should they?

**Richbart:** Speaking of vitality, you mention that for believers the Bible is one of its main sources. In my commentary I highlight the different kinds of emphases that seem to be placed on the Old and the New Testaments in Eternal Hope and the African American churches. Can you say more about this?

**Klaits:** You raise a really fascinating set of issues concerning the Old Testament's stress on obedience and covering and the New Testament's emphasis on grace. That broad distinction is certainly one that all of these believers would recognize. In Eternal Hope, they say that the Old Testament is the New Testament concealed, and that the New Testament is the Old Testament revealed. All of these believers place a great deal of emphasis on the epistles of Paul, in particular the distinctions he draws between the obediently willing and the disobediently willful self. Pastor Charles at Eternal Hope often remarks that you need to read the Gospels and the book of Acts to get saved, and the epistles to keep you saved. I do want to emphasize, though, that the members of the African American churches would not associate covering and obedience solely with the Old Testament. In fact, one of their favorite passages about covering comes from the New Testament: "Charity shall cover the multitude of sins" (1 Pet. 4:8). That said, there is a greater stress on the dangerous consequences of disobedience in the African American churches.

I can illustrate this point by telling you about a Bible study led by Elder Rebecca in Heaven's Tabernacle on the sixth chapter of Romans. Over the course of the study, she drew on a set of millennia-old Christian tropes associating Judaism with literalism and adherence to external forms—tropes that Christians have historically used to accuse one another of privileging fleshly over spiritual perception, and the letter of the law over grace (Nirenberg 2015). Elder Rebecca pointed out that Paul is trying to give his readers "an understanding about the law." She said, substantially:

> You need to know you're a sinner, and that's what the law tells you. There had to be a name for sin to make people feel accountable. The Jews' mindset was, if I sin, I'll just make a sacrifice. But mercy is pardoning for guilty acts and grace is a free gift that's unmerited. So Paul had to de-program the minds of people he's writing to away from religion and ritual, which was the Old Testament idea. But it's important not to take advantage of grace. I should not want to sin because Jesus paid a debt He didn't owe.

Elder Rebecca then told a story about how she had been at the bus stop a few days previously and met someone she knew "from her past," when she had been addicted to crack cocaine. This person said to her: "There's something different about you," and she replied, "Yes, I've been clean for twenty-two years. It's easy because my mind is made up. I'm not a recovering addict, I'm recovered. I don't do this walk with God because I'm scared of being in the wrong place. I do it because He loved me enough to pick me up from where I was." And I think everything Elder Rebecca said up to this point dovetails with the emphasis that you identify in the New Testament on grace. But her next statement was, "I'm not going to let one second cost me forever." In other words, she is not going to allow one second of giving into a temptation to do drugs to cost her eternal life – she is not going to "take advantage of grace." Elder Rebecca's gloss on Romans does not lead her to associate the dangers of disobedience only with the Old Testament dispensation. She does not see any contradiction between speaking of God's grace in conjunction with the dangers of disobedience.

**Richbart:** Was there the same level of emphasis placed on obedience at Eternal Hope? Was it talked about? Did they associate obedience with works?

**Klaits:** I don't recall believers at Eternal Hope drawing distinctions between faith and works. There was talk about obedience in that they said you have to be obedient to the laws of the church. You have to obey the pastor when he tells you it's time to fast. You have to stay away from sinful activities. Those things are very important. But there was much less discussion of the consequences of disobedience than in the African American churches. There was much less overt talk about the problems that are apt to arise if you get out from under God's covering. At Eternal Hope those problems were presented largely, I think, in the context of backsliding (that is, sinning deeply or leaving church entirely). For instance, Arlene said to me, "I've known people who have learned the truth and then backslid and terrible things have happened." But what Pastor Charles was *not* doing was telling believers that they themselves were continually disobedient, as Pastor John and Pastor Hadley did. It's certainly partly a function of precarity. Members of these African American churches know that one misfortune or one mistake can have devastating consequences for their lives, so that part of the appeal of faith for them has to do with staying protected, staying under God's covering.

For my part, I'd like to ask you to elaborate on your point that for the white middle-class Pentecostal treasure hunters you mention, "certain potential ethical discoveries remain closed off" given the stereotyped "clues" that God gives them about the people they ought to encounter. I'm wondering what you would like to tell them, if given the chance, about what the African American believers whom I've described see as God's designs for their vitality.

**Richbart:** I think the most striking difference I would try to explain is what you discuss in Chapter 3. For the African American believers, God's designs have less to do with emotional openness than with receiving protection from various harms. For them, the consequences of not abiding by God's designs are severe, reflecting the precarity and difficulty that many African American believers must "go through" to receive a blessing. I think this is where your book can be most helpful to believers, giving clear examples of how African American and white Pentecostal churches find life in Jesus in different ways. What gives me life as a Christian may not be the same thing that gives someone else life. The key point I was trying to make about Treasure Hunters' clues is that they characterize a certain type or kind of person who is in need of God's love, a certain kind of "lost person." This isn't to say Treasure Hunters don't believe that everyone is God's Treasure, but that there is a tension between the perceived universality of the Christian message and individual lived situations or life chances. At the center of various forms of Christian discernment is an assumption concerning how people should live: believers assign differential value to particular life trajectories. But this position begs questions about why the "world system," which Treasure Hunters often talk about, is more exploitative of some people than others. This interpretive gap is easily overlooked and even exacerbated when Christians insist on a singular vision of vitality.

## Commentary by LaShekia Chatman

*LaShekia Chatman holds a BA in Communication Studies and a BS in Medical Anthropology. As of this writing, she has completed her first year of coursework in the PhD program in Anthropology at SUNY-Buffalo, where she plans to explore how African American perinatal narratives may serve as qualitative ethnomedical interventions. She has worked extensively in education, holding multiple roles in International Education and English as a Second Language interventions at higher educational institutions. She has also worked with primary- and secondary-school students, leading programs in writing and literature, community health, religious education, youth ministry, and visual arts. For over twenty years, she has had a career as a culinary entrepreneur, leading her to develop programs in New York City focused on food justice advocacy, culinary arts education, and school nutrition.*

"Never grieve an opportunity to give your testimony" was among the many tropes on replay throughout my teenage years, and is a testament to the indelible mark left from a maturation in youth church and ministry grooming. At a time when I was seeking confirmation for my decision to enroll in a PhD program in Anthropology at SUNY-Buffalo where I met Fred Klaits, my arrival at these personal spiritual conclusions about a divine design in my life resounded both loudly and familiarly through the words of his interlocutors. In Chapter 5 dealing with confirmation, Klaits states, "Because Pentecostal believers locate the source of vitality beyond the self even as they insist that their vitality depends on their own responsiveness to that source, they express a need to be sure that they are apprehending God correctly in order to properly receive his care and extend it to others" (135). Klaits's project led me to reflect on some ambivalence I have come to feel about how other believers have identified the sources of my own vitality, often to my displeasure. I felt I had long since put those thoughts to rest, especially as I continue to work on developing Christian curricula for youth focused on social justice issues. Yet growing up in Baptist and Charismatic congregations in Buffalo, I found that however much care I devoted to crafting each aspect of my life through planning, thought, and research, this proved to be insufficient to those who felt it their charge to judge whether these actions were "God-ordained." During my upbringing, I was encouraged to feel that ways of worshipping God other than those practiced in Black Charismatic Baptist congregations did not enable believers to approach God in the most intimate ways. The experience of reading this ethnographic text has enriched my understanding of how and why I have felt that God has a design for my life.

I have hesitated to share my personal experiences of grappling with faith. After much introspection, I realized that my fear had to with the ambivalence I have come to feel about the judgmental aspects of church, together with my concern about ensuring a respectful hearing for African American Pentecostalism. I initially approached this project for the sake of practicality in enhancing my own skills as a reader of an ethnographic text, and began to unpack it with a twinge of skepticism about whether Klaits would be able to convey the sometimes self-contradictory aspects of Black Pentecostalism: the coexistence of the idea of a loving God with fears about disobeying His will. Klaits's remarks about "church hurt" resonate with my own experiences of incorrect assessments of my character and motivations. Yet church has for so many provided a gracious context for translating pain, encouraging endurance, and sparking social and spiritual emancipatory movements. I was drawn to Klaits's ethnography out of curiosity about what an anthropological analysis of an intimate aspect of my personal experience might look like, but ultimately my reading became a deeper probing of my own spiritual evolution. My experiences with not only Christianity but Islam and African spirituality continue to guide me toward the same self-truth that I call eternal wisdom, and that Klaits refers to as "insight." Klaits's account of speaking in tongues, tarrying and fasting, spiritual discernment, visions, prophecy, and revelation speaks to fundamental truths about my contemporary spiritual life. I firmly believe that it was in God's greatest design for me to candidly share my journey along my life's pathway toward this revelation—namely, before reading this text, I had never thought of myself as ambivalent about my faith.

I experienced a working-poor childhood in the East Side of Buffalo that contrasted with the social idealism of a grade 5–12 prep school experience at City Honors School, one of the most prestigious institutions in the country. These experiences contributed to strikingly different realities in our "talkin' proud" yet clearly dilapidated city.[2] The vibrant bustling downtown scene of my elementary school years began to fade with the luster of the granite and marble of M&T Plaza, AM&A's department store, and the Main Place Mall, which by the end of my high school years more rightfully resembled a ghost town. Growing up in a redlined city like Buffalo, whose suburbs still wield "sundown" signs prohibiting entrance between dusk and dawn, and where generations of children are all instructed along with their driving lessons of "where not to drive," I learned early on that most formal institutions were not designed for my benefit.

I can recall sensing a slow erosion of myself while shifting between three worlds: my school, my church, and my home. This ability to "shift" between roles (Jones and Shorter-Gooden 2003) was supposed to build character—for instance, family members discouraged me from attending a historically Black college on the assumption that I would not become sufficiently adept at "shifting." Everything was performative—especially church, including God, and the respectability politics formed through continual demands for physical manifestation of a supernatural interference were exhausting and emotionally debilitating and confusing. If I weren't a "Super Christian," then who or where or what would I be, other than doomed? Although my activities in our family's church took up a great deal of my time—I was an officer for several years in the citywide chapter of the Church Ushers Association, a youth liturgy speaker, an Eastern regional delegate to the National Baptist Association, and a liturgical dance team choreographer—I knew that there was more, and that this was not who I was.

The test would come when I decided to make "my own decision," one outside of what everyone thought I should make, namely to leave Buffalo and move to New York City. As with every other decision running against popular opinion, it prompted the question "Did God actually instruct me to do this or not?" If things worked out, either it was by some stroke of luck or I had actually heard God correctly. If they did not—well, then clearly I lacked all discernment. By

October of that year, I was forced to return to Buffalo, deathly ill, unable to walk, disgusted at the church as a whole, and, most notably, angry at God. I was eighteen years old. I had devoted my life to God, vowed chastity and purity in action and thought, resigned all honor to Him, read, studied, taught, prayed, repented and repeated, and spent my weekends and some weekday evenings in church services or ministry work without even so much as asking for special favor, on the understanding that my reward, if I sought His approval, and His mercy, and His guidance would be mine. Very soon afterward, I would arrive at the belief that most of the time, God was intentionally negligent, flippant, and quite possibly willfully ignorant, and the grace and preference which He'd extended to others in return for their work far exceeded that which He had extended to me. I really believed that there must have been something wrong with what I was doing, or perhaps it was all a lie. I felt the same kinds of self-accusation and disapproval from others when I left my abusive marriage eighteen years later. If my experiences were not the result of anything I had done, then there had to be a greater, more humane truth which everyone else experienced when they sang of the God who granted "liberty" from one bondage or another, but which I was missing. I'd always deeply known that there was something far greater to be experienced which required doing much less.

It would be years and several hundreds of miles away in my current home of New York City where I could find a more familiar God experience whose comfort extended beyond my home and into the sanctuary. For one whose membership and activity for over the past fifteen years has been with congregations in Harlem entrenched in a legacy of sociopolitical justice, the church as a springboard for human equity and civil rights sustains my moral edification as much if not more than my spiritual needs. In churches in New York City, I encountered a radicalized, inclusive, and practical-minded Jesus who was not foreign but a welcome adaptation befitting my personal idealization of Christ. By contrast, in the Buffalo congregations where I had been raised, conformity with God's perfection took precedence over the social ministry of Jesus.

Many of the acts of obedience that Klaits describes, such as tithing, avoiding retaliation, and accepting a job loss as God's will made me think, "Oh this is so ridiculous and illogical, but I've done it too! We do it, and somehow it works." My reaction resonates with Klaits's point that believers at Victory Gospel and Heaven's Tabernacle pay close attention to the rhythms of God's timing, expecting blessings as a result of their obedience. While I desired to relinquish myself to God's timing in this way, I came to feel slighted by the finger-pointing that ensued when things did not turn out as I had hoped. It was a way of thinking that put too much onus on myself, on my lack of obedience or discernment. I was reminded of this dynamic when reading Christine's remark "It's all on me," recounted in Chapter 4, that she made because she felt she had misinterpreted a dream about which apartment to rent. I can see the appeal of the emotional support that members of the suburban church of Eternal Hope derive from laying on hands in a group, an activity they call intercession.

In the African American churches I have known, praying intercessors occupy revered senior positions because they "cover" their pastors in prayer, together with saints or their relatives who are injured or grievously ill. In this respect, their roles are similar to those of "armor bearers" who are designated by the pastor to carry his or her Bible, vestments, and other pulpit accoutrements. Klaits mentions these offices held by senior members known as "leaders" in passing but might have dealt with these roles and political hierarchies more extensively. In many of the congregations I am familiar with, "Mothers" and "Elders" are prestigious designations, not solely honorific titles based on age. These senior women play important roles in regulating courtship and marriage, organizing child-rearing and baby blessings, managing pastoral operations and relations with homebound and ill congregation members, and approving social events. In addition, other officers such as trustees and deacons play vital roles and are a staple even within smaller congregations, carrying out administrative functions and community outreach in accordance with church bylaws. Deacons' executive functions sometimes balance or offset the authority of the church leader or pastor. Women who occupy roles of Mother and Elder, which in my experience do not exist in northern white Pentecostal congregations or Black conservative Baptist congregations, take on central roles in assessing believers' spiritual maturity.

These positions of female authority are often signaled by aesthetics of sanctification within Black churches, aesthetics whose distinguishing features have shifted over time. Modesty understood as bodily covering is a prevailing factor in dress for many Black Pentecostal women. During my upbringing in the 1980s and 1990s, I noticed that female congregants in Pentecostal churches did not wear makeup but had on signature long skirts with long-sleeved shirts regardless of the occasion. For Sunday church services, more mature worshippers would wear large ornately adorned hats with matching lace-edged handkerchiefs, large hand fans, and opaque hosiery. Percussion instruments such as tambourines, shekeres, and maracas that coordinated with Bible cases and handbags were also popular. In some churches, even lipstick was not allowed. When I was younger, I saw Pentecostal women dress in these distinctive ways while they were "out in the world" in public, though this is less common today.

This aesthetic was and still is known as looking "sanctified," and although dress regulation has become more casual in most congregations especially among younger parishioners, the regulation and standard of appearing "sanctified" remains a means of policing women in contemporary settings. These modesty regulations generally have to do with skirt length, tightness of clothing, how much cleavage or other bodily parts are revealed, and even how one sits within the sanctuary. Within some Baptist churches women may be given a "modesty handkerchief" to be placed on her lap at the discretion of a senior elder woman, often a Mother of the church, which creates a new floor-length hem when she is seated. Although Klaits mentions that blankets are placed over worshippers who have literally fallen to the floor in the Spirit, in my own experience the role of the cloth extends beyond maintaining modesty into policing sexuality.

Policing in the Pentecostal church in my experience does not stop at bodily modesty and sexuality. Regular admonishment, as Klaits indicates, is seen as vital within Black Pentecostal congregations. These reproaches are to be welcomed as "corrections" that create a keener sense of discernment in the believer until the point where she or he begins to "self-regulate through the Holy Spirit" to reach a point of absolute holiness.

One of the most striking episodes of the book to me was Kathy's narrative of ethical discovery recounted in Chapter 5. Her experience of dissatisfaction with God's plans for her vitality, which she expressed by questioning why she had been placed in a vulnerable and unsafe condition on a mission trip, differed greatly from Mother Smith's account of how she had only herself to blame for cosigning a car loan with her son in disregard of God's warning. In her narrative, Kathy did not present herself as accountable for possibly misunderstanding whether God really intended her to go to the Middle East. Instead, her questioning consisted of expressing confusion about what she felt God was doing to her, and searching for clarity. Mother Smith's comments on the need to seek confirmation, by contrast, consistently reflect an understanding that the onus is on believers to examine their thinking and behavior to assess whether they conform to God's timing. The two appear to have different understandings of the roles they are to play in bringing God's designs to fruition: Mother Smith has to examine herself for signs of obedience or disobedience, whereas nobody ever seems to have suggested to Kathy that her own powers of discernment might be at fault. While at age eighteen I would have appreciated it if some of my elders had been less judgmental to me about the qualities of my own discernment, it strikes me that Kathy's experience reflects her comparative privilege in the sense that most members of Eternal Hope do not continually feel a need to discern and avoid exploitative situations.

## Conversation between Fred Klaits and LaShekia Chatman

**Fred Klaits:** One of the many things that impresses me about your commentary is how poignantly you show how burdensome it can be to have to demonstrate discernment. When you were eighteen years old, you were subject to criticism from elders in your family and your church who felt that you had not shown discernment in your decisions—and by implication that you had not been properly "obedient" to God. It strikes me that their reactions were premised on a particular theory of justice, namely that justice consists of obedience. As I understand their view, a just act is one that is obedient to God. At this point in your life, you have joined faith communities that stress working for social justice. I'm wondering how you would compare the social-justice approaches of your current faith communities with the theory of justice as obedience that was prevalent in the churches where you were raised.

**LaShekia Chatman:** In the Charismatic Baptist church I attend now in New York City there's far more room for individual expression and for ideas of what was once considered alternative living. There is a huge LGBTQ community, and they receive respect that wasn't available to them in the churches I grew up in. The church supports school nutrition, food justice, housing justice, and they have a huge mental health outreach program of a kind that still doesn't exist in the congregations where I was raised in Buffalo. A lot of the things that were stigmatized as unholy or sinful in my other congregations are welcomed as expressions of just being you. You use your power to fortify the kingdom—it's a complete shift.

**Klaits:** Could you help me to understand how those concerns get articulated in theological terms, for instance about how the life of Jesus teaches us to have respect for others?

**Chatman:** In the church where I worship now, Christ is referred to as The Carpenter. It's a reframing of Him. He's still Savior, He's still Lord, Son of God. But there's more of an emphasis on His lifestyle being accessible wherever you are in your faith walk. You can live a life as Christ would, of loving acceptance, of giving, of teaching, full of loving people who are society's outcasts. That's a huge part of their outreach.

**Klaits:** How do you think that people like Pastor Hadley or Pastor John or others whom you might know who share their general orientation would react if you explained to them your revised understandings of justice?

**Chatman:** I would hate to stereotype them, but my immediate thought is that they might feel that the congregation I worship with now is more worldly, or secular. I'd be curious to know if they felt that the Word of God was watered down at all, because of the delivery. It's still a very Charismatic type of worship—I don't want to call it informal but it's more open. We have a pastor and other leaders who carry out administrative functions, but there's a much more general sense of equality.

**Klaits:** Why do you think they might consider the Word of God to be watered down?

**Chatman:** Because there's not the demand for holiness centered around decorum. And I happen to like it very much. Even though I followed those holiness rules, it just feels like I can breathe now. And I feel that everyone else feels that way too, and so it makes for such a beautiful experience when you go. You're just more able to be yourself.

**Klaits:** How do you think people like Pastor John or Pastor Hadley would react to the teachings in your current church about obedience, or to the lack thereof?

**Chatman:** I think they would see the lack of teaching about obedience as problematic, as leaving the congregation more vulnerable to the devil intervening in and compromising the Word of God. I could be wrong; I hope I am. But in my experience, there seems to be a concern with making Jesus or God too casual—I think there's a fear that that kind of intimacy is disrespectful.

**Klaits:** Do you think Pastor Hadley and Pastor John would be concerned that you might be being left exposed to various physical or moral dangers?

**Chatman:** Possibly. I think that would be more of a question they would have for my pastor, about his ideas about covering. That's not really something that we go deeply into in the congregations that I work with in New York. That might be a definite concern for Pastor John and Pastor Hadley. They might feel that because I follow that [socially progressive] tradition, I'm naive and unable to have proper covering for myself.

**Klaits:** On the subject of covering, thank you for prompting me to say more about church offices and issues of dress and comportment. You're quite right to draw attention to the importance of offices and titles. I think the reason I don't dwell on them is that I wished to draw attention to the differences between the concentrated and dispersed locations of charisma in the urban and suburban churches respectively. Let me give you an example. Just a few days ago, Pastor John was ordained as a Bishop by his own Overseer, a pastor based in another US state who supervises a network of churches. There was a big celebration at which Pastor John was dressed in a Bishop's vestments. Not only was he elevated, as they say, to the position of Bishop, but a number of the other leaders of Victory Gospel were elevated as well, including Mother Smith and other Ministers who lead Bible studies and engage in intercessory prayer for the sick and injured in ways that you mention. Mother Smith was ordained as an Elder, and a number of Ministers were elevated to positions of Deacons and Deaconesses. I'm sure that in the larger-scale congregations you're familiar with, the duties attached to those offices proliferate along the lines you discuss.

But what struck me about this arrangement is that it reflects the ways charisma is concentrated in Pastor John. It's because he was being elevated that the saints were elevated too. This is in keeping with the idea he has often expressed that the anointing drips from the head down to the rest of the body. Clearly, while all the leaders are being elevated, they derive their anointing and their covering from the anointing and the covering on Pastor John, which he derives in turn from his past and present spiritual mentors. And these concentrated forms of charisma are really quite different from the dispersed charisma operating during intercession events at the suburban church of Eternal Hope, where anybody can come and lay hands on anyone else (though usually of the same gender). It's a point in the service when charisma is not confined to Pastor Charles, notwithstanding the fact that Eternal Hope is part of a national denomination with a formal bureaucratic hierarchy.

You also bring up the subject of covering in relation to clothing and comportment, and I wanted to address some of the points you made about modesty. In some ways, Pastor John and Pastor Hadley actually set themselves against the kinds of "holiness" standards that you mention. Pastor John in particular often ridicules those standards in his preaching, saying that they are an aspect of a "religious mindset" that privileges external forms over a relationship with God. We're not a church, he often says, where people will make a young woman feel uncomfortable by telling her, "Let me help you cover up" and draping a blanket over her legs. It's perfectly acceptable in both of these churches for a woman to attend service in a tie-dyed T-shirt. Pastor Hadley wears artificial lashes and has highlights in her hair, and Elder Rebecca wears lipstick. Pastor Hadley says that the devil is perfectly happy if we all come to church dressed up and sit and do things the usual way. In fact, in some ways she sees the work of the Holy Spirit as counteracting appearances of holiness.

"It's okay to come to church lookin' cute," she often tells her congregation, "but you need to leave to' up"—disheveled by the activity of the Spirit. This said, Pastor Hadley does express pride in the wisdom and sensitivity God has given her to know how and when to speak to a young woman who might be dressed inappropriately.

These issues of comportment bear on the ways that holders of church offices are supposed to conduct themselves in relation to the charisma that's concentrated in Pastor Hadley. She gives instruction to the Ministers in Heaven's Tabernacle who preach sermons every couple of months about how and where to position themselves at particular points in a service. When someone is "giving their life to the Lord," she tells them, they need to be standing. They need to be in the front of the sanctuary, looking both at the Pastor who is leading the newly saved person through the confession of faith and out at the congregation, because the devil is particularly angry on these occasions and might attack one of the saints.

To give a further example, Pastor Hadley reproved the Ministers as a group for not having enough insight to be immediately aware of a couple of demonic attacks that took place in the sanctuary on the same day—attacks, she explained, caused by the devil's anger at the impending spiritual elevation of the church. First, right after a Bible study preceding the service proper, people were beginning to chat with each other but did not notice that one of the Ministers, a senior woman, was in distress. This woman later testified that she felt she was having a stroke—her arms and legs were going numb, but "I told myself, I just need to get to Pastor," who was sitting nearby at the time, "and it will be all right." Pastor Hadley took her in her arms and brushed the evil spirits off her body with forceful strokes of the hand while speaking in tongues. A few hours later, when service had been officially dismissed, Elder Rebecca collapsed and again, Pastor Hadley was one of the first to notice. Everyone was very alarmed and the paramedics were called. Elder Rebecca later said that she had felt the devil snatching at her breath and that she was going. As Pastor Hadley took her in her arms, Elder Rebecca told her to say goodbye to her daughter for her. Again, Pastor Hadley spoke in tongues until Elder Rebecca recovered somewhat, at which point she anointed her head with one of the bottles of oil that Apostle Cooper had recently blessed and that he had asked Pastor Hadley to distribute to the congregation. Finally, Pastor Hadley had to "lay out" on her stomach on the altar for several minutes to recover the strength that had gone out of her.

What was so clear in these episodes is that the body of the pastor really is God's vessel, and that the physicality of this contact among women is holy in a way that has little to do with concerns about respectability.

**Chatman:** Those relationships are very much like mother–daughter relationships. It's not just spiritual responsibility but a social responsibility that women have for younger women, especially when it comes to sexual modesty. They take a lot of care in protecting that. When a man lays hands on me there's always a female intercessor present, standing off to the side but in close proximity. There is a different kind of intimacy in the exchanges among women. It's always difficult to explain, but men and women have different kinds of vulnerabilities in the spirit realm. I've heard it explained that your gender leaves you vulnerable in different ways, makes you susceptible to different sorts of negative spirits. This justifies a type of policing.

**Klaits:** If that's the case, how would you characterize the kind of protection Pastor Hadley is providing to other senior women who are perhaps less spiritually mature than she is, since you are saying that women and men are vulnerable in different ways?

**Chatman:** Well, I think there's a mutual understanding that another woman has more of an empathy for the types of physical pain women experience, so they feel they have more license to touch you. As a woman who's receiving that deliverance or that healing, you also have to be open to allowing it to happen. You have to believe that you have this empathy with this other person who has the capacity to help you in your vulnerability. If a man is going to touch you even with the best of intentions, you are interested in your intimate space and you are more likely to feel vulnerable. In my experience, dealing with vulnerability is an important part of a successful healing or spiritual experience.

**Klaits:** Would you be willing to speak about your own experiences?

**Chatman:** I've had a lot of experiences with spiritual interventions and laying on of hands over almost thirty years. I have a very long history of autoimmune illnesses that develop into other things. I've had masses in my stomach, I've had issues with my heart and lungs and my GI tract, and I've had a type of mass in my breast—and they literally, I'm not kidding you, they disappeared. And during those experiences of laying on hands, or in other types of spiritual interventions, I know, to be completely honest, that I wasn't in full agreement—I don't want to say that I wasn't in spiritual alignment—but there was cynicism on my part about what was going on. Why lie about it? But I will say that in those moments when these transformations were happening I was fully conscious that something was happening in the spirit. And you can feel your body shifting. It sounds ridiculous, it sounds unbelievable, but I promise you it's absolutely true.

**Klaits:** And on those occasions, did you feel a kind of personal connection to the person laying hands on you such as I've described?

**Chatman:** I have, and sometimes it was honestly unwarranted. It wasn't that it was a horrible person, it's just that I don't like being that vulnerable. I like to suffer with some dignity but at some point, there is no more dignity in some of these things that are happening to your body. The people who are healing you sincerely want you to feel better, but part of participating is admitting that you're fallible or weak or that something's wrong and I did not like that. So that's where my resistance came from. And someone might say, oh that's the devil making you resist. Okay, whatever but in some cases it felt like a forced intimacy on their part because they very much wanted this for me and they did it with all good intentions because these are people who love me. I just didn't want to be vulnerable. This is really just a me thing. Most people are grateful and they love it and they go up to the altar for healing if they have a migraine.

**Klaits**: I understand it's hard to be called out. Like the time when a prophet asked me to stand up and told me that the devil is after my mind.

**Chatman:** Right.

**Klaits:** The thing is, I didn't need her to tell me that—I knew perfectly well. But I just want to conclude by saying how moved I am by the fact that you felt that reading my text helped you to reflect in new ways on your own faith journey.

**Chatman:** Thank you for chatting with me about this, no one asks. It's really helpful to be asked. It's been a trying time lately spiritually, so it's like therapy to check in.

# Notes

## 1 Designs for Vitality

1 The capitalization of racial/ethnic designations is a contested issue in the contemporary United States. I have opted not to capitalize the term "white" in keeping with the work it performs in designating a comparatively unmarked, hence privileged, social category. I capitalize "Black" in accordance with Lori Tharps's argument (2014) that "Ever since African people arrived in this country, we have had to fight for the right to a proper name." For the most part, I use the designations "Black" and "African American" interchangeably.

2 I follow the usual academic practice of not capitalizing pronouns referring to the divinity because I do not wish to impose upon readers who do not share Christian beliefs. However, I do capitalize these pronouns in direct quotes from believers, who use capitals in this fashion, though not all of them do so consistently. They rely on the King James Version of the Bible, which does not capitalize such pronouns. All biblical quotations are taken from the King James Version unless noted as NIV (New International Version), to which these church members also refer at times to elucidate the King James.

3 In conceptualizing enfleshment, Crawley follows Fred Moten's argument (2003) that because Black radical aesthetics dwell "in the break" between words, shouts, and shrieks of pain, they counter the Sausurrean abstraction of language from sounds, together with the forms of propriety and proprietorship that underpin that abstraction (see also Barrett 1999).

4 Such an awareness may not pertain in the same way in other Christian contexts. Apostolic Christians in Botswana, for instance, are acutely aware of how their well-being depends on how other people perceive them. For them, believing in God entails fostering love and countering possibilities of jealousy, which poses a continual danger to bodies and relationships (Klaits 2010). In this respect, theirs is a more socialized God than the transcendent being whom Hunt envisions.

5 By convention, the designation "first-wave" or "classical" refers to Pentecostal denominations founded in the first few decades following the Azusa Street revival in Los Angeles in 1906.

6 By contrast, Webb Keane (2016) argues on the basis of literature on child development that the capacity to adopt a third-person perspective, facilitated by linguistic and other semiotic forms, is essential to the ability to track one's "own

actions and purposes and those of another, to remain aware of the differences between them, and to grasp how they fit together" (64). Keane also points out that third-person stances are central to "morality systems" (Williams 1985), including piety movements, which are constructed by "self-conscious people who aspire to stand apart from the taken-for-granted flow of life in order to act upon it" (200).

7  I am employing the term "misrecognition" in a different way than Pierre Bourdieu (1990), although his treatment of symbolic violence is very apposite in this connection. My usage here is in line with Emmanuel Levinas's (1969) discussion of how one becomes a person by properly recognizing the other, acknowledging "You are, therefore I am." "You" might be God.

8  Anthony Pinn (2003) makes a similar point in writing of Black religion, Christian and otherwise, as a "quest for complex subjectivity" in the face of dehumanizing assaults. See CERCL Writing Collective (2017) for treatments of embodiment and lived religion from this perspective.

9  Hochschild depicts Jackie Tabor's faith as an aspect of an "endurance self." Faith induces Jackie to renounce what she might want at the present moment, and to leave eventual fulfillment to God. Hence she acknowledges the desirability of a clean environment but remarks, "You have to put up with the way things are … Pollution is the sacrifice we make for capitalism" (2016: 179).

10  Elisha describes the wonder that a pastor working in social outreach in Knoxville expressed when he told him of his research project: " 'You're blowing my mind here!' he kept saying … He relished the fact that someone other than himself was interested in studying 'what God is trying to do in Knoxville,' as he phrased it" (2011: 5).

11  A fruitful approach has been to examine how Christian temporalities of giving, asking, and receiving make relations of care visible and otherwise apprehensible to the senses (Klaits 2011; Scherz 2014, 2017; Zoanni 2019).

12  Intercession can take place outside the context of altar calls, for instance when God lets a believer know to pray for others in their absence. Further, not all laying on of hands constitutes intercession, which involves response to a need. For instance, believers may lay hands on one another to help them receive the Holy Ghost, a purpose distinct from recognizing their needs for prayer.

13  Pentecostal believers on the Copperbelt of Zambia articulate similar imperatives to "move by the Spirit," by which they mean to act in accordance with God's timing as distinct from their own will (Haynes 2017).

14  For a recording, consult https://www.youtube.com/watch?v=34GsV2bITzg (accessed January 29, 2020).

15  For a recording, consult https://www.youtube.com/watch?v=h-nviU6fUOs (accessed February 12, 2020).

16  For a recording, consult https://www.youtube.com/watch?v=CpBDxwCRbzk (accessed February 12, 2020).

17 Writing from a womanist theological standpoint, Douglas presents a "blues slant" on Jesus' life and teachings, arguing that "he refused to be domesticated" (2012: 143). She advances a trenchant critique of the exclusionary attitudes within many African American churches toward LGBTQ people, making the point that these tendencies derive from a broader "narrative of civility" that "is far too compatible with the very culture, systems, and ideologies that have disrespected black bodies" (xiii). For a foundational statement of womanist theology, see Grant (1989).

18 "Church mother" is an honorific title bestowed on the most elder and respected women, who like Mother Smith often sit at the rear of the church during services, observing saints' reactions from a perspective unavailable to the pastor at the front. C. Eric Lincoln and Lawrence Mamiya (1990) point out that the "phenomenon of the 'church mother' has no parallel in white churches; it is derived from the kinship network found within black churches and black communities" (275).

19 The Pentecostal believers among whom Elaine Lawless (1988) worked in rural Indiana made the same comparison.

20 In a culminating episode of *Go Tell It on the Mountain* ([1952] 2013), James Baldwin powerfully depicts a trance state in which the central character John Grimes hears a voice telling him to "go through" suffering so that he may be saved.

21 Some of the political contours of these designs for vitality begin to emerge when viewed in conjunction with those advanced in other religious movements that developed during the period of the Great Migration—including Father Divine's Peace Mission, the Commandment Keepers Ethiopian Hebrew Congregation, the Nation of Islam, and the Moorish Science Temple of America—which Judith Weisenfeld (2016: 5) characterizes as "religio-racial" in that practitioners "believed that understanding black people's true racial history revealed their correct and divinely ordained religious orientation" (see also Curtis and Sigler 2009). In each, leaders "worked to reshape racial meaning by challenging racial hierarchy, or sought to dismantle race altogether, seeking other bases for collective identity still rooted in shared African descent" (7). For adherents of these and comparable movements such as the African Hebrew Israelites of Jerusalem (Jackson 2013; Rouse, Jackson, and Frederick 2016), sustaining the vitality of the religio-racial body through healing and dietary practices has been key to maintaining sacred forms of ancestry and time. Writing of a non-Abrahamic religious movement, Elizabeth Pérez (2016) shows that as Lucumí initiates in Chicago prepare food, they recall and undergo forms of passage into captivity, being "made into the slaves of the spirits in order to be affirmed as priests" (201). Signaling the pervasiveness of tropes of "going through" in Afro-Diasporic religious traditions, Pérez (161–5) indicates the parallels between testifying about struggle before witnesses in Black churches and storytelling by Lucumí elders who tell initiates about how they have exacerbated their own difficulties by misunderstanding the will of the orishas.

The many controversies between and among leaders of these various movements and those of African American Pentecostal-Holiness churches reveal how dialogues about the sources and nature of vitality have shaped religio-racial pluralism. For example, Father Divine promoted vitality by providing sumptuous banquets to followers during the Great Depression as evidence of God's bounty, and by maintaining that "sin is the cause of all sickness and death. When one becomes afflicted and dies he has separated himself from God" (quoted in Weisenfeld 2016: 159). During the 1930s, Bishop Robert Lawson, founder of the COOLJC, consistently denounced Divine's "false promise of 'live and never die' " (270). This promise underpinned the obligations of Divine's followers to renounce familial attachments as a source of "physical, mental, and spiritual disease" (205) and to commit to celibacy and communal living. Lawson himself had broken in 1918 with G. T. Haywood, his mentor in the PAW, over Holiness standards concerning divorce and women's attire. Lawson insisted that women wear head coverings in church, and that a divorced person who remarried while his or her spouse was alive was guilty of adultery (Alexander 2011: 222–3). Lawson's thoughts about "producing a holy Black female personhood" (Casselberry 2017: 5) were an important basis for his argument that "God had deliberately created a mixed bloodline in Jesus—Hamitic, Semitic, and Japhetic" (56) through Mary. At the height of the Jim Crow era in 1925, Lawson advanced this claim in a work strikingly entitled *The Anthropology of Jesus Christ Our Kinsman (Dedicated to the Glory of God and to the Help of Solving the Race Problem)*. Reworking hegemonic "one drop of blood" ideologies of race and gender (Davis 1991), he placed "Black women *in* the body of Christ. … Black women did not merely have access to salvation; rather, the blood Jesus shed on the cross *was* their blood" (Casselberry 2017: 57).

22  For a recording of this song by Matt Redman, consult https://www.youtube.com/watch?v=frcVMNviUFI (accessed September 27, 2021).

23  I received all relevant permissions to carry out ethnographic research from the Institutional Review Board at the State University of New York at Buffalo.

24  In carrying out interviews during this phase of the project, we used a modified version of an approach adopted by Mary Abrums (2000, 2010) from Kristina Minister (1991). We distributed to participants a sheet of paper on which we had arranged a number of topics and invited them to discuss these topics "as if you were telling a testimony about your life." The topics included Spirituality, Development as a Woman/Man of God, Development as a Woman/Man, Sacrifice, Will of God, Finances, Tithes, Favor, Offering, Blessings, Who Do You Trust?, Illness, Disobedience, Healing, Racism, Who Helps You Manage?, Prayer, Generational Blessings and Curses, Trials and Tribulations, and Obedience.

25  For Pastor John, the term "spiritual parents" refers to elders in the faith, both male and female, in whom he confides and who have authority to discipline him (see

Chapter 2). He has been intrigued by my descriptions of my work in Botswana because of his interest in African history and society. He points out that one source of alienation for many Black youth is lack of knowledge about their African heritage.

26 For a report on this event, see https://www.new-directions.sps.ed.ac.uk/interview-klaits-pastor-john/ (accessed September 7, 2020).

27 Women in the African American community who are asked by friends to become their children's godmothers play important roles in childcare but do not necessarily provide spiritual insight. However, Pastor Hadley recounted in an interview how her own godmother's discernment helped to authorize the prayer group she led before becoming a pastor. Her account illustrates some of the careful linguistic moves through which believers indicate that they have attained positions of authority by God's will rather than their own. She had informed her godmother that she would be traveling from Buffalo to another city for a revival with two other women. Her godmother replied, "I don't see just two women—I see a line of women." She did not want to be burdened, so she demurred:

> "Oh no, you don't see no line of women with me." I said, "Uhn uhn. I don't need it." But it was a total of eighteen women that followed me out of the city and they had an awesome experience so when we came back—and I was very careful, I only asked them what the Lord led me to ask—when we came back they gathered together and because they had such an awesome time they said, "Sister Hadley, why don't you have a conference [a revival] in Buffalo?"

28 In African American Pentecostal churches, the prestigious title "Apostle" is usually reserved for pastors who have trained ministers with congregations of their own. Subordinate pastors, together with members of their congregations, commonly attend revivals sponsored by their Apostles each year. Every pastor, Apostles included, is said to need an "Overseer," another minister who will advise them, "cover" them in prayer, and "correct" them when necessary. For a discussion of women's ordination in Black churches, see Fry Brown (2003).

## 2 Being in the World but Not of It in Buffalo: Insights Derived from Places

1 While only 13.5 percent of housing stock in the United States as a whole was constructed before 1940, 63 percent of homes in the city of Buffalo are of that age or older. By comparison, the proportion of housing built before 1940 in Baltimore is 44 percent, in Boston 55 percent, in Cleveland 54 percent, in Chicago 46 percent, and in New York City 42 percent. Source: https://www.governing.com/gov-data/tra

nsportation-infrastructure/age-year-built-for-homes-in-cities.html (accessed August 10, 2020).

2 Source: https://www.infoplease.com/us/us-cities/population-20-largest-us-cit ies-1900-2012 (accessed June 28, 2020).

3 Source: https://en.wikipedia.org/wiki/Demographics_of_Buffalo,_New_York (accessed August 13, 2021).

4 Source: https://www.wgrz.com/article/news/local/erie-county-populat ion-grew-for-first-time-in-decades/71-84df3983-72c5-4fce-b804-2c727219ea37 (accessed August 13, 2021).

5 Source: https://ppgbuffalo.org/files/documents/data-demographics-history/demogr aphics_and_data/datademographicshistory-_profile_of_buffalo_and_its_region.pdf (accessed June 28, 2020).

6 An index of dissimilarity is an assessment of the evenness with which two groups are distributed across components of a given geographic area. Source: http:// www.censusscope.org/us/rank_dissimilarity_white_black.html (accessed June 28, 2020).

7 Source: https://www.census.gov/quickfacts/buffalocitynewyork (accessed August 13, 2021). These figures add up to more than 100 percent, perhaps because some respondents classified themselves in multiple ways.

8 The officially recorded wage gap between formally employed white and Black male workers in the United States has narrowed since 1950, shrinking substantially during the 1960s and 1970s but remaining largely stable afterward. In 1950, the median wage of Black male workers was 57 percent of the median wage of white male workers, while by 2014 that ratio had increased to 67 percent. However, these measures do not include people who are unemployed or incarcerated. More comprehensive analyses taking these groups into account show that for every $1 earned by white men in 2014, Black men were earning $0.51, shockingly the same ratio as in 1950. High incarceration rates contribute to high unemployment rates, since it is often difficult for people with criminal records to find jobs (Fader 2013). The period when the comprehensively measured wage gap expanded most dramatically was in the aftermath of the housing crisis of 2008, when people of color suffered disproportionate job losses (Leonhardt 2020).

9 Kraus argues (2000: 7):

The Great Migration of southern blacks to northern cities, post-World War II suburbanization, and deindustrialization, all became important factors in shaping the evolution of urban politics. But there is no necessary connection between these macro-population and economic changes and the development of ghetto neighborhoods, nor indeed do these trends suffice to account for ghetto development without the decisive influence of local politics.

10 Source: https://nlihc.org/resource/report-shows-african-americans-lost-half-their-wealth-due-housing-crisis-and-unemployment (accessed June 29, 2020).

11 A more inclusive antidiscrimination ordinance was finally passed in 2006, but it continues to make exemptions for rentals in owner-occupied properties, as well as for rentals to same-sex partners. Source: Buffalo City Code Part II, Article IV, §154–18, https://ecode360.com/13584190 (accessed July 8, 2020).

12 While Pastor John and Pastor Hadley readily let others know that they are saved, they are more reluctant to inform acquaintances in non-church contexts that they are pastors. This reticence stems from their understanding that God will "send a messenger" appropriate for a given person, and that they are not called to minister to everyone. However, they do approach strangers if they feel led by God to speak to them about their circumstances.

13 For instance, Christine recalled that First Lady had advised her not to become upset at a scolding Tony had given her two children from her first marriage:

> I might not agree with a certain way that he'll talk to the kids, and she'll just basically tell me like, you know: "The Lord's not gonna let anything happen to these children. They're His children. He's not gonna let anyone hurt them." … It's not to harm them, it's just, you know, to make them stronger. To teach [my son] how to be a man of God, and teach him how to act right and not be acting a fool. There's kids out here that act horrible.

14 Pastor Hadley preaches that the legalization of same-sex marriage unleashed "the spirit of murder" in that such unions do not (in her view) produce children. Mainly concerned about women who have relations with other women, she suggests that they are not giving birth to the children whom they might have conceived with men.

15 Source: https://www.thepartnership.org/wp-content/uploads/2019/01/Opioid-Epidemic-Final-Presentation.pdf (accessed July 16, 2020).

## 3 Openings and Enclosures: Designs for Communication and Care

1 Writing of African American praise dancers in New York City, Elisha (2018) notes that "smiles and facial manipulations are performative devices, but they do not violate Christian ethics of transparency. Their purpose is to make visible a higher level of intention, one based not just on how a dancer feels but on how she is being moved and directed to make others feel" (387).

2 This particular style of laying on hands is not considered "intercession," but rather a means of inviting the Holy Ghost. Intercession involves asking God to fulfill a

particular need, whereas trying to "receive the Holy Ghost" entails a more general expression of repentance and willingness to devote one's life to God.

3   At Eternal Hope, believers usually refer to adults as "Brother" or "Sister" followed by a surname. At Victory Gospel and Heaven's Tabernacle only pastors and other leaders are called by their surnames, while ordinary saints address one another as "Brother" or "Sister" followed by a first name. In this text, I retain prestigious titles such as Pastor, Apostle, Mother, or Elder, but in order to prevent awkwardness have opted not to refer to ordinary saints by the titles Brother or Sister.

4   I am grateful to an anonymous reviewer for making this point clear to me.

5   While members of Eternal Hope likewise commonly pray so as to "cover in Jesus' blood" those who are in need, they do not attribute a special role to Pastor Charles in extending covering.

6   Those who give gifts of money and labor are very often described as "being a blessing" to the recipient. As I understand it, this phrasing conveys the humility of the giver by framing the act more in terms of God's purposes than in terms of individual volition.

7   Using a metaphor of policing to describe deliverance, Pastor John explains that having spiritual "power" is like possessing a gun, while the office of pastor is the badge that gives him the "authority" to use it.

8   Source: https://aandbcounseling.com/10-indicators-spirit-of-rejection-tormenting/ (accessed April 3, 2020).

9   A New Orleans resident named Danielle told Rebecca Carter (2019) that she had been expecting the incarceration or death of a son who was involved in drug dealing, so that she "prayed and asked God to give me the strength when that phone rang." Carter comments:

> As she continued to speak, it became apparent that the source of Danielle's strength was also tied to the knowledge she possessed, gained from experience and an awareness of how the world worked … This was not separate from the strength and knowledge she attributed to God; rather, it stemmed from a belief that God supported her through death and mourning, and this gave her the capacity to stand and to support and strengthen others. (36)

10  Pastor Hadley works to establish comparable forms of "connection." Toward the end of a service at Heaven's Tabernacle, she told a musician: "The devil tried to afflict you with the spirit of depression because he knows if he can block the ministry of music, nothing can happen in the temple" (see Chapter 5). "But what the devil didn't know is that you're connected with me!" After speaking with and laying her hands on a female visitor who approached the altar, she announced, "If you're a woman and have lumps, the Lord is trying to get your attention!" She told this woman to go to the bathroom; when she returned, she reported that she could not

feel a lump anymore. Pastor Hadley then asked her daughter Cheryl, a prophet, to come forward and praise God for the visitor; Cheryl held her hand and began to dance a rapid, forceful two-step. Afterward, Cheryl explained to me that because the visitor did not have a relationship with God, she needed someone to praise him on her behalf, an act that required a tactile connection. Likewise, when a believer wishes to make a monetary offering but has no money with her, another person may offer to hold some cash with her as they approach the collection basket together.

11 A large popular Christian literature highlights how dangerous spiritual connections may be forged not only in "the world" but within the church as well, for instance *Seductions Exposed* (Greenwald 1988), *Witchcraft in the Pews* (Bloomer 1996), and *Pastor or Pimp?* (Matthews 2013).

## 4 Depending on God: Designs for Personal Value

1 I am grateful to Hillary Kaell for making this point clear to me.
2 The Catholic Charismatic believers described by Csordas (1994) likewise regard prayer as a means of alleviating painful childhood memories.
3 Commenting on a white working-class woman's narrative about African American men "using" white women in Detroit, John Hartigan Jr. (2005) points out that while the "racial aspect of her reading is evident, … it is subsumed within a more fundamental class logic of treating all social relations as manipulative" (223–4).
4 Hunt (1995) encourages readers to evaluate their "mental state" on a set of continuums, for instance, "Wanting to get even—Praying for enemies," "Reliance on self—Reliance on God," and "Addicted to television—Devoted to prayer" (4–5). He then provides a set of "Indications of Continuing Growth," including "I am becoming more conscious of God throughout the day," "I interpret my circumstances in the realization that God is always with me," and "I respond immediately when God speaks to me" (15).

## 5 Seeking Confirmation: Designs for Events

1 In *Black Gods of the Asphalt*, Woodbine refers to Donna Haskins as Dora.
2 In *Take Back What the Devil Stole* (2021), Woodbine quotes Donna Haskins's account of how she questioned her own motives upon first hearing the Holy Ghost speak to her through a Baptist minister's sermon:

> "He said, 'If that man ain't treating you no good, kick him to the curb. If you've done all that you can, then they don't deserve you.' Then I heard him

say, 'Did you stop to think, to see if he's worthy of you?' Made me question me! I questioned me!" Donna exclaimed, surprised by the first time she questioned gendered constructions of herself and the world. (111)

3 For a recording of "I Love You Lord Today," consult https://www.youtube.com/watch?v=_zj5nQ04sWM. For "Here I Am to Worship," consult https://www.youtube.com/watch?v=YXg2ztge8f0 (accessed September 20, 2020).

4 For a recording of this song by Israel Houghton, consult https://www.youtube.com/watch?v=QWQ6Z8LpPso (accessed October 18, 2020).

5 This question is a slight alteration of Ps. 11:3, "If the foundations be destroyed, what can the righteous do?"

6 The minister here made implicit reference to a passage in Martin Luther King Jr.'s "I Have a Dream" speech (1963).

7 Elsewhere (Klaits 2017a) I elaborate on this point in light of David Graeber's (2005) discussion of "fetishism" as social creativity.

8 Woodbine (2021: 175–8) relates how the prophet Donna Haskins needed to learn how to discern future, past, and present events she perceives in the spirit world.

9 US Federal Trade Commission, Consumer Information. Source: https://www.consumer.ftc.gov/articles/0215-co-signing-loan (accessed August 18, 2020).

10 Buffalo is well known as a center of the quasi-legal debt collection industry (Halpern 2014).

## Conclusion: Ethics and Politics of Pious Vitality

1 This point has been made in many critical treatments of secularism, for instance Lucinda Ramberg's (2014) discussion of how the Indian state has criminalized marriages to the goddess Yellamma in an effort to create "proper subjects of privatized sex, personal devotion, and respectable religion" (221).

2 To be sure, Arlene's struggles with her "manipulative" ex-husband were central to her account of how she developed a relationship with God. Far from understanding divine presence as unequivocally soothing, she attributed a key episode in her divorce, namely her decision to look inside her ex-husband's briefcase, to God's instructions. Yet in contrast to Pastor Hadley, who spoke of her pain at her ex-husband's betrayal as having been designed by God as a comeuppance for her own previous sins, Arlene narrated her suffering over the course of her divorce not as a central element so much as a by-product of divine plans. For instance, God revealed to Arlene that her relationship with her ex-husband had been "idolatrous." She did not conclude, however, that God intended her to reap what she had sown in her "idolatry," but rather that God was showing her that her relationship with him needed to take precedence over her marriage.

3 In contrast with Povinelli, Mattingly (2010) discerns connections between present suffering and prospects for future betterment in practices of hope, which constitute "an imaginative space marked by temporal uncertainty. One waits in a [hospital] lobby not only for a person, a place, an activity, or some news, but for the future itself" (14). While the eschatological frames always present in Pentecostal churches do diminish "temporal uncertainty," such moves as seeking confirmation, sowing into people, and learning how to make requests of God call the nature of time consistently into question. The element of salvation, though, induces believers to assess the legitimacy of their practices of hope (cf. Mattingly 2014b) with an eye to the divine third person, whose designs lend these assessments a specific set of critical casts.

4 I am grateful to Gillian Feeley-Harnik for bringing this point to my attention.

5 Ideals of positive liberty have historically provided justifications for modern authoritarianism. To quote Laidlaw's summary (2014: 144) of Berlin's argument:

> Once the idea of the self that is to realize the objective good is subjected to "metaphysical fission" into higher and lower parts ([Berlin] 2002: 36), and the former identified with some "greater" entity such as the state, society, race, or common good ([Berlin] 2002: 37, 180), then the concept of positive liberty becomes an astonishingly reliable and flexible resource in the justification of tyranny.

In US political discourse, the metaphysical fission of the self into "responsible" and "irresponsible" elements has provided a highly reliable tool for justifying oligarchical and white-supremacist power (MacLean 2017).

On the other hand, Wendy Brown (2015) also argues that religious commitments foster aspirations for positive freedom, but the conclusions she derives have quite different political implications. Like Laidlaw, she points out that "religious freedom is not freedom in the liberal sense but instead a switch point between submission to political and religious authority, or political and religious communities" (326). Yet Brown demonstrates that the examples of the political freedom fighters Socrates and Martin Luther King, Jr. "problematize the classic liberal binary between freedom and authority and the secular line between private and public" (331). For both Socrates and King, freedom "is exercised in the choice of virtuous or ethical existence over everyday comforts, satisfactions, and feeding of desires ... Those who remain enslaved to concern with comfort or personal desires will neither be free nor set the world free" (330). At least for King, though, both "the authority of the divine and the 'common sense' of democracy ... test any given law's justice or rightness. This, of course, converts God to being a democrat and promulgating democracy, which is no minor conversion" (329).

# Appendix: Commentaries and Conversations

1 Source: https://www.youtube.com/watch?v=hHm-rJ_VmmE (accessed January 27, 2021).

2 "Talkin' proud" was the slogan of a 1980s-era public relations campaign sponsored by the city of Buffalo intended to boost the economy following the closures of local steel mills.

# References

Abrums, M. (2000), "'Jesus Will Fix It after Awhile': Meanings and Health," *Social Science and Medicine*, 50 (1): 89–105.

Abrums, M. (2010), *Moving the Rock: Poverty and Faith in a Black Storefront Church*, Lanham, MD: AltaMira Press.

Alexander, E. (2011), *Black Fire: One Hundred Years of African American Pentecostalism*, Downers Grove, IL: IVP Academic.

Alexander, M. (2010), *The New Jim Crow: Mass Incarceration in the Age of Colorblindness*, New York: New Press.

*American Gospel: Christ Alone* (2019), [Film] B. Kimber (dir.), USA: American Gospel Motion Picture, LLC, AG2 Motion Picture, LLC.

Anderson, E. (1999), *Code of the Street: Decency, Violence, and the Moral Life of the Inner City*, New York: W. W. Norton.

Anderson, R. M. (1979), *Vision of the Disinherited: The Making of American Pentecostalism*, New York: Oxford University Press.

Badiou, A. (2003), *Saint Paul: The Foundation of Universalism*, trans. R. Brassier, Stanford, CA: Stanford University Press.

Badiou, A. (2006), *Being and Event*, trans. O. Feltham, London: Continuum.

Baker, K. (2011), *Gospel according to the Klan: The KKK's Appeal to Protestant America, 1915-1930*, Lawrence: University Press of Kansas.

Baldwin, J. (1963), *The Fire Next Time*, New York: Dial Press.

Baldwin, J. ([1952] 2013), *Go Tell It on the Mountain*, New York: Vintage International.

Baradaran, M. (2017), *The Color of Money: Black Banks and the Racial Wealth Gap*, Cambridge, MA: Belknap Press of Harvard University Press.

Barrett, L. (1999), *Blackness and Value: Seeing Double*, Cambridge: Cambridge University Press.

Bassett, L. (1995), *From Panic to Power: Proven Techniques to Calm Your Anxieties, Conquer Your Fears, and Put You in Control of Your Life*, New York: HarperCollins.

Bear, L. (2016), "Time as Technique," *Annual Review of Anthropology*, 45: 487–502.

Beauboeuf-Lafontant, T. (2007), "'You Have to Show Strength': An Exploration of Gender, Race, and Depression," *Gender and Society*, 21 (1): 28–51.

Beauboeuf-Lafontant, T. (2009), *Behind the Mask of the Strong Black Woman: Voice and the Embodiment of a Costly Performance*, Philadelphia, PA: Temple University Press.

Berlin, I. (2002), *Liberty*, Oxford: Oxford University Press.

Best, W. D. (2005), *Passionately Human, No Less Divine: Religion and Culture in Black Chicago, 1915–1952*, Princeton, NJ: Princeton University Press.

Bialecki, J. (2014), "Does God Exist in Methodological Atheism?: On Tanya Lurhmann's *When God Talks Back* and Bruno Latour," *Anthropology of Consciousness*, 25 (1): 32–52.

Bialecki, J. (2017), *A Diagram for Fire: Miracles and Variation in an American Charismatic Movement*, Oakland: University of California Press.

Bielo, J. S. (2009), *Words upon the Word: An Ethnography of Evangelical Group Bible Study*, New York: New York University Press.

Bielo, J. S. (2011), "'How Much of This Is Promise?': God as Sincere Speaker in Evangelical Bible Reading," *Anthropological Quarterly*, 84 (3): 631–53.

Bjork-James, S. (2018), "Training the Porous Body: Evangelicals and the Ex-Gay Movement," *American Anthropologist*, 120 (4): 647–58.

Bloomer, G. (1996), *Witchcraft in the Pews*, Lanham, MD: Pneuma Life Publishing.

Bourdieu, P. (1990), *The Logic of Practice*, trans. R. Nice, Stanford, CA: Stanford University Press.

Bourgois, P. I. (1995), *In Search of Respect: Selling Crack in El Barrio*, Cambridge: Cambridge University Press.

Bowler, K. (2013), *Blessed: A History of the American Prosperity Gospel*, New York: Oxford University Press.

Brahinsky, J. (2012), "Pentecostal Body Logics: Cultivating a Modern Sensorium," *Cultural Anthropology*, 27 (2): 215–38.

Brown, W. (2015), "Religious Freedom's Oxymoronic Edge," in Winnifred Fallers Sullivan, Elizabeth Shakman Hurd, Saba Mahmood, and Peter G. Danchin (eds.), *Politics of Religious Freedom*, 324–34, Chicago: University of Chicago Press.

Bullard, R. D., G. S. Johnson, and A. O. Torres, eds. (2004), *Highway Robbery: Transportation Racism and New Routes to Equity*, Cambridge, MA: South End Press.

Butler, A. D. (2007), *Women in the Church of God in Christ: Making a Sanctified World*, Chapel Hill: University of North Carolina Press.

Butler, A. (2021), *White Evangelical Racism: The Politics of Morality in America*, Chapel Hill: University of North Carolina Press.

Calvin, J. (1960), *Institutes of the Christian Religion*, trans. F. L. Battles, J. T. McNeill (ed.), Philadelphia, PA: Westminster Press.

Calvin, J. (1996), *The Second Epistle of Paul the Apostle to the Corinthians and the Epistles to Timothy, Titus and Philemon*, trans. T. A. Smail, D. W. Torrance, and T. F. Torrance (eds.), Grand Rapids, MI: William B. Eerdmans.

Calvin, J. (2008), *Institutes of the Christian Religion*, trans. H. Beveridge, Peabody, MA: Hendrickson Publishers.

Cannon, K. G. ([1988] 2006), *Black Womanist Ethics*, 2nd ed., Eugene, OR: Wipf and Stock Publishers.

Cannon, K. G., E. M. Townes, and A. D. Sims, eds. (2011), *Womanist Theological Ethics: A Reader*, Louisville, KY: Westminster John Knox Press.

Carothers, S. (1990), "Catching Sense: Learning from Our Mothers to Be Black and Female," in F. Ginsburg and A. L. Tsing (eds.), *Uncertain Terms: Negotiating Gender in American Culture*, 232–47, Boston, MA: Beacon Press.

Carter, R. L. (2019), *Prayers for the People: Homicide and Humanity in the Crescent City*, Chicago: University of Chicago Press.

Casselberry, J. (2017), *The Labor of Faith: Gender and Power in Black Apostolic Pentecostalism*, Durham, NC: Duke University Press.

CERCL Writing Collective (2014), *Breaking Bread, Breaking Beats: Churches and Hip-Hop—A Basic Guide to the Key Issues*, Minneapolis, MN: Fortress Press.

CERCL Writing Collective (2017), *Embodiment and Black Religion: Rethinking the Body in African American Religious Experience*, Sheffield, UK: Equinox Publishing.

Chappell, D. L. (2004), *A Stone of Hope: Prophetic Religion and the Death of Jim Crow*, Chapel Hill: University of North Carolina Press.

Chipumuro, T. T. (2014), "Pastor, Mentor, or Father?: The Contested Intimacies of the Eddie Long Sex Abuse Scandal," *Journal of Africana Religions*, 2 (1): 1–30.

Coates, T.-N. (2015), *Between the World and Me*, New York: Spiegel & Grau.

Cole, J. B., and B. Guy-Sheftall (2003), *Gender Talk: The Struggle for Women's Equality in African American Communities*, New York: Ballantine Books.

Coleman, S. (2004), "The Charismatic Gift," *Journal of the Royal Anthropological Institute*, 10 (4): 421–42.

Coleman, S. (2006), "Materializing the Self: Words and Gifts in the Construction of Charismatic Protestant Identity," in F. Cannell (ed.), *Anthropology of Christianity*, 163–84, Durham, NC: Duke University Press.

Coleman, S. (2011), "Prosperity Unbound? Debating the 'Sacrificial Economy'," *Research in Economic Anthropology*, 31: 23–45.

Coleman, S. (2015), "Borderlands: Ethics, Ethnography, and 'Repugnant' Christianity," *HAU: Journal of Ethnographic Theory*, 5 (2): 275–300.

Coleman, S., and J. Dulin (2020), "Secrecy, Religion, and the Ethics of Discernment," *Ethnos*, 1–14.- DOI: 10.1080/00141844.2020.1765831.

Collier-Thomas, B. (2010), *Jesus, Jobs, and Justice: African American Women and Religion*, New York: Alfred A. Knopf.

Collins, P. H. (1994), "Shifting the Center: Race, Class, and Feminist Theorizing about Motherhood," in E. N. Glenn, G. Chang, and L. R. Forcey (eds.), *Mothering: Ideology, Experience, and Agency*, 45–65, New York: Routledge.

Collins, P. H. (2000), *Black Feminist Thought: Knowledge, Consciousness, and the Politics of Empowerment*, New York: Routledge.

Collins, P. H. (2004), *Black Sexual Politics: African Americans, Gender, and the New Racism*, New York: Routledge.

Cone, J. H. (2011), *The Cross and the Lynching Tree*, Maryknoll, NY: Orbis Books.

Coontz, S. (1992), *The Way We Never Were: American Families and the Nostalgia Trap*, New York: Basic Books.

Crawford, E. E. (1995), *The Hum: Call and Response in African American Preaching*, Nashville, TN: Abingdon Press.

Crawley, A. T. (2017), *Blackpentecostal Breath: The Aesthetics of Possibility*, New York: Fordham University Press.

Crumbley, D. H. (2012), *Saved and Sanctified: The Rise of a Storefront Church in Great Migration Philadelphia*, Gainesville: University Press of Florida.

Csordas, T. J. (1994), *The Sacred Self: A Cultural Phenomenology of Charismatic Healing*, Berkeley: University of California Press.

Csordas, T. J. (1997), *Language, Charisma, and Creativity: The Ritual Life of a Religious Movement*, Berkeley: University of California Press.

Csordas, T. J. (2004), "Asymptote of the Ineffable: Embodiment, Alterity, and the Theory of Religion," *Current Anthropology*, 45 (2): 163–85.

Currid-Halkett, E. (2017), *The Sum of Small Things: A Theory of the Aspirational Class*, Princeton, NJ: Princeton University Press.

Curtis, E. E. IV, and D. B. Sigler, eds. (2009), *The New Black Gods: Arthur Huff Fauset and the Study of African American Religions*, Bloomington: Indiana University Press.

Curtis, J. (2021), *The Myth of Colorblind Christians: Evangelicals and White Supremacy in the Civil Rights Era*, New York: New York University Press.

Darity, W. J., D. Hamilton, M. Paul, A. Aja, A. Price, A. Moore, and C. Chiopris (2018), *What We Get Wrong about Closing the Racial Wealth Gap*, Samuel DuBois Cook Center on Social Equity at Duke University and Insight Center for Community Economic Development. Available online: https://socialequity.duke.edu/wp-content/uploads/2019/10/what-we-get-wrong.pdf (accessed October 25, 2020).

Daswani, G. (2015), "A Prophet but Not for Profit: Ethical Value and Character in Ghanaian Pentecostalism," *Journal of the Royal Anthropological Institute*, 22 (1): 108–26.

Davis, D.-A. (2006), *Battered Black Women and Welfare Reform: Between a Rock and a Hard Place*, Albany: State University of New York Press.

Davis, F. J. (1991), *Who Is Black?: One Nation's Definition*, University Park: Pennsylvania State University Press.

Davis, G. L. (1985), *I Got the Word in Me and I Can Sing It, You Know: A Study of the Performed African American Sermon*, Philadelphia: University of Pennsylvania Press.

Day, K. (2014), *Faith on the Avenue: Religion on a City Street*, New York: Oxford University Press.

Deleuze, G. (2001), *Pure Immanence: Essays on a Life*, New York and Cambridge, MA: Zone Books and MIT Press.

Desmond, M. (2016), *Evicted: Poverty and Profit in the American City*, New York: Crown Publishers.

Dickinson, M. (2016), "Working for Food Stamps: Economic Citizenship and the Post-Fordist Welfare State in New York City," *American Ethnologist*, 43 (2): 270–81.

Douglas, K. B. (2012), *Black Bodies and the Black Church: A Blues Slant*, New York: Palgrave Macmillan.

Du Bois, W. E. B. ([1903] 1990), *The Souls of Black Folk*. New York: Vintage Books.

Du Mez, K. K. (2020), *Jesus and John Wayne: How White Evangelicals Corrupted a Faith and Shattered a Nation*, New York: Liveright Publishing Corporation.

Duck, W. (2015), *No Way Out: Precarious Living in the Shadow of Poverty and Drug Dealing*, Chicago: University of Chicago Press.

Dupont, C. R. (2013), *Mississippi Praying: Southern White Evangelicals and the Civil Rights Movement, 1945–1975*, New York: New York University Press.

Elisha, O. (2008), "Moral Ambitions of Grace: The Paradox of Compassion and Accountability in Evangelical Faith-Based Activism," *Cultural Anthropology*, 23 (1): 154–89.

Elisha, O. (2011), *Moral Ambition: Mobilization and Social Outreach in Evangelical Megachurches*, Berkeley: University of California Press.

Elisha, O. (2018), "Dancing the Word: Techniques of Embodied Authority among Christian Praise Dancers in New York City," *American Ethnologist*, 45 (3): 380–91.

Ellison, R. ([1952] 1995), *Invisible Man*, New York: Vintage Books.

Emerson, M. O., and C. Smith (2000), *Divided by Faith: Evangelical Religion and the Problem of Race in America*, Oxford: Oxford University Press.

Engelke, M. (2004), "Discontinuity and the Discourse of Conversion," *Journal of Religion in Africa*, 34 (1/2): 82–109.

Engelke, M. (2007), *A Problem of Presence: Beyond Scripture in an African Church*, Berkeley: University of California Press.

Erickson, M. J. (1998), *Christian Theology*, Grand Rapids, MI: Baker Academic.

Fader, J. J. (2013), *Falling Back: Incarceration and Transitions to Adulthood among Urban Youth*, New Brunswick, NJ: Rutgers University Press.

Feeley-Harnik, G. ([1981] 1994), *The Lord's Table: The Meaning of Food in Early Judaism and Christianity*, 2nd ed., Washington, DC: Smithsonian Institution Press.

Fernandez, J. (1982), "The Dark at the Bottom of the Stairs: The Inchoate in Symbolic Inquiry and Some Strategies for Coping with It," in J. Maquet (ed.), *On Symbols in Anthropology: Essays in Honor of Harry Hoijer*, 13–43, Malibu, CA: Undena Publications.

Forman, J. Jr. (2017), *Locking Up Our Own: Crime and Punishment in Black America*, New York: Farrar, Straus and Giroux.

Foucault, M. ([1984] 1990), *The History of Sexuality, Volume 2: The Use of Pleasure*, trans. R. Hurley, New York: Vintage.

Frederick, M. F. (2003), *Between Sundays: Black Women and Everyday Struggles of Faith*, Berkeley: University of California Press.

Frederick, M. F. (2016), *Colored Television: American Religion Gone Global*, Stanford, CA: Stanford University Press.

Fretheim, T. E. (1996), *The Pentateuch*, Nashville, TN: Abingdon Press.

Fry Brown, T. L. (2003), *Weary Throats and New Songs: Black Women Proclaiming God's Word*, Nashville, TN: Abingdon Press.

Gates, H. L. (1988), *The Signifying Monkey: A Theory of Afro-American Literary Criticism*, New York: Oxford University Press.

Gilkes, C. T. (2001), *If It Wasn't for the Women...: Black Women's Experience and Womanist Culture in Church and Community*, Maryknoll, NY: Orbis Books.

Gilpin, D. R. (2020), "NRA Media and Second Amendment Identity Politics," in A. Nadler and A. J. Bauer (eds.), *News on the Right: Studying Conservative News Cultures*, 84–105, Oxford: Oxford University Press.

Goldberg, M. (2006), *Kingdom Coming: The Rise of Christian Nationalism*, New York: W. W. Norton.

Goldman, M. (2007), *City on the Edge: Buffalo, New York*, Amherst, NY: Prometheus Books.

Goluboff, S. (2011), "Making African American Homeplaces in Rural Virginia," *Ethos*, 39 (3): 368–94.

Gorman, T. J. (2017), *Growing Up Working Class: Hidden Injuries and the Development of Angry White Men and Women*, New York: Palgrave Macmillan.

Graeber, D. (2005), "Fetishism as Social Creativity: Or, Fetishes Are Gods in the Process of Construction," *Anthropological Theory*, 5 (4): 407–38.

Grant, J. (1989), *White Women's Christ and Black Women's Jesus: Feminist Christology and Womanist Response*, Atlanta, GA: Scholars Press.

Greenwald, G. L. (1988), *Seductions Exposed: The Spiritual Dynamics of Relationships*, New Kensington, PA: Whitaker House.

Griffith, R. M. (1997), *God's Daughters: Evangelical Women and the Power of Submission*, Berkeley: University of California Press.

Griffith, R. M. (2004), *Born Again Bodies: Flesh and Spirit in American Christianity*, Berkeley: University of California Press.

Griffith, R. M. (2017), *Moral Combat: How Sex Divided American Christians and Fractured American Politics*, New York: Basic Books.

Guyer, J. (2007), "Prophecy and the Near Future: Thoughts on Macroeconomic, Evangelical, and Punctuated Time," *American Ethnologist*, 34 (3): 409–21.

Halpern, J. (2014), *Bad Paper: Chasing Debt from Wall Street to the Underworld*, New York: Farrar, Straus and Giroux.

Hammond, F., and I. M. Hammond ([1973] 2010), *Pigs in the Parlor: A Practical Guide to Deliverance*, Kirkwood, MO: Impact Christian Books.

Hannah-Jones, N. (2020), "What Is Owed," *New York Times Magazine*, June 30. Available online: https://www.nytimes.com/interactive/2020/06/24/magazine/repa rations-slavery.html?searchResultPosition=3 (accessed December 17, 2021).

Hardin, J. A. (2019), *Faith and the Pursuit of Health: Cardiometabolic Disorders in Samoa*, New Brunswick, NJ: Rutgers University Press.

Harding, S. F. (2000), *The Book of Jerry Falwell: Fundamentalist Language and Politics*, Princeton, NJ: Princeton University Press.

Harrison, F. V. (2008), *Outsider Within: Reworking Anthropology in the Global Age*, Urbana: University of Illinois Press.

Harrison, M. F. (2005), *Righteous Riches: The Word of Faith Movement in Contemporary African American Religion*, Oxford: Oxford University Press.

Hartigan, J. J. (2005), *Odd Tribes: Toward a Cultural Analysis of White People*, Durham, NC: Duke University Press.

Harvey, J. (2014), *Dear White Christians: For Those Still Longing for Racial Reconciliation*, Grand Rapids, MI: William B. Eerdmans.

Haynes, N. (2013), "On the Potential and Problems of Pentecostal Exchange," *American Anthropologist*, 115 (1): 85–95.

Haynes, N. (2015), "Egalitarianism and Hierarchy in Copperbelt Religious Practice," *Religion*, 45 (2): 273–92.

Haynes, N. (2017), *Moving by the Spirit: Pentecostal Social Life on the Zambian Copperbelt*, Oakland: University of California Press.

Haynes, N. (2020), "The Expansive Present: A New Model of Christian Time," *Current Anthropology*, 61 (1): 57–76.

Higginbotham, E. B. (1993), *Righteous Discontent: The Women's Movement in the Black Baptist Church, 1880–1920*, Cambridge, MA: Harvard University Press.

Hinson, G. (2000), *Fire in My Bones: Transcendence and the Holy Spirit in African American Gospel*, Philadelphia: University of Pennsylvania Press.

Hirschkind, C. (2006), *The Ethical Soundscape: Cassette Sermons and Islamic Counterpublics*, New York: Columbia University Press.

Hochschild, A. R. (2016), *Strangers in Their Own Land: Anger and Mourning on the American Right*, New York: New Press.

Hodges, B. (2020), "As Mayor of Minneapolis, I Saw How White Liberals Block Change," *New York Times*, July 9. Available online: https://www.nytimes.com/2020/07/09/opinion/minneapolis-hodges-racism.html (accessed December 17, 2021).

hooks, b. (1992), *Black Looks: Race and Representation*, Boston, MA: South End Press.

hooks, b. (2004), *We Real Cool: Black Men and Masculinity*, New York: Routledge.

Hovland, I. (2016), 'Christianity, Place/Space, and Anthropology: Thinking Across Recent Research on Evangelical Place-Making', *Religion* 46 (3): 331–58.

Humphrey, C. (2008), "Reassembling Individual Subjects: Events and Decisions in Troubled Times," *Anthropological Theory*, 8 (4): 357–80.

Hunt, T. W. (1995), *The Mind of Christ: The Transforming Power of Thinking His Thoughts*, Nashville, TN: B & H Publishing Group.

Jackson, J. L. Jr. (2001), *Harlemworld: Doing Race and Class in Contemporary Black America*, Chicago: University of Chicago Press.

Jackson, J. L. Jr. (2013), *Thin Description: Ethnography and the African Hebrew Israelites of Jerusalem*, Cambridge, MA: Harvard University Press.

Jackson, J. L. Jr. (2015), "Peter Piper Picked Peppers, but Humpty Dumpty Got Pushed: The Productively Paranoid Stylings of Hip-Hop's Spirituality," in M. R. Miller and A. B. Pinn (eds.), *The Hip-Hop and Religion Reader*, 86–98, New York: Routledge.

Jackson, M. (1983), "Knowledge of the Body," *Man*, 18 (2): 327–45.

Jones, C., and K. Shorter-Gooden (2003), *Shifting: The Double Lives of Black Women in America*, New York: HarperCollins.

Jones, G. (2014), "Secrecy," *Annual Review of Anthropology*, 43: 53–69.

Jones, R. P. (2020), *White Too Long: The Legacy of White Supremacy in American Christianity*, New York: Simon & Schuster.

Katznelson, I. (2005), *When Affirmative Action Was White: An Untold History of Racial Inequality in Twentieth-Century America*, New York: W. W. Norton.

Keane, W. (2002), "Sincerity, 'Modernity', and the Protestants," *Cultural Anthropology*, 17 (1): 65–92.

Keane, W. (2016), *Ethical Life: Its Natural and Social Histories*, Princeton, NJ: Princeton University Press.

King, M. L. Jr. (1963), "I Have a Dream." Available online: http://www.americanrhetoric.com/speeches/mlkihaveadream.htm (accessed October 25, 2020).

Klaits, F. (2010), *Death in a Church of Life: Moral Passion during Botswana's Time of AIDS*, Berkeley: University of California Press.

Klaits, F. (2011), "Asking as Giving: Apostolic Prayers and the Aesthetics of Well-Being in Botswana," *Journal of Religion in Africa*, 41 (2): 206–26.

Klaits, F. (2017a), "'Catch the Word': Violated Contracts and Prophetic Confirmation in African American Pentecostalism," *HAU: Journal of Ethnographic Theory*, 7 (3): 237–60.

Klaits, F., ed. (2017b), *The Request and the Gift in Religious and Humanitarian Endeavors*, New York: Palgrave Macmillan.

Klaits, F., and S. A. McLean (2015), "Valuing Black Lives: Pentecostalism, Charismatic Gifts, and Human Economies in a U.S. Inner City," *American Ethnologist*, 42 (4): 610–23.

Klin-Oron, A. (2014), "How I Learned to Channel: Epistemology, Phenomenology, and Practice in a New Age Course," *American Ethnologist*, 41 (4): 635–47.

Kochman, T. (1981), *Black and White Styles in Conflict*, Chicago: University of Chicago Press.

Kohut, H. (1971), *The Analysis of the Self: A Systematic Approach to the Psychoanalytic Treatment of Narcissistic Personality Disorders*, New York: International Universities Press.

Kostarelos, F. (1995), *Feeling the Spirit: Faith and Hope in an Evangelical Black Storefront Church*, Columbia: University of South Carolina Press.

Kraus, N. (2000), *Race, Neighborhoods, and Community Power: Buffalo Politics, 1934–1997*, Albany: State University of New York Press.

Laidlaw, J. (2014), *The Subject of Virtue: An Anthropology of Ethics and Freedom*, New York: Cambridge University Press.

Lakoff, G. (2002), *Moral Politics: How Liberals and Conservatives Think*, 2nd ed., Chicago: University of Chicago Press.

Latour, B. (2005), "'Thou Shall Not Freeze-Frame'—or How Not to Misunderstand the Science and Religion Debate," in J. D. Proctor (ed.), *Science, Religion and the Human Experience*, 27–48, Oxford: Oxford University Press.

Lawless, E. J. (1988), *God's Peculiar People: Women's Voices and Folk Tradition in a Pentecostal Church*, Lexington: University Press of Kentucky.

Lee, G., and H. Lim (2009), "A Spatial Statistical Approach to Identifying Areas with Poor Access to Grocery Foods in the City of Buffalo, New York," *Urban Studies*, 46 (7): 1229–315.

Lee, T. (2016), *Catching a Case: Inequality and Fear in New York City's Child Welfare System*, New Brunswick, NJ: Rutgers University Press.

Leonhardt, D. (2020), "The Black–White Wage Gap Is as Big as It Was in 1950," *New York Times*, 25 June. Available online: https://www.nytimes.com/2020/06/25/opinion/sunday/race-wage-gap.html?searchResultPosition=9 (accessed October 25, 2020).

Lester, R. J. (2017), "Self-Governance, Psychotherapy, and the Subject of Managed Care: Internal Family Systems Therapy and the Multiple Self in a US Eating-Disorders Treatment Center," *American Ethnologist*, 44 (1): 23–35.

Levinas, E. (1969), *Totality and Infinity: An Essay on Exteriority*, trans. A. Lingis, Pittsburgh, PA: Duquesne University Press.

Lewin, E. (2018), *Filled with the Spirit: Sexuality, Gender, and Radical Inclusivity in a Black Pentecostal Church Coalition*, Chicago: University of Chicago Press.

Lincoln, C. E., and L. H. Mamiya (1990), *The Black Church in the African-American Experience*, Durham, NC: Duke University Press.

Lindhardt, M. (2009), "More than Just Money: The Faith Gospel and Occult Economies in Contemporary Tanzania," *Nova Religio*, 13 (1): 41–67.

Lipsitz, G. (2006), *The Possessive Investment in Whiteness: How White People Profit from Identity Politics*, Philadelphia, PA: Temple University Press.

Luhrmann, T. M. (1989), *Persuasions of the Witch's Craft*, Cambridge, MA: Harvard University Press.

Luhrmann, T. M. (2004), "Metakinesis: How God Becomes Intimate in Contemporary U.S. Christianity," *American Anthropologist*, 106 (3): 518–28.

Luhrmann, T. M. (2007), "How Do You Learn to Know That It Is God Who Speaks?," in D. Berliner and R. Sarró (eds.), *Learning Religion: Anthropological Approaches*, 83–102, New York: Berghahn Books.

Luhrmann, T. M. (2012), *When God Talks Back: Understanding the American Evangelical Relationship with God*, New York: Alfred A. Knopf.

Luhrmann, T. M. (2020), *How God Becomes Real: Kindling the Presence of Invisible Others*, Princeton, NJ: Princeton University Press.

MacLean, N. (2017), *Democracy in Chains: The Deep History of the Radical Right's Stealth Plan for America*, New York: Viking Press.

MacRobert, I. (1988), *The Black Roots and White Racism of Early Pentecostalism in the USA*, New York: St. Martin's Press.

Magavern, S. (2018), *Evicted in Buffalo: The High Costs of Involuntary Mobility*. Available online: https://ppgbuffalo.org/files/documents/housing_neighborhoods/general/housingneighborhoods-_evicted_in_buffalo.pdf (accessed October 25, 2020).

Mahmood, S. (2005), *Politics of Piety: The Islamic Revival and the Feminist Subject*, Princeton, NJ: Princeton University Press.

Mann, T. W. (2013), *The Book of the Torah*, Eugene, OR: Wipf and Stock Publishers.

Marina, P. (2013), *Getting the Holy Ghost: Urban Ethnography in a Brooklyn Pentecostal Tongue-Speaking Church*, Lanham, MD: Lexington Books.

Matthews, D. H. (2013), *Pastor or Pimp?*, N.p.: CreateSpace Independent Publishing Platform.

Mattingly, C. (2010), *The Paradox of Hope: Journeys through a Clinical Borderland*, Berkeley: University of California Press.

Mattingly, C. (2014a), *Moral Laboratories: Family Peril and the Struggle for a Good Life*, Oakland: University of California Press.

Mattingly, C. (2014b), "The Moral Perils of a Superstrong Black Mother," *Ethos*, 42 (1): 119–38.

Mauss, M. ([1924–5] 2015), *The Gift: Expanded Edition*, trans. J. Guyer, Chicago: HAU Books.

McIntosh, K., E. Moss, R. Nunn, and J. Shambaugh (2020), *Examining the Black–White Wealth Gap*. Available online: https://www.brookings.edu/blog/up-front/2020/02/27/examining-the-black-white-wealth-gap/ (accessed October 25, 2020).

McKernan, S.-M., C. Ratcliffe, E. Steuerle, and S. Zhang (2013), *Less Than Equal: Racial Disparities in Wealth Accumulation*. Available online: https://www.urban.org/resea rch/publication/less-equal-racial-disparities-wealth-accumulation/view/full_ report (accessed May 22, 2020).

McRoberts, O. M. (2003), *Streets of Glory: Church and Community in a Black Urban Neighborhood*, Chicago: University of Chicago Press.

Meyer, B. (1999), *Translating the Devil: Religion and Modernity among the Ewe in Ghana*, Trenton, NJ: Africa World Press.

Miller, D. (2012), *Blue Like Jazz: Nonreligious Thoughts on Christian Spirituality*, Nashville, TN: Thomas Nelson.

Mills, C. W. (1997), *The Racial Contract*, Ithaca, NY: Cornell University Press.

Minister, K. (1991), "A Feminist Frame for the Oral History Interview," in S. Berger and D. Patai (eds.), *Women's Words: The Feminist Practice of Oral History*, 27–41, New York: Routledge.

Mitchem, S. Y. (2007), *Name It and Claim It?: Prosperity Preaching in the Black Church*, Cleveland, OH: Pilgrim Press.

Mittermaier, A. (2011), *Dreams That Matter: Egyptian Landscapes of the Imagination*, Berkeley: University of California Press.

Mittermaier, A. (2012), "Dreams from Elsewhere: Muslim Subjectivities beyond the Trope of Self-Cultivation," *Journal of the Royal Anthropological Institute* 18 (2): 247–65.

Moriarty, M. (2020), *Pascal: Reasoning and Belief*, Oxford: Oxford University Press.

Moten, F. (2003), *In the Break: The Aesthetics of the Black Radical Tradition*, Minneapolis: University of Minnesota Press.

Muhammad, K. G. (2010), *The Condemnation of Blackness: Race, Crime, and the Making of Modern Urban America*, Cambridge, MA: Harvard University Press.

Mullings, L. (1989), "Gender and the Application of Anthropological Knowledge to Public Policy in the United States," in S. Morgen (ed.), *Gender and Anthropology*, Washington, DC: American Anthropological Association.

Mullings, L. (2001), "Households Headed by Women: The Politics of Class, Race, and Gender," in J. Goode and J. Maskovsky (eds.), *The New Poverty Studies: The Ethnography of Power, Politics, and Impoverished People in the United States*, 37–56, New York: New York University Press.

Mullings, L. (2020), "Neoliberal Racism and the Movement for Black Lives in the United States," in Juliet Hooker (ed.), *Black and Indigenous Resistance in the Americas: From Multiculturalism to Racist Backlash*, 249–94, Lanham, MD: Lexington Books.

Mullings, L., and A. Wali (2001), *Stress and Resilience: The Social Context of Reproduction in Central Harlem*, New York: Kluwer Academic/Plenum Publishers.

Nelson, T. J. (2005), *Every Time I Feel the Spirit: Religious Experience and Ritual in an African American Church*, New York: New York University Press.

Nirenberg, D. (2015), *Aesthetic Theology and Its Enemies: Judaism in Christian Painting, Poetry, and Politics*, Waltham, MA: Brandeis University Press.

Obeyesekere, G. (1981), *Medusa's Hair: An Essay on Personal Symbols and Religious Experience*. Chicago: University of Chicago Press.

Omartian, S. (2005), *The Power of a Praying Parent*, Eugene, OR: Harvest House Publishers.

Orsi, R. A. (2005), *Between Heaven and Earth: The Religious Worlds People Make and the Scholars Who Study Them*, Princeton, NJ: Princeton University Press.

Orsi, R. A. (2016), *History and Presence*, Cambridge, MA: Belknap Press of Harvard University Press.

Pagels, E. H. (1979), *The Gnostic Gospels*, New York: Random House.

Pascal, B. (1995), *Pensées*, trans. A. J. Krailsheimer, New York: Penguin.

Pérez, E. (2016), *Religion in the Kitchen: Cooking, Talking, and the Making of Black Atlantic Traditions*, New York: New York University Press.

Pettit, B. (2012), *Invisible Men: Mass Incarceration and the Myth of Black Progress*, New York: Russell Sage Foundation.

Pfeil, G. (2011), "Imperfect Vessels: Emotion and Rituals of Anti-Ritual in American Pentecostal and Charismatic Devotional Life," in M. Lindhardt (ed.), *Practicing the Faith: The Ritual Life of Pentecostal-Charismatic Christians*, 277–305, New York: Berghahn Books.

Pinn, A. B. (1995), *Why, Lord?: Suffering and Evil in Black Theology*, New York: Continuum Publishing.

Pinn, A. B. (2003), *Terror and Triumph: The Nature of Black Religion*, Minneapolis, MN: Fortress Press.

Porter, C. R. (1999), *Imani All Mine*, Boston, MA: Houghton Mifflin.

Posner, S. (2021), *Unholy: How White Christian Nationalists Powered the Trump Presidency, and the Devastating Legacy They Left Behind*, New York: Random House.

Povinelli, E. A. (2011), *Economies of Abandonment: Social Belonging and Endurance in Late Liberalism*, Durham, NC: Duke University Press.

Premawardhana, D. (2018), *Faith in Flux: Pentecostalism and Mobility in Rural Mozambique*, Philadelphia: University of Pennsylvania Press.

Price, E. G. III, ed. (2012), *The Black Church and Hip Hop Culture: Toward Bridging the Generational Divide*, Lanham, MD: Scarecrow Press.

Ralph, L. (2014), *Renegade Dreams: Living Through Injury in Gangland Chicago*, Chicago: University of Chicago Press.

Ramberg, L. (2014), *Given to the Goddess: South Indian Devadasis and the Sexuality of Religion*, Durham, NC: Duke University Press.

Reeves, R. V. (2017), *Dream Hoarders: How the American Upper Middle Class Is Leaving Everyone Else in the Dust, Why That Is a Problem, and What to Do about It*, Washington, DC: Brookings Institution Press.

Reinhardt, B. (2018), "Waiting for God in Ghana: The Chronotopes of a Prayer Mountain," in M. K. Janeja and A. Bandak (eds.), *Ethnographies of Waiting: Doubt, Hope, and Uncertainty*, 113–37, London: Bloomsbury Press.

Republican National Committee (2016), *Republican Platform 2016*. Available online: https://prod-cdn-static.gop.com/media/documents/DRAFT_12_FI NAL%5B1%5D-ben_1468872234.pdf (accessed May 30, 2020).

Richbart, M. (2019), *Christian Treasure Hunting: Counterpublics and Semiotics*, unpublished M.A. Project, Department of Anthropology, State University of New York at Buffalo.

Rios, V. M. (2011), *Punished: Policing the Lives of Black and Latino Boys*, New York: New York University Press.

Robbins, J. (2001), "God Is Nothing but Talk: Modernity, Language, and Prayer in a Papua New Guinea Society," *American Anthropologist*, 103 (4): 901–12.

Robbins, J. (2004), *Becoming Sinners: Christianity and Moral Torment in a Papua New Guinea Society*, Berkeley: University of California Press.

Robbins, J. (2010), "Anthropology, Pentecostalism, and the New Paul: Conversion, Event, and Social Transformation," *South Atlantic Quarterly*, 109 (4): 633–52.

Robbins, J. (2013), "Beyond the Suffering Subject: Toward an Anthropology of the Good," *Journal of the Royal Anthropological Institute*, 19 (3): 447–62.

Roediger, D. R. (2005), *Working toward Whiteness: How America's Immigrants Became White: The Strange Journey from Ellis Island to the Suburbs*, New York: Basic Books.

Roose, K. (2009), *The Unlikely Disciple: A Sinner's Semester at America's Holiest University*, New York: Grand Central Publishing.

Rothstein, R. (2017), *The Color of Law: A Forgotten History of How Our Government Segregated America*, New York: Liveright Publishing.

Rouse, C. M., J. L. Jackson Jr., and M. Frederick (2016), *Televised Redemption: Black Religious Media and Racial Empowerment*, New York: New York University Press.

Sandel, M. J. (2020), *The Tyranny of Merit: What's Become of the Common Good?*, New York: Farrar, Straus, and Giroux.

Sanders, C. J. (1996), *Saints in Exile: The Holiness-Pentecostal Experience in African American Religion and Culture*, New York: Oxford University Press.

Scherz, C. (2014), *Having People, Having Heart: Charity, Sustainable Development, and Problems of Dependence in Central Uganda*, Chicago: University of Chicago Press.

Scherz, C. (2017), "Seeking the Wounds of the Gift: Recipient Agency in Catholic Charity and Kiganda Patronage," in F. Klaits (ed.), *The Request and the Gift in Religious and Humanitarian Endeavors*, 47–64, New York: Palgrave Macmillian.

Scherz, C. (2018), "Enduring the Awkward Embrace: Ontology and Ethical Work in a Ugandan Convent," *American Anthropologist*, 120 (1): 102–12.

Seeman, D. (2018), "Divinity Inhabits the Social: Ethnography in a Phenomenological Key," in J. D. Lemons (ed.), *Theologically Engaged Anthropology*, 336–54, Oxford: Oxford University Press.

Sennett, R., and J. Cobb (1972), *The Hidden Injuries of Class*, New York: Knopf.

Shabazz, R. (2015), *Spatializing Blackness: Architectures of Confinement and Black Masculinity in Chicago*, Urbana: University of Illinois Press.

Silverman, R., H. Taylor, L. Yin, C. Miller, and P. Buggs (2018), "Perceptions of Residential Displacement and Grassroots Resistance to Anchor Driven Encroachment in Buffalo, NY," *Urbanities*, 8 (2): 79–86.

Silverman, R. M., H. L.Taylor Jr., L. Yin, C. Miller, and P. Buggs (2019), "There Goes Our Family Friendly Neighborhood: Residents' Perceptions of Institutionally Driven Inner-City Revitalization in Buffalo, NY," *Journal of Community Practice*, 27 (2): 168–87.

Smith, C. (1998), *American Evangelicalism: Embattled and Thriving*, Chicago: University of Chicago Press.

Smith, C. (2000), *Christian America?: What Evangelicals Really Want*, Berkeley: University of California Press.

Smith, J. K. A. (2010), *Thinking in Tongues: Pentecostal Contributions to Christian Philosophy*, Grand Rapids, MI: William B. Eerdmans.

Smitherman, G. (1977), *Talkin and Testifyin: The Language of Black America*, Boston, MA: Houghton Mifflin.

Snorton, C. R. (2014), *Nobody Is Supposed to Know: Black Sexuality on the Down Low*, Minneapolis: University of Minnesota Press.

Spencer, J. M. (1989), "God in Secular Music Culture: The Theodicy of the Blues as the Paradigm of Proof," *Black Sacred Music*, 3 (2): 17–49.

Stack, C. B. (1974), *All Our Kin: Strategies for Survival in a Black Community*, New York: Harper & Row.

Stewart, K. (2020), *The Power Worshippers: Inside the Dangerous Rise of Religious Nationalism*, New York: Bloomsbury Publishing.

Stewart, M. (2018), "The 9.9 Percent Is the New American Aristocracy," *The Atlantic* (June). Available online: https://www.theatlantic.com/magazine/archive/2018/06/the-birth-of-a-new-american-aristocracy/559130/ (accessed November 24, 2020).

Strings, S. (2019), *Fearing the Black Body: The Racial Origins of Fat Phobia*, New York: New York University Press.

Strings, S. (2020), "It's Not Obesity. It's Slavery," *New York Times*, May 25. Available online: https://www.nytimes.com/2020/05/25/opinion/coronavirus-race-obesity.html?searchResultPosition=1 (accessed October 25, 2020).

Sullivan, M. L. (1989), *"Getting Paid": Youth Crime and Work in the Inner City*, Ithaca, NY: Cornell University Press.

Sullivan, S. (2014), *Good White People: The Problem with Middle-Class White Anti-Racism*, Albany: State University of New York Press.

Sullivan, S. C. (2011), *Living Faith: Everyday Religion and Mothers in Poverty*, Chicago: University of Chicago Press.

Summers, B. T. (2019), *Black in Place: The Spatial Aesthetics of Race in a Post-Chocolate City*, Chapel Hill: University of North Carolina Press.

Taves, A. (1999), *Fits, Trances, and Visions: Experiencing Religion and Explaining Experience from Wesley to James*, Princeton, NJ: Princeton University Press.

Taylor, K.-Y. (2019), *Race for Profit: How Banks and the Real Estate Industry Undermined Black Homeownership*, Chapel Hill: University of North Carolina Press.

Taylor, K.-Y. (2021), "A Different Buffalo Is Possible," *New Yorker*, October 29. Available online: https://www.newyorker.com/news/the-political-scene/another-buffalo-is-possible (accessed October 29, 2021).

Tharps, L. L. (2014), "The Case for Black with a Capital B," *New York Times*, November 18. Available online: https://www.nytimes.com/2014/11/19/opinion/the-case-for-black-with-a-capital-b.html?searchResultPosition=1 (accessed October 25, 2020).

Thomas, T. (2021), *Kincraft: The Making of Black Evangelical Sociality*, Durham, NC: Duke University Press.

Thornton, B. J. (2016), *Negotiating Respect: Pentecostalism, Masculinity, and the Politics of Spiritual Authority in the Dominican Republic*, Gainesville: University Press of Florida.

Tisby, J. (2019), *The Color of Compromise: The Truth about the American Church's Complicity in Racism*, Grand Rapids, MI: Zondervan.

Townes, E. M. (1995), *In a Blaze of Glory: Womanist Spirituality as Social Witness*, Nashville, TN: Abingdon Press.

Tranby, E., and D. Hartmann (2008), "Critical Whiteness Theories and the Evangelical 'Race Problem': Extending Emerson and Smith's *Divided By Faith*," *Journal for the Scientific Study of Religion*, 47 (3): 341–59.

Traub, A., L. Sullivan, T. Meschede, and T. Shapiro (2017). *The Asset Value of Whiteness: Understanding the Racial Wealth Gap*. Available online: https://www.demos.org/research/asset-value-whiteness-understanding-racial-wealth-gap (accessed May 22, 2020).

Turner, E. (1992), *Experiencing Ritual: A New Interpretation of African Healing*, Philadelphia: University of Pennsylvania Press.

van Wyk, I. (2014), *The Universal Church of the Kingdom of God in South Africa: A Church of Strangers*, Cambridge: Cambridge University Press.

Venkatesh, S. A. (2006), *Off the Books: The Underground Economy of the Urban Poor*, Cambridge, MA: Harvard University Press.

Wacquant, L. (2009), *Punishing the Poor: The Neoliberal Government of Social Insecurity*, Durham, NC: Duke University Press.

Walton, J. (2009), *Watch This!: The Ethics and Aesthetics of Black Televangelism*, New York: New York University Press.

Washington, H. A. (2006), *Medical Apartheid: The Dark History of Medical Experimentation on Black Americans from Colonial Times to the Present*, New York: Doubleday.

Weber, M. (2003), *The Protestant Ethic and the Spirit of Capitalism*, trans. T. Parsons, Mineola, NY: Dover Publications.

Webster, J. (2013), *The Anthropology of Protestantism: Faith and Crisis among Scottish Fishermen*, New York: Palgrave Macmillan.

Weisenfeld, J. (2016), *New World A-Coming: Black Religion and Racial Identity during the Great Migration*, New York: New York University Press.

Werbner, P., and R. Werbner (forthcoming), "Charisma," in S. Coleman and J. Robbins (eds.), *The Oxford Handbook of the Anthropology of Religion*, Oxford: Oxford University Press.

Werbner, R. (1997), "The Suffering Body: Passion and Ritual Allegory in Christian Encounters," *Journal of Southern African Studies*, 23 (2): 311–24.

Whitehead, A. L., and S. L. Perry (2020), *Taking America Back for God: Christian Nationalism in the United States*, New York: Oxford University Press.

Williams, B. (1985), *Ethics and the Limits of Philosophy*, Cambridge, MA: Harvard University Press.

Williams, B. (1993), "Moral Incapacity," *Proceedings of the Aristotelian Society*, 93: 59–70.

Williams, D. S. (1993), *Sisters in the Wilderness: The Challenges of Womanist God-Talk*, Maryknoll, NY: Orbis Books.

Williams, L. S. (1999), *Strangers in the Land of Paradise: The Creation of an African American Community, Buffalo, New York, 1900–1940*, Bloomington: Indiana University Press.

Wilson, W. J. (1987), *The Truly Disadvantaged: The Inner City, the Underclass, and Public Policy*, Chicago: University of Chicago Press.

Wood, J. (2020), "Does Knowing God Just Take Practice?," *New Yorker*, November 2. Available online: https://www.newyorker.com/magazine/2020/11/09/does-know ing-god-just-take-practice (accessed November 19, 2020).

Woodbine, O. X. O. (2016), *Black Gods of the Asphalt: Religion, Hip-Hop, and Street Basketball*, New York: Columbia University Press.

Woodbine, O. X. O. (2021), *Take Back What the Devil Stole: An African American Prophet's Encounters in the Spirit World*, New York: Columbia University Press.

Yancy, G. (2012), "Introduction: Framing the Problem," in G. Yancy (ed.), *Christology and Whiteness: What Would Jesus Do?*, 1–18, Abingdon, VA: Routledge.

Zanfagna, C. (2017), *Holy Hip Hop in the City of Angels*, Oakland: University of California Press.

Zoanni, T. (2019), "Appearances of Disability and Christianity in Uganda," *Cultural Anthropology*, 34 (3): 444–70.

# Index

Note: Endnotes are indicated by the page number followed by "n" and the endnote number e.g., 20 n.1 refers to endnote 1 on page 20.

www.ingramcontent.com/pod-product-compliance
Lightning Source LLC
Chambersburg PA
CBHW050426280326
41932CB00013BA/2010